REPORTING BACK:

Notes on Journalism

ALSO BY LILLIAN ROSS

REPORTING BACK:

Notes on Journalism

LILLIAN ROSS

COUNTERPOINT
WASHINGTON, D.C.

Library of Congress Cataloging-in-Publication Data
Ross, Lillian, 1927–
Reporting Back : notes on journalism / Lillian Ross
p. cm.
ISBN 1-58243-109-4
1. Journalism. 2. Reporters and reporting. 3. Ross, Lillian, 1927– .
I. Title.
PN4733 .R59 2002
070.4—dc21
 2002003709

FIRST PRINTING

Text design by Amy Evans McClure

Printed in the United States of America on acid-free paper that meets the American National Standards Institute Z39–48 Standard.

COUNTERPOINT
P.O. Box 65793
Washington, D.C. 20035–5793
Counterpoint is a member of the Perseus Books Group

10 9 8 7 6 5 4 3 2 1

To *The New Yorker's* Editors—Past and Present

CONTENTS

INTRODUCTION

THIS BOOK IS about the journalism that I love and work at. It is not about newspaper reporting or television anchoring or radio newscasting or Internet magazines. It is not about "*investigative* journalism," "*confrontational* journalism," "the *new* journalism," or any other jargon-journalism. Journalism to me is factual writing, and the highest kind of it comes in the form of good writing, and often writing that, at its best, is witty. Every now and then, journalism has been found to be timeless; and its writers have been considered to be on a par with the best in literature. I subscribe to the classic who-what-when-where-why-and-how guidelines in my journalism, and I follow them carefully, along with some basic traditions in the service of laughter and truth. But I also enjoy the challenge of pushing traditional structures. For me, there has always been satisfaction and joy in finding or even inventing new ways of telling a story.

I don't know whether journalistic stories contribute to any kind of social history. They might. With the terrorists' horrifying destruction of New York's World Trade Center and the murderous attack on the Pentagon on September 11, 2001, the initial response

of so many journalists was astonishing to see and hear. Every journalist I know relied on his expertise to meet the challenge of providing important information, understanding, consolation, and guidance to confused and heartbroken people all over the world. We know that the Second World War and the Vietnam War left us journalistic legacies of many kinds. It may take years to sort out the journalistic contributions brought forth by this still overwhelming, on-going phenomenon. The war on terrorism, in all its complicated aspects, is one I'm not equipped to write about head on. For my stories now, I've been playing it by ear. However, I do know that each one of us does whatever he or she was born to do.

In any case, it is invariably fun, and no hardship, for me to write my stories. My focus in this book is on what journalistic stories can be in themselves; where the material for them may be found; and how they may be written with clarity and humor. My purpose is to spell out some of my ideas, as they developed over fifty years, about writing these stories. To illustrate my points, I'll use excerpts from my own writing. Every good reporting writer is different from every other; every good story is different from every other. So there should be no doubt about the singularity of my point of view in doing reportorial stories in general and mine in particular.

My starting point is *The New Yorker* magazine, where I have been doing most of my reporting and writing since 1945. That is where I grew up journalistically. Initially, the freedom and support and wherewithal for doing the work came from *The New Yorker*, originally from its first and second editors, Harold Ross and William Shawn, and later on, from their successors.

My ideas for what I do in journalism were formed at the age of eight when my older sister, Helen, told me that, when she grew up, she was going to be "a travelling correspondent." She said, "I'll go all over the world, and I'll write about the way everything looks or sounds or seems to me." That was it. I absorbed her ideas, and they've never changed. I asked no questions; I merely accepted my lowly sibling role and did what Helen bade me to do and the way she bade me to do it. Wherever I've gone since, whatever I've seen or heard or felt, and however I've reported and written, I've done

it all using these borrowed sensibilities. To me, Helen was the authority on everything. She was beautiful and original and intuitive and loving and funny and smart, and she was always right. I tried to imitate her in almost every way. Helen gave me a special way of seeing and hearing that has always stayed with me. I became simultaneously detached yet empathetic. It was a generous and special working gift, and I'm forever grateful to Helen for it. When people asked me from time to time about the strongest literary influences in my work, I would give various names, including Ivan Turgenev, Laura Lee Hope, Joseph Mitchell, J. D. Salinger, and Ernest Hemingway ("The old simple words are the best," he repeatedly told me). The work of those writers indeed had a profound effect on me. The first and deepest and lasting influence to this day, however, was that of my sister Helen. She taught me to see and sense what is in people. From her, I learned what is basic to my work: my reporting is subjective in selecting facts. The clear indulgence of subjectivity in the process of selection and the objective need of factuality are absolute twin elements in my journalism. They stem from the formative powers in my own life.

I've tried to find the facts and tell the truth. Helen had a wry, sharp, original, warm, perceptive humor, about herself and everybody else she knew. Her humor echoed my father's, which was always his own. Helen also taught me irony, before I even knew the word. Among other things, our lives evolved ironically, with my continuing enjoyment of her discoveries and her premature death when she was in her forties.

The source of the other single influence on my work was William Shawn, with whom I was wholly and happily engaged in my life, personally and professionally, for almost five decades. He was the editor-in-chief of *The New Yorker* from 1952 to 1987. What he gave me before and during that stretch of time and until his death in 1992, went far beyond the editorial realm. He gave me a complete life. With Bill Shawn, daily, I developed tolerance, judgement, and taste. All of it operated in a delicate balance with our mutual appetite for discovering those most precious things— laughter and humor. William Shawn encouraged me to distill my

own sense of humor in my work. I loved making him laugh. He not only gave me the confidence to do the reporting and writing, but he also gave me a sense of life. It seems to me that every journalist needs, in addition to talent, in whatever he or she sets out to do, three clear elements: confidence, proof of being loved and needed, and a passion for life. Bill Shawn indisputably gave me all of these. A reporter who has them is completely independent and free of such needs when he or she goes out to report. That reporter asks only for his story.

In 1981, I wrote in the Introduction to my book *Reporting,* "Every reporter must work in his own way, speak with his own voice, find his individual style." There is no avoiding the fact that the very nature of a reporter, of every writer, is revealed in his writing. What you are as a human being shows up in your work. In my case, I am keenly and consciously aware of what I know are my borrowed sensibilities.

The journalists whose work I seek out and respond to are mostly at *The New Yorker,* now more than ever. In fact, I find myself reading the magazine far more today than I did in the past. I don't see what a few of my older colleagues peculiarly pine for, in what they call "the good old days" under the editorship of Harold Ross and William Shawn. These two were indeed fascinating personalities. Both were also geniuses: Ross in his inventiveness and the uniqueness of what he created; and Shawn, who fostered the emergence and continuing viability of so many diverse talents.

There is no getting away from the fact, however, that Tina Brown, who took over the job of Editor of the magazine in 1992, contributed indelibly to the continuing and growing vitality of its reporters, writers, and artists, including me. Moreover, she made many brave and ingenious personnel changes at the magazine. She found some of the best new young writers and artists and editors of our time and opened the magazine to them. She published photography for the first time. Many of my colleagues at *The New Yorker* feel as I do; we admire her and are greatly indebted to her. I worked for her very much in the same way as I had with William Shawn.

Since 1998, *The New Yorker* has had, as its editor, David Remnick, who, at forty-three, knows and understands the past mysteries of *The New Yorker* as well as the traditions. He quickly made additional changes and innovations and found interesting and exciting new writers, artists, and photographers. He has already become an original and dependable fixture. It's not easy to take over a whole institution, populated by a bunch of sensitive, self-aware egos—some of them still viable and volatile oldsters and middle-agers—and make them feel needed just as much as a bunch of wonderfully talented kids. Like Bill Shawn, he very carefully selects the editors who help him, and he fully understands and appreciates their particular brilliance and their essential modesty. There's no point in my dissembling my feelings about *The New Yorker;* it's been my journalistic home.

My kind of journalism is never created by the writer alone. There is always, for me, an editor, or a subeditor, who helps, in hundreds of ways. The credit, the acclaim, the admiration, and other rewards, without exception, always go to the writer, while the editor fades to black. A great editor—in an unsolicited parental role—leads a writer to feel he "did it all by himself." The more insecure the writer is, the more he takes the help for granted. I prefer to have my editors stay collectively in the picture. It's more fun that way. I enjoy doing my writing for them. I do it now in practically the same way, and for the same reasons, as I did it in the very beginning.

Somewhere along the line, a critic used the phrase "fly on the wall" to describe my journalistic "technique." Bill Shawn called it "a silly and meaningless phrase." He said, "It's for people who don't understand that every writer is different from every other writer, the way every human being is different from every other." Today, there are journalism teachers who actually "teach" their students to "be a fly on the wall." Even I, to my amazement, was asked, as late as the 1990's, by a former editor at *The New Yorker* to do a certain story and, to "do it as a fly on the wall." What craziness! A reporter doing a story can't pretend to be invisible, let alone a fly; he or she is seen and heard and responded to by the people he or she is writing about; a reporter is always chemically

involved in a story. Any editor instructing a reporter to be a fly—on or off the wall—is misguided.

Often, when I write my stories, it feels a bit like creating a short story, but it's more difficult, because I'm working with facts. I don't believe a reporter has the right to say what his subject is thinking or feeling. Furthermore, thoughts and opinions and feelings, including those of a reporter, should be demonstrated in the reporting of quotes and actions. As I write, I'm always trying to build scenes into little story-films. Whether I'm writing a short piece for The Talk of the Town (about a thousand words) or a long one (4,000 to 8,000 words), I always think of it visually, like a film, that tells a story with a beginning, a middle, and an end.

In my introduction to *Reporting*, I tried to outline some of my guidelines—I called them "principles," a word I acquired in my life with William Shawn. Today, I still try to follow these principles. I still abide by them. I've repeated some of them here; I've also amplified them.

Here are my working guidelines:

I try to write as clearly and simply and straightforwardly as possible. In poetry and fiction, there may be a place for ambiguity, but there isn't in reporting.

I choose to write only about people, situations, and events that appeal to me. Every editor I've worked with believed, as I did, that the only reason to write a story—especially a story about a person—was to shed some light on what that individual is in relation to the work he does. Fame or sensationalism alone are never appealing; in fact, they're deadening.

I don't want to write about anybody who doesn't want me to.

I don't want to write about anyone I don't like.

I trust my response to a person in the first few minutes of meeting him. The first experience—of anything, to me—is the most significant and the most memorable. It's that sense—of a person or an event or a situation—that leads me, in the act of writing, to my story. Recognition of that sense is immediate.

If another person permits me to write about him, he is opening his life to me, and I have a responsibility to him. Even if that per-

son is indiscreet about himself, or invades his own privacy, I use my own judgement in deciding what to write. Just because someone "said it" is no reason for me to use it. My obligation to people I write about doesn't end once my piece is in print. Anyone who trusts me enough to talk about himself is giving me a form of friendship. I am not doing him a "favor" in writing about him, even if he values publicity. A friend is not to be used and abandoned. A friendship established in writing about someone often continues to grow after a piece of writing is published. Although I don't want to write about people I dislike, I certainly use common sense if I write about a friend. Common sense dictates that the writer has no self-serving or self-aggrandizing motive for selecting the subject.

The old fictional portrayal of the journalist—at his desk, fedora on his head, pecking away at the typewriter, cigarette drooping from a corner of his mouth, a half-full whiskey bottle near at hand—is for the birds. Some of my former colleagues who followed that way of life found that it was damaging to their work, to their productivity, to their lives. A marvelously talented tennis player, Monica Seles, was asked recently why she goes on playing competitive tennis. She replied: "It's what I love to do, and it's given me a special and wonderful life." That's the way I feel.

I resist taking a writing assignment for financial reasons. Earning money is often mentioned as a way to "free you to do what you want to do later on." One certain way of blocking you from doing what you want to do later on is to do something else now for the money alone.

I don't use a tape recorder when I report. To me, the machine distorts the truth. It's a fast, easy, and lazy way of eliciting talk, but a conversationalist is not necessarily a writer. Tape-recorded interviews are not only misleading; they are unrealistic; they are lifeless. I don't want a machine to do my listening for me. Literal reality rarely rings true. It is not interesting. Among other things, the reporter hears too much of his own voice. Tape-recorded interviews by newspaper reporters covering straight news stories are obviously necessary. That is a different kind of journalism, the kind I don't do.

As soon as I started reporting, I started taking my notes in small, 3 x 5-inch spiral Clairefontaine notebooks. I have thousands of these notebooks filled with my scribbling. Most of the time, I use a Uni-Ball pen with a micro point; it's fast moving. I try to listen while I write, and if I can't do both simultaneously, my listening takes priority. *Listening* is the quintessential word. I make sure to write down key, identifying phrases and words that help me remember the rhythm and context of what I'm hearing. Then I'm able to reproduce long exchanges. When I'm working against an imminent deadline, I have the theme of the story in mind as I report, and I'm able to write my story from my notes. Often, I prefer to transcribe my notes as soon as possible in a way that makes it easier for me to remember exactly the way the talk, especially the dialogue, went. Invariably—and from the time I started doing this work—I found that I've had a sense of what the "story" should be right away, and, as I'd go along in writing it, there has been a certain mystical force—something outside of myself—that takes over and the story seems to write itself. Once that force takes over, it makes the work seem delightfully easy and natural and supremely enjoyable. It's sort of like having sex.

Like most of my colleagues, I do my own research, whatever the story calls for. In order to proceed quickly, I include such matters as historical facts, dates, spellings, titles, institutions, and scientific, political, economic, and social material in the course of writing a story. Before going to press, however, we at *The New Yorker* are blessed with an assemblage of fact-checkers who are the best ever. When I first came to the magazine, there were about five checkers, and they were elegant, highly cultured, esoteric, and somewhat intimidating, but kindly, middle-aged gentlemen. Their lives seemed to be devoted solely to checking. Gradually, over the years, women were admitted to the checking bastion, and they seemed to get far younger, too. These days, there is a veritable army of male and female checkers, and they are often just out of college, every one a hard-working, smart, informed potential editor or reporter. I depend on them for accuracy, and with each new story, I'm gratefully indebted to them.

What about quoting? I have to find the quotes that work for me, quotes that reveal the truth. In over fifty years of reporting, I've never had anyone I've written about question the accuracy of my quotes. One reason for my dislike of the tape recorder is that it actually interferes with one's listening to the rhythm and to the essence of what a person says and how the person says it and how the person feels and who the person is. The person is responding to the machine and not to the reporter. Furthermore, that tape-recording reporter is not being asked to be a writer. A machine is not a writer.

What I see and hear when I begin to report almost immediately leads to my finding a theme; I then know what to look for. I find the significant and revealing facts and quotes to support the theme of the story; then nothing else matters (nothing) until I've written it.

Reporters to me are writers, and the best reporters are often outstanding writers. It is with reluctance that I accept the word "journalist," even though "journalism" is supposed to be what journalists write. And the fancy word "reportage" actually gives me the creeps. The appropriate word is "reporting." The word "reportage" seems to have been taken up in the last century by people who wanted to be thought of more highly. The finest practitioners of reportorial writing are "writers."

The finest reportorial writers are truth tellers. There is a magical power in factual details. Here is an example of how factually detailed reporting at its best can be beautiful writing. It is over fifty years old, but it is indeed timeless, which is due to the writing and only the writing. The author is Joseph Mitchell, who is among the best reporters ever. The following bit from the story called "Mazie" was originally published in *The New Yorker,* and it has been a steady inspiration to me and to countless other reporters:

> Mazie has presided for twenty-one years over the ticket cage of
> the Venice Theatre, at 209 Park Row, a few doors west of
> Chatham Square, where the Bowery begins. . . .
> Sitting majestically in her cage like a raffish queen, Mazie is
> one of the few pleasant sights of the Bowery. She is a short,

bosomy woman in her middle forties. Some people believe she
has a blurry resemblance to Mae West. Her hair is the color of
sulfur. Her face is dead white, and she wears a smudge of rouge
the size of a silver dollar on each cheek. Her eyes are sleepy and
droopy-lidded. On duty, she often wears a green celluloid eye-
shade. She almost always has a cigarette hanging from a corner
of her mouth, and this makes her look haughty. Like a movie
croupier, she can smoke a cigarette down to the end and not take
it from her mouth once, even while talking. She has a deep ciga-
rette cough; she smokes three and a half packs a day and says
tobacco is murdering her. On her right hand she wears four dia-
mond rings. She likes vigorous colors, and her dresses are spectac-
ular; they come from shops on Division Street. The glass-topped
Bowery and Chinatown rubberneck wagons often park in front
of the Venice, and now and then a band of sightseers stands on
the sidewalk and stares at Mazie. She despises sightseers and says
they give the Bowery a black eye. Sometimes she thumbs her nose
at them. Actually, however, she does not mind being stared at.
"People walk past here just to give me the eye," she once said. "I
got a public of my own, just like a god-damn movie-pitcher star."

Reporting is not about the reporter, even though he is always
revealed in the writing. If one is the kind of person who needs
attention from others—who prefers talking to listening, who wants
to be the star of a situation or important to the situation, who
essentially wants to show off—reporting is not a choice line of
work. One should not use reporting as a way of getting noticed. If
the work is original and solid and true, it will make its mark, and
the creator of it will automatically be recognized.

Courtesy is all important. I resent people who feel that the
power of a publication behind them gives them license to bully
people or lie to them. It does not give them free rein to be insolent
or impatient with people who are being asked for information nec-
essary for the story. People one is writing about may not fully
understand what I do in the writing, but if the reporter is honest
with them, they will respond honestly on their own terms. I have

found usually that being honest and open with people always leads to having them cooperate with me. And usually, they appreciate what one writes about them. They may take the writing for granted. Often, they may say: "Well, of course, that's true, and all you did was come in and write it down as it happened." That has always been OK with me. I don't look for the kind of understanding and appreciation of my writing from them that I get from my editor. An editor's response is enough for me.

I have consistently learned more and more about writing from all the great writers I admire, especially at *The New Yorker,* from writers like James Thurber, S. J. Perelman, John Hersey, E. B. White, A. J. Liebling, J. D. Salinger, John McCarten, and Joseph Mitchell. I adore the writing of such colleagues as Mark Singer, Hendrik Hertzberg, Roger Angell, Nancy Franklin, John Cassidy, Anthony Lane, Jeffrey Toobin, Susan Orlean, Malcolm Gladwell, David Owen, Bruce McCall, Hilton Als, Ian Frazier, Larissa MacFarquhar, John Seabrook, Adam Gopnik, Ken Auletta, Rebecca Mead, Philip Hamburger, Calvin Trillin, and David Remnick. Off the top of my head, I haven't named even half of them. Each of these writers is unique. One learns from them but is never compelled to imitate them. When the writers are great, their originality is inspiring and thrilling.

Even small touches were always noticed and understood by William Shawn. The same is true today of David Remnick. Shawn would say, with respect and wonder to many of his writers and artists: "Nobody else can do what you can do." Among the artists, there is only one Steig or Arno or Petty or Sempé or Addams or Birnbaum or Hokinson or McCall or Spiegelman or Koren or Chast or Steinberg or Booth. Originality is a pretty special phenomenon; those who understand it treasure it. Genuine talent resists any hint of imitation, of borrowing even one noticeable touch. When an original piece of writing is imitated, the telltale imitation hangs on that writer the way a string bikini would hang on Mother Teresa.

I cherish my memories of Joseph Mitchell in particular. I feel blessed not only to have his writings, but to have had him as a friend. Shortly after I joined the staff in 1945, I met him at a party,

and he immediately welcomed me into the fold by talking about "our paper." The expression was thrilling to me. To this day, whenever I think of the way he said "our paper," I get weepy. For years, he loved to talk about what he called "the mystique of our writing" giving me a dizzy feeling of mutual appreciation. He talked, in his soft, charming North Carolina accent, without embarrassment and without any of the self-conscious grim theorizing of pretentious literary folks. Every time I had a piece published in the magazine, he would come into my office, shake his head, and screw up his face in that familiar expression of puzzlement and admiration. He would then recite bits from the story, and laugh with unconcealed generosity and enjoyment. When I read anything of his, I was often unable to speak; I would look at him in awe. We could talk endlessly about writing. At that point in my life, it was inconceivable that there was anything else to being alive.

I would say that I could feel the writing coming from somewhere but couldn't say where. He never made me feel that I sounded silly or outlandish. "Damn!" Joe would say. "It's the damndest thing." Then we would talk about the "mystique," the way it felt, while writing, that someone else was doing it for you. "It's that thing, that thing that takes hold of your fingers? It's doin' it for you, isn't it?" And he would shake his head from side to side and laugh in wonder.

What Joe Mitchell called "that thing" is indefinable. Readers, I know, respond to it. The nicest compliments have come from readers who say: "You make me feel that I am right there with you."

KINGS OF QUEENS

TO FIND OUT WHAT is going on in China or in Israel or in California or in Kansas, I need and depend on the work of other journalists. My admiration for what I read in *The New York Times* or in *The Nation* or in the *Wall Street Journal* is unbounded. I could never do what their reporters do. I am overwhelmed by Marie Brenner's hard, factual reporting in *Vanity Fair*. I compulsively open *The New York Times* first thing every Wednesday and Sunday to Maureen Dowd's column. My Saturday doesn't start until I've read what Frank Rich in that newspaper has to say about what's going on in the USA. I listen reverently to what National Public Radio reporters and commentators come up with. In the *Times,* I used to look for Deborah Sontag's reports from Israel, but I would never be able to go there to do her kind of work. I depend on Rick Hertzberg or Joe Klein of *The New Yorker* or on Jim Hoagland in the *Washington Post* for insight into political machinations. I read newspaper stories about the entertainment business that give me background information for what I might want to do. But the stories I write grow only out of what I see and hear myself.

A straight news story in *The New York Times* (the kind I don't write) not only tells me the basic facts I want to know, but it also often sets me off to report and write a piece that intrigues *me*. From that aforementioned newspaper:

> March 8, 1995. Late Edition. Final. Page 1.
> Headline: DEATH PENALTY IN NEW YORK REIN-
> STATED AFTER 18 YEARS; PATAKI SEES JUSTICE
> SERVED
> ALBANY. MARCH 7.
> Gov. George E. Pataki fulfilled one of his central campaign vows today by signing a death penalty bill into law, making New York the 38th State with capital punishment.
> Mr. Pataki used two pens that belonged to slain police officers in a bill-signing ceremony with all the choreographed flourish of one of his stump events. . . .
> The measure passed by a 94–52 vote in the Democratic-controlled Assembly at 4:37 this morning after nearly 12 hours of debate. It passed in the Republican-controlled Senate by a 38–19 vote. . . .

Accompanying the 1,024-word story was a photograph of Governor Pataki signing the bill and another photograph with the following caption:

"Assemblyman Anthony S. Seminerio, a Queens Democrat, arguing in support of a death penalty bill early yesterday at the Capitol in Albany. The Assembly passed the measure shortly after 4:30 A.M."

The New York Times didn't say anything else about Assemblyman Seminerio. To me, the story would be about Seminerio, as a politician, as a man, in his milieu. That morning I telephoned him in his Albany, N.Y., office. He told me he was being given a party in Queens the next day and invited me to attend. So I did. Here is the story I wrote for The Talk of the Town, published in *The New Yorker*—"In Queens, a King and His Courtiers" (1995):

> Last week, a day after watching Governor Pataki sign the death penalty into law, Anthony Seminerio, the Democratic state

assemblyman from Queens (Ozone Park, Richmond Hill, Glen-
dale, etc.) and a co-sponsor of the bill, drove his Ford Crown
Victoria in the pouring rain from Albany to Queens, where,
at La Bella Vita restaurant and catering hall, on Rockaway
Boulevard, his election committee was giving its annual fund-
raising dinner for him. In the state legislature, Seminerio—sixty,
a former corrections officer, very friendly, very popular, very
ample in girth—is given to saluting his colleagues (Democrats,
Republicans, and Conservatives alike) on both cheeks with kisses.
In Queens, where he maintains two district offices, with coffee
and doughnuts available throughout the day and evening to all
who enter, and where, he says, "when someone walks in off the
street he's treated the same like if I knew him for twenty years,"
he is called "our most beloved assemblyman." In his assembly
district of the past seventeen years, the thirty-eighth, every-
body refers to him as Tony. And nobody ever assumes you might
be talking about any of the thousands of other Tonys in the
neighborhood.

In La Bella Vita, with the dinner scheduled to start at six,
Tony was there half an hour early. His campaign treasurer, Arlene
Pedone—cheerful, energetic, hoarse-voiced, eyeglassed, earringed,
with freshly coifed graying brown hair—sat at the entrance table,
opposite mirrors on a red brick wall and facing one stairway lead-
ing up and another one down to the rooms of the dinner. Arlene
was assisted by a couple of duplicates of herself with lists in
hand for checking off the names of the arrivals. Even as the con-
stituents opened their mouths to announce to Tony their names
and their organizations, Tony was hugging every man and every
woman and kissing each one on both cheeks. Arlene was accept-
ing happily presented checks ("No cash. Never give us cash.")
for tickets at a hundred and twenty-five dollars each. The con-
stituents crowded in, many of them also ample in girth and wear-
ing shiny suits, walking in a rocking, sidewise gait, as though
stepping, football-training style, amid tires.

"This is party time!" Tony said exuberantly. "Everybody's com-
ing! Three hundred and seventy people are coming to pay their

respects! The Corrections Captains Association! The Jamaica
Hospital Medical Center. The New York Center P.B.A. The
Continental Post of the American Legion. The Forest Park
Jewish Center. The Knights of Pythias! Judges! Retired judges!
Ex-district leaders! Only, my wife had to stay home with the
flu. But they're all here, my son, two daughters, my son-in-law,
my other son-in-law, my brothers, my sisters, my Aunt Betty,
my granddaughter, four months old!" To the President of the
Sergeants Benevolent Association he said, "Go upstairs and hold
my four-month-old granddaughter. She'll love you. . . ."

Upstairs, the constituents visited the bar, attacked giant
tureens of spaghetti, penne, mussels, meatballs, beef stew, egg-
plant parmigiana, and salad, and listened to someone bang out
"I've Got You Under My Skin" on an electronic keyboard. . . .
Tony found his granddaughter, wearing a white dress and a white
tiara, uncomplaining and politically cooperative as he handed her
around from one constituent to another.

"Tony, where's Giuliani?" someone asked.

"He had a function, otherwise he'da been here," Tony said. "He
worked for me in the election when I needed him. I worked for
him, he worked for me."

"Tony's people cut across all lines," Arlene said.

"Tony!" someone said. "I hear you had a rough session. An all-
nighter."

"Only till four-thirty in the morning. It was nothing," Tony
said. It was the evening's only reference—and an oblique one, at
that—to the passage of the death-penalty bill.

"We don't have to talk about it," Arlene said. "Everyone knows
Tony is reflecting the will of his constituents."

Then Tony took the microphone from the electronic-keyboard
man and addressed his constituents. "Without you lovely people,
there's no Tony Seminerio," he said. "Now I'm gonna sing." And
he did. He sang "Heart of My Heart."

Every word of the story above is selected carefully. The first
paragraph identifies Seminiero, indicating his role in the passage of

the death penalty bill; his political personality; his local base of power. Then he's shown in action at his party in relation to his constituents as he uses even his baby granddaughter to ingratiate himself with his supporters. Finally, his attitude toward the death penalty bill is characterized. The story ends with his singing "Heart of My Heart." All elements are revealed with facts, quotes, and actions; my own views are implied in what I chose to use.

New York has many power-figures, heads of large corporations and enterprises whose personalities and characters paradoxically camouflage their expertise, their finesse, their wiliness, and even their wealth. I like them. So many of them are funny, and they make me laugh. What they do in their work makes me laugh. They often remind me, one way or another, of L. B. Mayer. I liked him, too.

Here's part of a Talk story from 1986 entitled "Sam," about a real estate mogul originally from Queens, another kind of king and his courtiers.

Samuel Jayson LeFrak, the chairman of the Lefrak Organization, which is the nation's largest private developer and builder of apartment houses, is sixty-eight, fast-talking, loud-talking, and hardworking, with a heavy appearance, vaguely suggestive of an ex-fullback, and with the refreshingly self-appreciative manner of one who clearly likes what he is doing and the way he is doing it. He wears silver-framed aviator-style bifocals, sports on his left little finger a gold college ring with an almost dime-size ruby in the middle (University of Maryland, Class of '40), keeps a long cigar in his mouth ("I'm a chewer, not a smoker"), dresses conservatively (navy-blue blazer, matching pants, too tight shirts, bright knit ties), and tears around the metropolitan area in a telephone-equipped car from one to another of his three offices (Forest Hills, West Fifty-seventh Street, Battery Park City) and to his buildings.

He escorts on tours of his properties ambassadors, opera singers, friends, and relatives—wife, Ethel; grown children Denise, Richard (president, as of 1975, of the L.O.), James, twelve ("Richard's sons; they're already reading leases"); and

granddaughters Allison, twenty, and Jennifer, seventeen—and
trailing behind, usually, are one or more of his seventeen vice-
presidents (in charge of engineering and construction, in charge
of management, in charge of finances, etc.).

Mr. LeFrak ("Call me Sam," he says to anyone who spends
more than five minutes with him and still addresses him as Mr.
LeFrak, and "Call me anything, but don't call me late for break-
fast" to anyone asking whether the name should be pronounced
*Lef*rak, as in the Organization, or Le*Frak,* as after Sam, the latter
being the original pronunciation of the family name in Paris,
from which Harry LeFrak, Sam's father and the Organization's
founder, migrated) is very fond of all his apartment houses,
including those built by Harry before 1948, when Sam took
over as president. It was Sam who gave names to the houses.
When the L.O. was building apartment houses in Queens, Sam
started naming them after states. "After I used up the states,
through the Hawaii, I went to trees—The Elm, The Beech,
The Walnut, The Maple, eleven trees—and then I started on the
colleges—Harvard, Colgate, Cornell, Oxford, through twenty-six
colleges. Then I went to the Presidents and used them all, but
only through The Lincoln, to avoid the modern."

The other afternoon, in the Battery Park City office of the
L.O., Mr. LeFrak waited with Maxwell Goldpin, his vice-
president in charge of acquisitions, for the arrival of Frank
K. Takabe, who is the president of the North America Taisei
Corporation, a Japan-based engineering and construction firm
that had expressed interest in the possibility of participating in
the L.O.'s current project: Newport City, where the L.O., with
the help of associates, built six huge apartment buildings, all with
uniform window-wall façades and classical architecture, of dark
brown and beige exposed concrete. The office that Mr. LeFrak
and Mr. Goldpin sat in—across from each other at a long
mahogany conference table capable of seating twenty—was
on the first floor, directly over a parking garage and adjoining
St. Joseph's Chapel, a part of the edifice, and under thirty-three
stories of apartments, all with large closets and all with built-in

computers. Mr. Goldpin is a neat, pleasant man in his late fifties who has worked for the L.O. for thirty-six years. . . . Before buying a house in Roslyn, Mr. Goldpin lived in The Washington, in Forest Hills. They ate lunch: tuna and sliced tomato on a kaiser roll with poppy seeds for Mr. LeFrak, and American cheese and tomato on rye for the vice-president, with a Tab for each.

Outside four huge windows was the Liberty Street Esplanade (skateboarders, baby carriages, strollers, picnickers), which looks out on a splendid view of the Statue of Liberty, Ellis Island, the Hoboken Terminal, the New Jersey Turnpike, and, along the six-mile waterfront area on the west bank of the Hudson, the beginnings of Newport City, spotted with cranes, pile drivers, the outlines of the first six concrete floors of a planned thirty-four story office center, and the outlines of the first three floors of the initial thirty-four-story apartment house, which Mr. LeFrak has already named The George Washington of New Jersey.

"The Japanese are coming over, Mac, and I tell you," Mr. LeFrak said, chewing on his tuna-and-tomato with zest. "I don't need their money."

"You always told me the greatest privilege a person can have is to say no," Mr. Goldpin said.

"I like to serve the mass, not the class," Mr. LeFrak said. "I'm pleased that I can serve the people. Larger closets for less money! That's an achievement. Where I'm going you can't take stocks and bonds. What was Battery Park in 1968, before we got here? Rotting piers! We built Battery Park City. I gave fifteen years of my life to this." He waved at the windows. "Now across the river we'll have Baghdad on the Hudson. Twenty times the size of what we've built here. The largest development in the world! Affordable housing! A place for the Yuppies! We'll build a hundred and twenty-one million square feet of buildings. That's thirty World Trade Centers."

"Certain people are motivated mainly by money," Mr. Goldpin said. "Not you."

"What's my objective?" Mr. LeFrak asked, and answered himself: "Heaven!"

"Sam, you're a genius," Mr. Goldpin said. "You know it. I know it, everybody knows it."

. . . They finished their lunch and gazed out the windows toward the rising Newport City. . . .

Frank K. Takabe arrived, shook hands with Mr. LeFrak and Mr. Goldpin, and handed each of them, with a very slight bow, his card. A stocky, strong-looking gentleman, gray-haired, with heavy sideburns and heavy eyebrows, he, too, had on silver-rimmed aviator-style spectacles, but his were tinted. With Mr. LeFrak, it was immediately "Frank," and with Mr. Takabe, minutes later, "Sam." Mr. Goldpin left.

"Frank, we're going to create the eighth wonder of the world," Mr. LeFrak said. . . .

VISITORS

MY STORY "The Yellow Bus" (1960), about a group of high school seniors from Indiana visiting New York, was a new kind of hill to climb, requiring some shifting of gears in the approach. As I went along in reporting it, I felt that I was being handed glorious gifts in the form of jigsaw puzzle pieces, very similar to shots for a movie that had to be edited together to make a whole. It taught me to watch for a situation, involving a sizeable group of people unknown to me, who were going to participate in a common experience unknown to them. Doing "The Yellow Bus" taught me how to handle action. Permission to replicate copies of the piece, in the intervening decades, is still requested several times a year by journalism teachers. Apparently, I'm pleased to hear, it's called a "cult" piece.

I had been alerted by an acquaintance to a plan of eighteen seniors from the Bean Blossom Township High School, in the village of Stinesville, about twenty miles from Bloomington, Indiana, to come to New York as a group on a bus in order to celebrate their graduation. All were coming to the city for the first time, chaperoned by their twenty-eight-year-old English teacher. The bus driver

and the teacher's husband, a thirty-two-year-old political science graduate student at Indiana University in Bloomington, were the only others in the party.

In order to get the story moving, I first had to establish a solid factual basis; I found the necessary facts as I got to know the students and their chaperone. But I wanted to write this one in the third person, with action, and I wanted it to be visual for the reader, like a film. Also, I wanted the eighteen characters to reveal, in their quotes, how they responded to the new stimulus of the big city of New York.

To learn when they were coming, I telephoned the teacher, and arranged to meet the bus. Thus, I was able to start my story this way:

> A few Sundays ago, in the late, still afternoon, a bright-yellow school bus, bearing the white-on-blue license plate of the State of Indiana and with the words "BEAN BLOSSOM TWP MONROE COUNTY" painted in black letters under the windows on each side, emerged into New York City from the Holland Tunnel. Inside the bus were eighteen members of the senior class of the Bean Blossom Township High School, who were coming to the city for their first visit. The windows of the bus, as it rolled out into Canal Street, were open, and a few of the passengers leaned out, dead-pan and silent, looking at each other.

Then, I quickly sketched in the essential facts as background for the ensuing action and quotes to play against.

> Stinesville has three-hundred and fifty-five inhabitants and a town pump. The visitors had driven eight hundred and forty miles in thirty-nine and a half hours. Each senior had fifty dollars to spend, and the group had a fund of $957.41, which they had saved up for six years from profits on candy concessions at basket-ball games and other activities. The money would cover the cost of motels and hotels. Earlier that year, they had voted for the trip. Some of the boys had wanted to go to New Orleans instead, but they were out-voted by all the girls and the rest of the boys, who wanted New York. The chaperone/English teacher said that the

Bean Blossom school was the most democratic school she had ever seen. "They vote on everything," she said. "We have an average of two votes on something or other every day." The senior class president was in charge of all the voting on the trip. He was one of the two members of the senior class who planned to go to college. The other class members expected, for the most part, to get secretarial or clerical jobs, or to work in automobile or electronic parts factories in Bloomington. The New York trip was in the nature of a first and last fling. The lone veteran visitor among them was the bus driver, who was also their advice-giver on where to stay (the Hotel Woodstock on West Forty-third Street) and where to eat (Hector's Cafeteria, around the corner from the hotel).

The facts are essential as a cushion for the action. The story gave an account of where the visitors ate (unhappily, at Hector's): "My ma cooks better than this" or "I like the kind of place you just set there and decide what you want" or "Man, you can keep this New York. This place is too hustly, with everybody pushin' and no privacy. Man, I'll take the Bib Boy any old day."

The class president polled his classmates on what they wanted to do on their first night.

At first, nobody wanted to do anything special. Then they decided that the only special thing they wanted to do was to go to Coney Island, but they wanted to save Coney Island for the wind-up night, their last night in New York. However, nobody could think of anything to do that first night.

In a re-vote, everybody voted to go to Coney Island right away.

They stayed in Coney Island about an hour. Nobody went up to the boardwalk to take a look at the ocean, which none of the class had ever seen. They didn't feel they had to look at the ocean. "We knew the ocean was there."

There were passages of interchanges among the visitors that I chose to write. Here's one:

The next morning, a meeting of the class was held in the hotel lobby to take a vote on when to leave New York. Jay Bowman reported that they had enough money to cover an extra day in the city, plus a side trip to Niagara Falls on the way home. Or, he said, they could leave New York when they had originally planned to and go to Washington, D.C., for a day before heading home. . . . The class voted for the extra day in New York and Niagara Falls.

"I'm glad," Becky Kiser said, with a large, friendly smile, to Dennis Smith. Several of her classmates overheard her and regarded her with a uniformly deadpan look. "I like it here," she went on. "I'd like to live here. There's so much to see. There's so much to do."

Her classmates continued to study her impassively until Dennis Smith took their eyes away from her by saying: "You get a feeling here of goin' wherever you want to. Seems the city never closes. I'd like to live here, I believe. People from everyplace are here."

"Limousines all over the joint," Albert Warthan said.

"Seems like you can walk and walk and walk," Dennis went on dreamily. "I like the way the big buildin's crowd you in. You want to walk and walk and never go to sleep."

"I hate it," Connie Williams said with passion.

"Oh, man, you're just not lookin' ahead," Mike Richardson said to Dennis. "You got a romantic notion. You're not realistic about it."

"This place couldn't hold me," Larry Williams said. "I like the privacy of the farm."

"I want to go to new places," said Becky, who had started it. "I want to go to Europe."

"Only place I want to go is Texas," Larry said. "I got folks in Texas."

"There's no place like home," Mike said. "Home's good enough for me."

"I believe the reason of this is we've lived all of our lives around Stinesville," Dennis said. "If you took Stinesville out of the country, you wouldn't be hurt. But if you took New York out of the country, you'd be hurt. The way the guide said, all our clothes and

everything comes from New York. . . ."

"I hate New York," Connie said.

The story ended as follows:

> On their last evening in New York, all the boys and girls, accompanied by the Wattses, went to the Radio City Music Hall, making it in time to see the stage show. Then they packed and went to bed. . . .
>
> Next morning, at five-forty-five, the Bean Blossomers assembled in the lobby; for the first time since the trip had started, nobody was late. The bus pulled out at exactly 6 A.M., and twenty minutes after that, heading west over the George Washington Bridge, it disappeared from the city.

Unlike other stories, the characterization of individuals in "The Yellow Bus" was very light, just enough to support the characterization of the group as a whole in their limited capacity to respond, or pitiful inability to respond, to what was being offered to them. Perhaps this piece is a kind of Profile of a part of U.S. society that is closed off—or that closes itself off—from feelings of curiosity and wonder and excitement in life. Still, there is humor in the way these high school kids resisted being touched by New York. To me, it's funny to hear Connie say, "I hate New York."

Humor often makes my stories into stories. For me, it's the essential ingredient. Humor, after all, is pervasive in life. There is always truth in humor. If there's a point to be made by the writer in a story, it can be made with facts and with quotes that have humor and irony. It's humor that drives a story. It's the key to originality and power in reporting. This reporter couldn't live, let alone work, without laughing.

In 1945, I wrote my first Talk of the Town story, about another kind of visitor who made me laugh. It was called "One Man's Family," about twenty-four-year-old Ahmad-Abdul Jabbar, who was staying at the Waldorf with his Saudi Arabian United Nations delegation. I didn't know, when I set out to do the story, what a "sheik" was, so I came to this one without any preconceptions.

My ignorance made it possible to start laughing immediately, because Ahmad-Abdul Jabbar was a cynical, sophisticated, self-confident, upfront, English-speaking sheik, and he made no bones about how he was here to have a good time. He was. . .

> a short, chubby sheik . . . dressed in a white igal, white kufaya, white aba, white balto, maroon socks, and thick-soled maroon oxfords. He was humming "I'm the Sheik of Araby," as we arrived and a moment afterward broke into "Alexander's Ragtime Band." He was soon interrupted by music from another room. He smiled patiently. "Small Prince Nawaf is playing his records again," he said. "His Royal Highness discovered a music shop in Brooklyn that sells Arabic records. He has purchased a large collection. He plays them until three in the morning. Some of us cannot sleep. Personally, I would prefer to listen to hot jazz, but he is the Prince."

The humor was there—waiting for the writer.

The Sheik told me that he loved to go shopping at Brooks Brothers, as did the other sheiks and princes in the delegation.

> "We all bought pin-striped business suits. We were very uncomfortable when we wore the igal and aba in public. We would immediately be surrounded by several strange ladies. At least one of them was bound to tell us that we reminded her of Rudolph Valentino. As you know, it is not our custom to speak to strange ladies. Once I went three years without speaking to a single lady."
> . . . Sheik Jabbar told us that he had limited his shopping to inexpensive earrings, bracelets, and necklaces for his four sisters and shaving sets for his friends. "I'm no prince," he said. "I'd rather spend what money I have on cheeseburgers."
> We asked if we could meet the small Prince Nawaf. He was still in the next room under the guardian eye of a city detective. The Prince is thin, dark, and very active. He wears long pants and knows four words of English—"hello," "goodbye," "O.K.," and "cinema." Through an interpreter, he informed us that he is in the fourth grade at the School for Princes back home and that he

studies geography, history, geometry, and religion. When he was at the Waldorf, he spent a couple of hours every morning on his schoolwork, and then, accompanied by the detective, he got into a livery Cadillac and explored the city. Among the places he and the detective visited were Palisades Park, Jones Beach, Rockaway Beach, and Coney Island. At Coney Island, the Prince bought cotton candy, corn on the cob, whistles, dolls, and comic hats, and enjoyed eighteen consecutive rides on the Dodgem. Prince Nawaf went back to Coney Island so many times that his big brother, Prince Faisal, got curious and went out there too.

COME IN, LASSIE!

"**C**OME IN, LASSIE!" one of my first long reporting pieces for *The New Yorker*, appeared in February, 1948. What I learned about reporting in tackling this story has stayed with me to this day. It was the first of a line of mileposts that led me to a series of challenging subjects, each one of which added to a kind of storehouse of working patterns. In this first one, I came into unfamiliar territory, had to make contacts with people to provide required information, and found and developed a clear theme for my narrative. In all of this, I discovered literary forms that grew out of the nature of the material. I used those forms, and they were exciting and indispensable.

Several months earlier, newspaper stories had told about some Hollywood people in the movie business who had been blacklisted by the studios because they had been charged with contempt of Congress for refusing to tell the House Committee on un-American Activities what political party, if any, they belonged to. The newspaper stories told me what was happening in Hollywood, but I wanted to do my own story about what it felt like in that atmosphere; how the celebrated figures in the motion

picture industry were responding to the situation; whether the
kinds of movies being made might be different from those being
made before the HUAC investigation. So I went to Hollywood. I
telephoned Bill Shawn, and we talked about what I might find for
my piece in *The New Yorker.*

Although I had visited Hollywood for the first time as a student,
I had not had entrée to anything or anyone. Now I was still young
enough to be overwhelmed by the place. I had no contacts, so I
simply telephoned the studios and told their publicity people I was
in town to do a story. Heady stuff immediately came my way.
Everybody in the business, I learned, was eager to talk to me.
Movie stars. Directors. Producers. I was invited to big, lavish par-
ties. The display of wealth was mind-boggling. The film sets were
mesmerizing. Glamorous restaurants had fabulous food. Almost
immediately, wherever I turned, I sensed what my story would be.
Nervousness and uncertainty were all around me.

People in the movie business then were the same as they are
now; they had varying and interesting degrees of talent, skills,
charisma, intellect, egotism, affluence, power, stardom, visibility,
and success, all of which were attuned, in this small community, to
very big money and what big money buys. Somehow or other, folks
in the place—more than any other place—always seemed to har-
bor gigantic stores of self-preoccupation, slaphappy self-indul-
gence, ample hedonism, and a big concentration of neediness to be
loved. People wanted to talk about the political investigation. I
found my facts rather easily.

> Hollywood is baffled by the question of what the Committee on
> un-American Activities wants from it. People here are wonder-
> ing, with some dismay and anxiety, what kind of strange, brood-
> ing alienism the committee is trying to eliminate from their
> midst, and, in fact whether it was ever here. They are waiting
> hopefully for Chairman J. Parnell Thomas, or Congress, or
> God, to tell them.

Before proceeding further, I owed the reader a quick summary
of what had led up to the situation:

They have been waiting in vain ever since last November, when
eight writers, a producer, and a director—often collectively referred
to these days as "the ten writers"—were blacklisted. . . . In the
meantime, business, bad as it is, goes on. The place is more ner-
vous than usual, but it is doing the same old simple things in the
same old simple ways. The simplicities of life in Hollywood are
not, of course, like those anywhere else.

I was able to get the story moving quickly with some action. I
then gave examples of cowardice, weakness, self-deception, and
idiocy in past Hollywood (and perhaps present Hollywood, too) as
well as desperation to be "safe" and to find "safe" subjects for
movies. It doesn't work in good writing to make such observations
baldly. I like to make the statements with facts and with quotes.
The story stated this fact, for instance:

> Almost the only motion-picture star who is taking conditions in
> his stride is Lassie, a reddish-haired male collie (a movie star at
> M-G-M) who is probably too mixed up emotionally over being
> called by a girl's name to worry about the box office. Lassie is
> working more steadily, not only in films but on the radio, than
> anyone else in Hollywood.

Carefully selected quotes made important points:

> At an upper bracket party not long ago, a Selznick man intro-
> duced to me as Merve told me that he was appalled and outraged
> by the blacklisting of the ten writers. "It's a damn shame," Merve
> said, beaming at me. "Those human beings got a right to think
> or believe anything without letting Washington in on their ideas.
> They can't put their ideas into Hollywood pictures. Nobody can."

Then I quoted the *Gone with the Wind* producer Sam Wood:

> "I say make every damn Communist stand up and be counted.
> They're a danger and a discredit to the industry!"
> Merve continued to beam. "Make *every* radical, every Socialist,
> and every Anarchist stand up and be counted," he said expansively.
> "We ought to get every one of them out of the industry."

Using quotes in this way, I was able to characterize typical industry people who easily adjust to flip-flopping. I gave further examples. They were funny and surprising, demonstrating a kind of conduct that might in other circles be considered amoral.

The political self-consciousness at parties is, on the whole, rather cheerful. "I never cut anybody before this," one actress remarked happily to me. "Now I don't go anywhere without cutting at least half a dozen former friends."

To reinforce my characterization of the rampant mindless insecurities and fears caused by intimidation of people afraid of being called "communists," I told about the actor Fredric March having been called to account. . .

because he had given an ambulance to Loyalist Spain. Then it turned out that Mr. March had also given an ambulance to Finland when she was at war with Russia. "I was just a big ambulance-giver," March told the investigators. "I just like to give ambulances," he told a HUAC head, who replied firmly, "Well, then, Mr. March. Before you give any more ambulances away, you go out and consult your local Chamber of Commerce, or the American Legion, and they'll tell you whether it's all right."

Longtime fixtures in the movie business were up front and direct with me about what was happening to them:

Rumors that the F.B.I. is going to take over casting operations at the studios are discounted by those who lived in Hollywood for more than fifteen years. The casting director at Metro-Goldwyn-Mayer, a fidgety, cynical, sharply-dressed, red-cheeked man named Billy Grady, Sr., who has worked in Hollywood for nearly twenty years, thinks that it would serve J. Edgar Hoover right if casting of actors were handed over to the F.B.I. "Hoover thinks *he's* got worries!" Grady shouted at me in a Hollywood restaurant. "What does a G-man do? A G-man send guys to Alcatraz! Ha! I'd like to see a G-man find a script about Abraham Lincoln's doctor in which we could work in a part for Lassie. What do you find inside

of Alcatraz? Picture stars? Directors? Cameramen? No! The god-
dam place is full of doctors, lawyers, and politicians. This is the
fourth biggest industry in the country, and only three men in this
industry ever went to jail. There are fifty thousand people in this
industry, and all they want is the right to take up hobbies. Spencer
Tracy takes up painting. Clark Gable takes up Idaho. Dalton
Trumbo, who got the sack, takes up deep thinking. Take away their
hobbies and they're unhappy. For God's sake, Tracy doesn't paint
when he's acting. Gable doesn't shoot ducks. Trumbo doesn't think
when he's writing for pictures. I say let them keep their goddam
hobbies. They're all a bunch of capitalists anyway."

The story indicated that a number of actors and producers,
including Charlie Chaplin, said they were planning to go to
England, France, or Italy, where they believed they would be free
to make the kind of pictures they liked.

Jack L. Warner, busiest of the Brothers, is genially inclined to bol-
ster up the courage of those who are ready to throw in the towel.
"Don't worry!" he roars, slapping the backs of the lesser men
around him. "Congress can't last forever!"

In doing this story, I met for the first time the director John
Huston, about whom I would write in connection with his movie
adventures, here and there, over the next several decades. I liked
him and his movies, and I enjoyed being around him. He and his
entire family would eventually become my friends. In this initial
meeting, I had lunch with him and several cast members of *Key
Largo,* the movie he was then making. It was an adaptation of a
Maxwell Anderson play with Humphrey Bogart, Lauren Bacall,
Edward G. Robinson, and Lionel Barrymore. Bogart, one of the
stars of the movie, had announced a couple of months earlier, that
a recent trip he had made to Washington with others—to protest
against the methods of the un-American Activities Committee—
had been a mistake.

I made some exciting journalistic discoveries at the lunch that I
would use for years to come:

The actors were in a gay mood. They had just finished rehearsing a scene (one of the new economies at Warner is to have a week of rehearsals before starting to film a picture) in which Bogart is taunted by Robinson, a gangster representing evil, for his cowardice, but is comforted by the gangster's moll, who tells Bogart, "Never mind. It's better to be a live coward than a dead hero." Bogart had not yet reached the point where a guy learns he must fight against evil. Huston was feeling particularly good, because he had just won a battle with the studio to keep in the film some lines from Franklin Roosevelt's message to the Seventy-seventh Congress on January 6, 1942—"But we of the United nations are not making all this sacrifice of human effort and human lives to return to the kind of world we had after the last world war."

"The big shots wanted Bogie to say this in his own words," Huston explained, "but I insisted that Roosevelt's words were better."

Bogart nodded. "Roosevelt was a good politician," he said. "He could handle those babies in Washington, but they're too smart for guys like me. Hell, I'm no politician. That's what I meant when I said our Washington trip was a mistake."

"Bogie has succeeded in not being a politician," said Huston, who went to Washington with him. "Bogie owns a fifty-four-foot yawl. When you own a fifty-four-foot yawl, you've got to provide for her upkeep."

"The Great Chief died and everybody's guts died with him," Robinson said, looking stern.

"How would you like to see *your* picture on the front page of the Communist paper of Italy?" asked Bogart.

"Nyah," Robinson said, sneering.

"The *Daily Worker* runs Bogie's picture and right away he's a dangerous Communist," said Miss Bacall, who is, as everybody must know, Bogart's wife. "What will happen if the American Legion and the Legion of Decency boycott all his pictures?"

"It's just that my picture in the *Daily Worker* offends me, Baby," said Bogart.

"Nyah," said Robinson.
"Let's eat," said Huston.

That natural, revelatory interchange, happening right before me, with the participants knowing I was there to write about them, showed me a new way to report. I immediately knew on the spot what I was going to write and how I would write it. I learned how to set the stage with facts, find the essential characters and their dialogue, and Go! The tiny but essential "Let's eat" touch, to me, was, and remains, enormously important, wrapping up the scene with humor and simultaneously delineating the entire interaction of Huston and the other characters. The scene was a big hit with readers of *The New Yorker,* especially in Hollywood. The story is an example of how dozens of little touches pile up to give the reader a clear picture of a situation.

"Come In, Lassie!" taught me how to watch and wait for the interactions of my characters. A few years later, I had the technique of writing dramatic scenes with factual material well under control. For my first book, *Picture* (1952), for example, Shawn pointed out that "the story, while wholly factual, takes the form of a novel." I had told him when I started to report the story that it was exciting and challenging, because it was "novelistic." I told him at the outset that I was going to write a long piece—about the filming of Stephen Crane's *The Red Badge of Courage*—in the form of a novel. It eventually became the book *Picture.*

"Come In, Lassie!" was published in early 1948, and it marked the beginning of my forty-year-long friendship with John Huston, who was then forty-two years old. I admired and respected him enormously from the moment I heard him say, "Let's eat!" We remained friends—and his wife, Ricki, and children, Tony, Anjelica, Allegra, and Danny, also became my friends. In 1987, a few days before he died, John telephoned my son and me from his Newport, Rhode Island, location for *Mr. North,* the movie he was producing from a screenplay he wrote that his son Danny was going to direct. He had hoped to act in the movie, but had fallen ill, and his part would be played by Robert Mitchum. Huston left us a message on

our answering machine: "I'm all right," he said. "I'm just fine, dar-
lings!" he said, in his extraordinary, mellifluous voice.

Fifty-three years ago, when I first wrote about Huston, I didn't
know that our friendship would continue, that he would regularly
be available every few years or so as a subject. Working as a reporter
all these years has given me that very special kind of privilege, not
only with Huston but with others in ensuing years. For me it has
been a great and continuing gift, as well as wonderful fun.

"Come In, Lassie!" also was the beginning of heartening en-
couragement from Harold Ross, who had been admittedly skepti-
cal of having women at his magazine. In the recently published
Modern Library book of his distinctive, funny, spirited letters, the
editor, Thomas Kunkel, included a copy of one from Ross to me
dated March 4, 1948, saying:

> I have received the following telegram from Hollywood:
> "Dear Harold: Lillian Ross's superb job only serves to support
> my belief that that rag of yours is the best magazine ever published
> —Regards—John Huston."
> This kind of thing is no more than I expected. H. W. Ross

In the same book of letters, there is one replying to a query
from James M. Cain, who "had complimented the editor on Lillian
Ross's controversial Profile of Ernest Hemingway."

> Dear Jim: Thanks for the letter, on behalf of Miss Ross and the
> magazine. It has kicked up many expressions of admiration from
> writers, at least; God know what readers think of things, ever,
> but writers recognize great work.
> I'll tell Miss Ross, to whom I can claim no relationship,
> although I'm thinking of adopting her.
> Glad to have heard from you. Carry on.
> As ever, Ross

That kind of praise is what young talent needs and feeds on. I
would hope that anyone, especially under the age of thirty, reading
this book finds, or knows how to seek, that kind of editorial appre-
ciation. I've had more than my share. It is essential.

It has always seemed to me, in all my reporting years, that each succeeding story was different from the preceding ones, each requiring special preparation and thought, each presenting a new challenge. Creating a story, especially about real people and real events, is as necessary a part of my life as breathing, eating, walking in Central Park (and checking out everybody and everybody's babies, both known and unknown). It is, moreover, in a class with love and sex. It puts me, as they say, "in another zone." Each story, actually, is like a human being; of all the billions of people in the world, past and present, each one is different from the other. To me, so is each story.

A good half century after "Come In, Lassie!," I am still using essentially the same methods. In the waning hours of the first year of our new millennium, for example, I wrote the Talk story entitled "An Analog Toast to the Digital Age." It was about a party celebrating the fifth anniversary of the PBS talk show, with the lawyer James Goodale as host, called *The Digital Age*. The story began: "It was name-dropping paradise the other night in the Four Seasons Grill Room." It described the party floor as holding . . .

a lot of people who had appeared on the show discussing such *Digital Age* topics as "Is There a Place for Two Tabloids in N.Y.C.?" (Mort Zuckerman); "If I Were to Do It All Over Again in the Digital Age" (Dan Rather); and "Can an All-Newspaper Company Make It?" (Arthur Sulzberger, Jr.).

Right off the bat, the *Digital Age* alumna Robin Byrd turned up, grinning to beat the band and partaking of the lobster and caviar canapés. She was wearing an Austrian crystal-studded leather bustier, black leather pants, and black patent-leather mules with six-inch stiletto heels.

"This is a great mix," she said enthusiastically, looking around the room and spotting Dan Rather, William Bratton, Howell Raines, Mike Bloomberg, Charlie Rose, Peter Duchin, Carl Bernstein, and Kenneth Starr. "It looks like not many are under the age of fifty or sixty. Nobody's talking digital to me. . . . I

pioneered cable twenty-five years ago. . . . I have a Web site . . . all
that digital means to me is higher electric bills."

Victor Navasky, who is the publisher and editorial director of
The Nation, and who has an elegant, patriarchal white beard, said
he wasn't digital either. . . . He said he had assigned one of his
students at the Columbia School of Journalism to come to the
party. "I asked her to find out if the media elite go to parties with
each other in order to do business together," he said. "And, if so, is
that a good thing or a bad thing?"

Ben Bradlee said he was at the party because of his wife and
said, "It has nothing to do with the digital age, if that's what we're
in. I use my computer only as a word processor. I don't do E-mail
or go on-line."

"Me neither," said Morley Safer, the *60 Minutes* man. "I'm not
giving up my typewriter."

. . . Mr. Navasky paused at the head of the stairs leading to the
exit. He said that his student had reported back to him about
whether the media elite did business with one another at parties.
The answer, she had told him, was yes, and when she and Navasky
were back in class, somebody would decide whether this was a
good thing or a bad thing.

Listening with your own ears—and not turning the listening
over to a tape recorder—gives one fresh, interesting, and original
quotes that bring the person you're writing about alive. Often, a
reporter substitutes words from his own vocabulary in a quote. If I
find myself doing it—perhaps because, at first, I can't remember
the exact word that was used—it throws the story off balance for
me; it bothers me terribly until I make myself remember—or check
with the subject for—the true word. Quotes work in monologue or
in dialogue, depending on what the sense of the story calls for.
When the subject of a story is an occasion, involving many peo-
ple—a party, or a conference, etc.—all the quotes should serve the
theme of the story.

9/11, 2001

WHAT WAS THERE for journalists like myself to write when we were engulfed by the biggest and most important news story of the century—the tragic attacks of the terrorists in New York and Washington on September 11, 2001? Like most other Americans, I was horrified, stunned, and in tears. At *The New Yorker,* we, too, had friends and families who suffered death, injury, and loss. So it gave me some measure of comfort to be able to participate, with many of my colleagues, in the journalistic effort we at *The New Yorker* made in the coverage of this terrible event. On the morning that the hijacked planes hit the World Trade Center buildings, The Talk of the Town editor, Susan Morrison, suggested to me that I might find some kind of story involving children.

How does one look for such a story in the horror that had suddenly hit us? My mind was almost paralyzed by what was on our television screens. I went out to Central Park and looked around, seeing eerie normalcy in the way folks were going on with their running, giving directions to tourists, pushing the baby strollers, etc., and giving, as an only sign of alarm, response to the sound of a plane overhead by suddenly, in freeze-frame, stopping

and turning their heads to look up at the sky. That was one touch, not a story.

I headed for a nearby public school, and there I found my story, in the principal. His character and actions, relevant to the disaster, were admirable and significant, and I was drawn to him. My little story was published in *The New Yorker* in a somewhat abridged version, together with some remarkable reporting by other writers about the attack. The following is my bit:

When the planes hit the World Trade Center towers, Dan Feigelson, a genial forty-three-year-old six-footer with a dark graying beard, was in the first hour of his fourth day in his job as principal of P.S. 6, a grade school on the Upper East Side. By lunchtime, arrangements had been made to release the students— parents waited in the teachers' lounge while volunteers ferried the children from the classrooms.

"We decided we shouldn't be the first ones to tell the kids about the tragedy," Feigelson said. "We wanted to let the parents decide what and how to tell them."

So the principal and the assistant principal stayed in the school, watching as each child was picked up calmly and quick- ly—until 6 P.M., when the last child, a fourth grader, was finally called for by his aunt, who had to walk north from Twenty-third Street. Feigelson spent the next three hours in his car, getting home to Brooklyn. For twelve years, he had taught fourth grade at P.S. 321 in Brooklyn, a job he loved. "I was doing staff and cur- riculum development for three years, but I wanted to get back to working with kids," Feigelson said. "So now, here I am, with hun- dreds of kids, in addition to three at home."

The next morning, the schools were closed. Feigelson spent several hours at district headquarters—one of forty principals conferring with a study team of New York University psycholo- gists about how to talk clearly to the kids about the tragedy. "Very valuable!" Feigelson said. . . . "My big worry here is about the six- year-olds who sat in front of the TV watching people jumping out of windows. Six-year-olds don't understand death; they think

the dead come back, they want to put food in the coffins. Tomorrow, some of the principals are going to speak at their all-school assembly, but I've decided to go into every class and talk to everybody face to face. I want all the kids to know they're safe, and I want the older ones to be kind to the little ones."

Next day, at 8 A.M., dressed in a neat black suit, pearl gray shirt, and blue necktie, Mr. Feigelson was in his school office, waiting for his teachers. He made sure there were coffee and bagels in the teachers' lounge for the staff and teachers, all of whom had been asked to arrive a couple of hours before the children were due. A motherly-looking NYPD safety officer stationed regularly at the entrance, asked for her bagel to be toasted, and it was. Feigelson touched into place some books on his office shelves—*The Power of Reading* by Krashen; *The Art of Teaching Reading* by Calkins. He straightened a framed photograph on the wall of the Marx Brothers hugging Lou Gehrig in Yankee uniform. He checked a letter he had written that said, "Dear P.S. 6 Parents: We hope that you will help us impart to our precious children that they are safe and cared for."

It was warm in the school. Mr. Feigelson removed his jacket. He said he was a little nervous. With his teachers seated in the school auditorium, he told them, lightly and calmly: "Good morning, staff. Thank you for coming in early. Thanks so much for the impressive way you pulled together to help on Tuesday. You are amazing. . . . We need to help the children so that they feel safe. We'll tell them, 'The school is still here, it's starting two hours late, but everything is the same.'"

There were questions: "Will we have recess outside?" Answer "Yes." "What do you say to the children?" "First of all, be honest. Our kids were glued to the television news. They kept seeing the pictures of the collapse over and over again. We'll make it clear that this happened only once, that this was done by evil people. . . ."

When the children were settled—in twenty-six classrooms—Feigelson said he was going to visit them all, starting with the older children.

"Good morning. Welcome back," he began, with a class of
fifth graders, seated with their teacher in a circle on the floor. He
sat down with them. His face was damp with perspiration. "First
of all, I want to make sure everybody is OK. . . . I want to thank
you for the way you helped two days ago. . . . You guys were
incredible. . . . We're safe here. . . ." Out in the hall, he wiped
the back of a forefinger over his brow.

Next class: "We're here to protect you. . . . You're the fifth
graders. A lot of the little kids look up to you. . . . This is no time
to tease them or to say scary things to them. . . . They need you to
be supportive of them. . . . As our Mayor says, this is no time for
hate . . . we all have to help each other . . ."

The frame of reference of a little story can be immense, but a
little story can help define a particular human being in a bigger
picture, and that is often what I try to do.

ADLAI STEVENSON

T HERE ARE MANY exciting elements in reporting, not the least of which over the years for me has been the opportunity to get to know and write about some pretty special and wonderful people. Moreover, I've been able, after first writing about them, to catch up with a number of them years or decades later, to see what had happened with them, and to write about them again. I've done that, for example, with, among others, Charlie Chaplin, Benny Goodman, John Huston, Ernest Hemingway, François Truffaut, Federico Fellini, Robin Williams, William Alfred, Edward Albee, Harold Pinter, and Adlai Stevenson. Most of them became friends after our initial meeting, but I never experienced conflict of interest; I felt completely free to write as I chose about them. We always had a mutual trust, and the advantage of the familiarity was my having easy accessibility to them.

Adlai Stevenson was one of the famous figures about whom thousands of stories had been written in newspapers, magazines, and books. That didn't deter me. *The New Yorker* always had something new to say. We wanted to know what was going on with him in the years since he lost the presidential elections against

Eisenhower and had been named by President Kennedy as Ambassador to the United Nations.

In June, 1962, about a year-and-a-half after Kennedy named him as U.N. Ambassador, I attended a U.N. Correspondents Association luncheon, at which he informed the guests that he had discovered that his job was "the best in the world for free luncheons." He also said: "When I took the job, I was told I would have a few busy months until the autumn, and then I would be free to go to ball games."

I always felt joyous, listening to Stevenson, whether I wrote about him or not. Writing about him was double icing on the cake. Among his other attributes, he never talked down to people, and I was deeply affected by his eloquence, his warmth, and his wit. In addition to everything else, he was a brilliant and interesting writer; he always wrote his own speeches. He raised politicking in unprecedented ways to the highest level in history. To me, he was a unique politician. In the 1960's, I used to plead with Bill Shawn to invite Stevenson to write for *The New Yorker,* and Shawn was just getting around to it when Stevenson died (of a heart attack, in London, in 1965). I had never seen anyone else like Stevenson and still haven't. I watched him on television when he lost the 1952 election to Eisenhower, and I wept as he made his concession speech, saying, he felt, as Abraham Lincoln once said, like the little boy who had stubbed his toe in the dark: "He was too old to cry, but it hurt too much to laugh."

At the luncheon, he said, "I have to go to Washington at least once a week, and friends invariably ask me if I don't miss Washington. When I tell them how absorbing I find the United Nations, they nod their heads and evidently don't believe me. For politicians, any place out of Washington is exile, but I don't find it so."

In May of 1963, I wrote about Stevenson again in a story for The Talk of the Town. Did my strongly favorable attitude toward Stevenson disqualify me to report on him? Not at all:

> At the moment when Astronaut Cooper was firing his retro-
> rockets and heading back from space, we were entering the

Waldorf-Astoria with United Nations Ambassador Adlai
Stevenson, who was on his way to his ninety-first reception
of the year 1963 and what we have estimated to be his one-
thousand-one-hundred-and-seventy-sixth reception in the line
of duty since he assumed his present post. The occasion was a
party celebrating the admission of Kuwait to the United Na-
tions. Kuwait, No. 111 in the assembly of nations, is a very rich
oil country, of 5,800 square miles (approximately the size of
Connecticut), bordering on Iraq, Saudi Arabia, and the Persian
Gulf, and its ruler, His Highness Sheik Sir Abdullah al-Salim
al-Sabah, like other government employees, gets a salary—in his
case, twenty-eight million dollars a year. The country has a daily
income of one and a quarter million dollars, and just before join-
ing the United Nations it signed up for the purchase of a million
dollars' worth of United Nations bonds. His Excellency Sheik
Sabah al-Ahmad al-Sabah, who was giving the party, was at the
head of the receiving line. . . .

"Now you stick with me," Ambassador Stevenson told us,
making first for His Excellency the Foreign Minister. "I just go
in there, hands open, ears open. Expect a concentrated period of
hand-shaking and whispering." His Excellency gave Ambassador
Stevenson a great big happy grin and passed him along quickly
to the couple beside him—Talaat Ghoussein, Kuwait's Chargé
d'Affaires in Washington, and Mrs. Ghoussein—who, in turn,
passed him on to Saeed Yacoob Shammas, Kuwait's Consul
General in New York, and Mrs. Shammas. They all greeted
Ambassador Stevenson, it seemed to us, not in the usual formal
manner of present-credentials-and-hello-and-goodbye but in the
gemütlich -reunion manner of people who see each other every
day at the office but rarely meet outside it, and, when they do,
manifest a special joy, as though it were a couple of years since
they had seen each other last. "Now I just let myself be drawn in
here," Ambassador Stevenson told us, steering us toward the rest
of the party. "Ah! Sir Muhammad Zafrulla Khan," he said, shak-
ing hands with the President of the General Assembly. Sir
Muhammad, twinkle-eyed and twinkle-bearded, promptly

whispered a few things into Ambassador Stevenson's left ear. A couple of other diplomats, including Ernest Thalmann, the Permanent (U.N.) Observer from Switzerland (which is not a member of the U.N.), came over and rejoiced with Ambassador Stevenson at his being there. The Permanent Observer and Ambassador Stevenson plunged into what seemed to be a running exchange about the possibility of Switzerland's becoming, after all these years, a joiner. Then Ambassador Stevenson found himself in the custody of a very talkative young American, who, after whispering things into his right ear for about ten minutes, turned out to be a party crasher with strong diplomatic opinions.

"Do you really listen to everybody?" we asked after Ambassador Stevenson had disengaged himself from the crasher.

"I'm meat for those people," he said, with the well-known Stevenson laugh.

"Don't you have bodyguards or something?" we asked.

"I've never cared much for elbowmen," he said as the crush moved in on him.

Journalistically, this Talk story is an example of how *The New Yorker* reporters used "we" as a device for asking questions and giving a visual picture of the action. If that story were edited today, we wouldn't bother to diagram what "we" were doing or saying; most of the same quotes and the same action would be included, without spelling out what "we" did. Doing it this way makes the story shorter and usually easier to read.

This story demonstrates how the reporter can do a story about an important and well-publicized figure without wanting to elicit a news scoop or some sensational gossip. I wanted to show what Stevenson really had to go through at these receptions. Also, I was able, in this brief story, to reveal his personality, his sense of humor, his warmth, his goodwill, as well as the way the U.N. people adored him. The ending of this story shows, I think, the kind of human being he was:

A little while later, the Ambassador left the reception, and so did we. Someone in the lobby had a portable radio, and we heard an

announcer say that Astronaut Cooper had climbed out of his cap-
sule. "Thank goodness he's back with the rest of us," Ambassador
Stevenson said.

In December of 1963, I wrote about Stevenson again. Still at the
U.N., he was presiding over the Security Council. He was going to
make a statement on apartheid in South Africa; it would be his
third important policy speech since Johnson became President.
President Kennedy had been assassinated a few weeks earlier, and
Stevenson, in his address, referred to President Johnson's first
address to a joint session of Congress in which he rededicated
the U.S. Government "to the unswerving support of the United
Nations." Stevenson spoke of President Johnson's "urgent call for
action to wipe out the remnants of racial discrimination in this
country. No less firm is our opposition to racial discrimination
anywhere."

That morning, I had met Stevenson for breakfast at his Waldorf
headquarters, and he had told me the Security Council might be
taking a vote on a resolution against South African apartheid. He
said to me over his coffee: "Somehow, I still have a complete sense
of the importance of the United Nations, in spite of the frustra-
tions and the exhausting trivia. I think of the United Nations, in
the political field, as one of the great experiments of man." He also
told me: "In my own day-to-day life, it's very much the way it
was when I was campaigning for President; it's campaigning per-
petually. The worst thing about running for President, for me, was
that you had to shave twice a day, and you have to do that in this
job, too."

Here is the ending of my story. The newspapers, of course, cov-
ered this event, but this little Talk story alone gave the details of an
historic moment:

> At 12:28 P.M., Governor Stevenson began to speak. He started off
> by saying, "Inasmuch as all the members of the Security Council
> have now spoken, I shall exercise my privilege of speaking on behalf
> of the United States," and ended by quoting President Kennedy as
> having said, "Is not peace, in the last analysis, a matter of human

rights?" and declaring that the United States would vote for the draft resolution. (Eighteen minutes.) During the translation of his speech, there was a great deal of wandering around by the delegates and their aides, and several of them went over to Governor Stevenson and conferred with him. A few minutes later, Governor Stevenson announced that five more delegates had asked for, and been granted, time to speak. They were representatives of Liberia (". . . All that we ask is justice for the non-white majority. . . . In his recent, eloquent Thanksgiving Day address to the American people, President Lyndon B. Johnson declared, 'God made all of us, not some of us, in His image. All of us, not just some of us, are His children'"), Sierra Leone, Tunisia, India (". . . The resolution is, in our opinion, a step forward, perhaps a small one, but nevertheless a step forward"), and Ghana ("In view of our desire to coöperate with our Scandinavian friends . . . my delegation would not press its request"). Ambassador Nielson, of Norway, then spoke a few words of thanks to Ghana for "the new sign of coöperation." The Ambassadors of the United Kingdom and the Union of the Soviet Socialist Republics both declared that they withdrew their objections to the resolution.

At 1:27 P.M., Governor Stevenson asked if anyone else wished to be heard, and when it appeared that no one did, he asked if there was "any objection to proceeding forthwith to a vote."

No one objected.

"All those in favor, please raise hands," Governor Stevenson said.

All representatives on the Council raised their hands. The Security Council was thereby appealing for a worldwide embargo on the shipment to South Africa of equipment for arms, as part of the drive to force her to abandon her policy of apartheid, and was, for the second time, condemning her for that policy.

"The result of the vote is unanimity," Governor Stevenson said. "I would suggest, therefore, that we adjourn."

As the representatives on each side of him arose, looking pleased, he sat quietly for a moment and then quickly gathered up his papers and left the Chamber.

The passage above is long, and the story of which it is a part is very long—much longer than our Talk stories run today. The question is not whether the stories in the 1960's were better than the stories in the present century. They were different only in the matter of length. My purpose and intention are the same today as they were then. I wrote at a more leisurely pace then; the challenges in form today are greater. For one thing, the reader, like the writer, doesn't have the leisure or the patience, to go slowly along, step by step, with the writing until he gets to the point. So the demand on the writer is quickly to establish a situation or a picture and immediately engage the characters in an action or an exchange that will make the point. Then the writer must immediately go on to build another point. What is important about reporting on Adlai Stevenson or on somebody else these days is to find the facts, the quotes, the scenes that make for action—all of which will reveal the person.

In 1965, Adlai Stevenson died suddenly, on a London street. I had been preparing a Profile for *The New Yorker* on him. I had had many long talks with him, and he had graciously invited me to accompany him on official errands. At William Shawn's suggestion, I abandoned the Profile and wrote a tribute for the magazine's Notes and Comment section. As usual, Bill Shawn wrote the jacket copy when the piece was published as a book. It was written, in the first person singular, about my experience with Stevenson. Shawn wrote: "Miss Ross suspended time for a moment here and a moment there, and Adlai Stevenson was again in our presence, in life —the tone of his voice, the ring of his laugh, the play of his mind, the very arc he described as he spent himself on behalf of us all."

Here are some examples of quotes and facts I packed into the piece that I wanted to lead up to a final scene defining Stevenson:

"I had a taste for literature and the academic. It's been part of the luggage I've carried in public life which doesn't yield public dividends."

His answer to me, at one point in his public pressured life, to what he'd like above all else to be doing at that moment: "I'd like to be out on my farm, in Libertyville, pruning trees."

My reportorial observation: "As usual, there were interruptions for autographs, for the introduction of wives, and for announcements from citizens that they had voted for him in 1952 and/or 1956—information that was frequently offered in a near-recriminatory key, because, in a success-happy age, he had not won."

On when he said he did not want to run for President in 1952 and was nevertheless nominated at the Democratic Convention: ". . . I was told 'You're indecisive.' Nobody can believe you when you say you're not a candidate. It's a curious thing. The more decisive you are in not seeking an exalted office, the more they say you're indecisive. My very decisiveness was attributed to what they called indecision. Sometimes you look back at it all and it seems almost comic. I don't have any feelings of bitterness. Both times I ran, it was obviously hopeless. To run as a Democrat in 1952 was hopeless, let alone run against the No. 1 War Hero. Even so, if it hadn't been for that going-to-Korea business, I might have beaten him." There was no sound of regret or vanity in Mr. Stevenson's voice; he spoke with as much enthusiasm for the subject, and as much appreciation of its inherent interest, as if he had been discussing some episode in history that he just happened to know something about.

At the 1964 World's Fair in New York, Stevenson was tapped to appear on "Illinois Day" along with Robert Lincoln Beckwith, a great-grandson of Abraham Lincoln. (Stevenson was always proud of his ancestry: his grandfather, the first Adlai E. Stevenson, had served as Vice-president under Benjamin Harrison in his second term (1893–1897); his great grandfather, Jesse W. Fell, of Bloomington, Illinois, had persuaded Abraham Lincoln to run for the Presidency.) On "Illinois Day," Stevenson quoted Lincoln's warning to political leaders in a message to Congress in December, 1862—"If there ever should be a time for mere catch arguments, that time surely is not now. In times like the present, no man should utter anything for which he would not willingly be responsible through time and in eternity." My story continued: "The words of Lincoln as Mr. Stevenson spoke them

did not appear to make much of an impression. The audience
was evidently waiting for the mechanical Lincoln to speak. This
Lincoln—a Walt Disney creation, followed Mr. Stevenson, and
its speech was billed as "great Moments with Mr. Lincoln." Mr.
Stevenson listened to it in apparent fascination. The mechanical
Lincoln really did sit, stand up, and make a speech—by means
of a recording by an actor—in a very deep, melancholy, Lincoln-
esque voice. I thought that the robot was creepy, but Mr. Steven-
son admired it. "It's a marvel," he said. "In one speech, the quotes
put together ran all the way from 1838 to 1864."

The following passage, ending the Stevenson piece, shows that it
was possible to cast an emotional memoir in the form of a factual,
and accurate and honest, piece of reporting:

There was one hot, muggy night in the summer of 1964, during
the political campaign, when I rode back with Mr. Stevenson on
a shuttle plane at the end of one of his incredibly full working
days in Washington. It was late when we landed at La Guardia
Airport. The city was steaming. Mr. Stevenson was greeted by
his driver, who handed him a portfolio of emergency cables and
messages to be studied. He did the work in the car as he was rid-
ing toward his apartment, and then he remembered that Mayor
Wagner had wanted to talk to him about some local aspects of
the election campaign, so he asked the driver to stop at Gracie
Mansion. It was around ten-thirty when we got there, and we ran
into the fading moments of what had been a Young Citizens for
Johnson Barbecue, imported from Texas. The barbecue seemed
to be under the supervision of Lynda Bird Johnson, Robert F.
Wagner, Jr., and other very young, very attractive, very recently
well-fed Democrats, and they all greeted Mr. Stevenson cordially.

It happened that he hadn't had anything to eat since lunch,
which he had eaten at the State Department with Dean Rusk.
The Gracie Mansion lawn, under festive garden lighting, was
strewn with delicious-looking and aromatic-smelling remnants
of what had clearly been a great party. Robert Wagner, Jr., said
that his father was upstairs, and quickly led Mr. Stevenson up to

see the Mayor. Half an hour later, Mr. Stevenson came down. He
looked a little hungry but not a bit tired. The party was petering
out by then, and the Mayor's guards, who did look tired, were
encouraging guests to leave. Everybody assumed—wrongly, I
thought—that Mr. Stevenson wanted to get away as fast as possi-
ble. Mr. Stevenson seemed to be peering wistfully at the Gracie
Mansion lawn. It looked inviting, that hot, humid, misty night,
with the paper picnic plates dotted about, and with suntanned,
laughing young men and women standing about in clusters,
talking, presumably, about the campaign, and with President
Johnson's caterer—fat and jolly, wrapped in a huge white apron,
and wearing a chef's tall white hat—still overseeing a long table
laden with steaks, sweet corn, and spareribs. But the party
was technically over, and a solicitous guard was ushering Mr.
Stevenson out to his car. He went. The guard saluted and left
him. Mr. Stevenson's driver opened the car door. Just then, a
young couple, both tall and skinny and wearing sandals and blue
jeans, the girl with long blond hair falling loosely over the collar
of a shirtwaist blouse and the boy with a cultivated fringe of
beard, strolled over to Mr. Stevenson, holding hands. They
smiled at him and coolly asked him what was going on at Gracie
Mansion. A party, he told them. They looked happy and lazy
and not impressed, and strolled away, still holding hands. Mr.
Stevenson stood there a moment or two, looking down the street
after them, and as he got into his car he said, "Summer in New
York is pretty wonderful, isn't it?"

Presidents

T HE TALK OF THE TOWN made it possible for me to write
stories about former U.S. presidents. I was never drawn to
writing about most sitting presidents. I've tried to stay away
from polemics. I try to keep informed about what's going on in
the world, and I watch hearings and press conferences on C-Span.
But I'm not drawn to cover the big news of the moment. I started
writing about Adlai Stevenson long after he'd been a presidential
candidate and when the newspapers weren't paying much atten-
tion to him.

Political writers were, and still are, not only more knowledge-
able than I am but also more eager to jump in and have their say. I
like to give my views about political figures—but only by making
them implicit in my selection of facts. I try to get past the image of
a public person, no matter how fixed it might be, and see where my
own curiosity takes me.

Also, there's an area in everybody's life that I consider to be
none of my business. I've always felt, from the beginning, that my
role as a reporter did not give me the right to try to be a psychoan-
alyst or a judge or a gossip, let alone an expert on any subject. I

resist the work of bullying writers who call themselves "biographers" and bring out books about people who don't want to be written about.

My pieces about Harry S. Truman (1945), Herbert Hoover (1949), John F. Kennedy (1963), Richard M. Nixon (1968), and William Jefferson Clinton (2001) have not been political as such. When President Roosevelt died, Harold Ross asked me to do a factual piece about Truman in Missouri. I had heard that Truman had once been in the haberdashery business.

What I wanted to find out, for The Talk of the Town, was what kind of haberdasher Truman had been. In Kansas City, via telephone, I located Edward Jacobson, formerly of Truman & Jacobson, Shirts, Collars, Hosiery, Gloves, Belts and Hats. Back in 1917, Truman and Jacobson had operated an Army Canteen at Fort Sill, Oklahoma, for six months, at a profit to the military of fifteen thousand dollars. Jacobson was the sergeant in charge and Captain Truman, being the exchange officer, was his boss. After the war, the two men decided to be business partners.

"I'd sold shirts for eleven years before the war and knew all about the business," Jacobson told me,

"—and Harry liked that type work. That is, he liked clothes. He was a very fastidious dresser. Always wore a high collar. It was the silk-shirt era, but he never wore silk shirts. He wore plain white broadcloth. . . . A showcase up front held a large silver loving cup given Truman by the boys of Battery D, which he had commanded overseas. Our store was the headquarters for all the Battery D boys in town. They'd come in to borrow money, which they always paid back. We never lost a dime on the boys. They also came in to ask advice. They'd ask Harry everything. Harry caught on to the business pretty quick. He knew all the answers in a few days. . . . I did most of the buying, and he did the books. He kept the books fine. That's because he was always so methodical in everything. We both sold. Some pretty rough characters used to come into the store, and Harry didn't care to wait on them. He was too much of a gentleman. He couldn't talk their

language. He'd get a clerk to wait on them. But he took all the
others. He liked to sell."

Truman & Jacobson's window trimmer, a man named Gus
Bowman, told me about Truman the salesman. "He sure was a
smart fellow," Bowman said. "Many times I watched him sell a
twenty-dollar silk shirt. He didn't push it onto a customer or any-
thing like that—just made the man feel that if he'd been buying
a shirt, that was the kind of shirt he would buy."

After the store closed, Jacobson said he went back to being a
salesman. "Harry got right into politics—ran for country judge
and won. Funny thing, Harry never talked much about politics."

I'm interested in what's going on politically in this country and
the rest of the world, but I prefer to leave the writing about it to
Joe Klein or Hendrik Hertzberg at our magazine. I'm more inter-
ested, for my reporting, in finding out that Truman as a salesman
didn't push the silk shirt on a customer than in what made him
push the buttons to drop the atomic bomb on Hiroshima.

In 1949, what was of interest to me about Herbert Hoover? He
was living at the Waldorf-Astoria and took regular early morning
walks. Bill Shawn suggested that I assume the role of "our man
Stanley" one morning and trail him. I waited at the hotel's Park
Avenue entrance. At precisely 8:16 A.M.,

> . . . the revolving door spun and out came Mr. Hoover, in double-
> breasted blue suit, white shirt, solid-blue necktie, green felt hat,
> and black shoes.
>
> The doorman saluted, and Mr. Hoover nodded soberly to him.
> He then paused, appraised the sky, looked north, looked south,
> settled for south, and started out with short, firm steps, his arms
> stiffly at his sides, his gaze straight ahead. A Sanitation man was
> so occupied with a rolling Dixie cup that he didn't look up. At
> Forty-ninth, Mr. Hoover stopped, faced west, and waited for a
> green light. When it came, he crossed Park, meeting on the island
> in the middle, an elderly lady, in a wrinkled brown coat, carrying
> several wrinkled brown paper bags, who pegged him, looked
> back, and then winked at Stanley. Mr. Hoover continued on

Forty-ninth to Madison, meeting no one, stopped again, and
looked up, north, and south. This time, the decision was north.
He stopped before a silver shop and admired—or, at any rate,
studied—a display of platters and candelabra, and then proceeded
to Fiftieth Street, where he was halted by a red light. He had
passed several people in this block, none of whom had identified
him. He crossed Fiftieth with the light, faced west, waited for
the light to change again, crossed Madison, and continued along
beside St. Patrick's. The pigeons grudgingly yielded him the right
of way, and near the corner a cop gave him a short, surprised look
and then grinned at Stanley and said, "Looks good, huh? What
is he—seventy-five?"

Stanley's report continued in this vein, taking Mr. Hoover—
with about one out of thirty people recognizing him—to Grand
Central,

> . . . before which he stopped to examine an Army recruiting
> poster headed "Action Packed careers." . . . None of the people
> tearing this way and that around him recognized the only living
> former President of the United States. After a few moments of
> apparent indecision, Mr. Hoover pushed his way to a taxi and got
> in quickly. Stanley got into another cab and followed him back to
> the Waldorf, via Madison, Forty-sixth, and Park. His conclusion:
> Mr. Hoover is a born early-morning walker, fast and determined,
> and a match for Harry Truman any day.

By December of 1968, after my exhilarating exposure to the
one-of-a-kind, brilliantly literate Adlai Stevenson, I was more than
ready for the then President-elect Richard Nixon, who was still liv-
ing in his apartment at 810 Fifth Avenue and walking daily to his
pre–White House office at the Hotel Pierre. "Nixon's Walk"—in
counterpoint to Hoover nineteen years before—ran in The Talk of
the Town. I wrote my story as a parody of Nixon-speak. It was the
first time, actually, that the "perfectly clear, etc." Nixonese had
been lampooned this way. "We want to make one thing perfectly
clear," is the way the story began.

The walk, by our measurement, comes to two hundred and forty-
eight steps—more or less, that is, allowing for a few side steps
every once in a while to make way for some nursemaid pushing
a baby carriage or some boy or girl or other person walking a dog.
Now, to be specific, the two hundred and forty-eight steps include
twenty-one steps going west from Mr. Nixon's residence. . . . Mr.
Nixon takes exactly one hundred and sixty-nine steps going south
to the Fifth Avenue entrance of the Hotel Pierre. . . . Now, this is
what we mean: Mr. Nixon's walk is composed of two hundred and
forty-eight separate and distinct steps, and the steps are not too
long—roughly about fifteen, maybe sixteen, inches. What hap-
pens is that these steps take him to the Hotel Pierre, where he
goes into the lobby and into an elevator and up to his office, and
that's that. He's arrived. He's in his office. . . . First of all, we have
to say that Mr. Nixon may give the appearance of walking briskly,
but steps measuring fifteen or sixteen inches each step mean—
and we want to be perfectly clear about this—steps measuring
fifteen or sixteen inches mean that he is not stepping too quickly.
He is certainly stepping cautiously, and all the time he is stepping
he is moving his legs. He also happens to be moving his arms, but
we'll get to that in just a couple of minutes. All the time he is
stepping, he is looking, observing, staring, gazing, and we might
add, he is seeing what there is to be seen on the whole block—
block and a fifth, that is—from his home to his office. Now, bear
with us while we take just a minute to explain something that's
really quite important if we're going to give you the best possible
description of Mr. Nixon's walk to his pre–White House office.
. . . Now, bear with us while we get Mr. Nixon past the entrance
to the Pierre Café, which happens to come just before he reaches
the entrance to the Hotel Pierre. . . . When Mr. Nixon goes home
from his office, of course—and we'd like to especially emphasize
this last point—he sees pretty much the same things he saw on
his way from his home to his office.

Thirty-four years later, in a piece called "Bill and George" from
The New Yorker of July 9, 2001, in bounces former President Bill

Clinton—supposedly disgraced, supposedly disreputable, suppos-
edly about to be disbarred, and supposedly a dismal national fig-
ure a lot of people supposedly wished would go away. But for the
few hundred people gathered at George Plimpton's house it's a
great and happy pleasure to have a nice, close look at Bill Clinton.
Like everybody else present, I loved seeing him and let him know
it. He wasn't tired, strained, or discouraged, or valiantly putting
on a political performance.

Bill Clinton came to George Plimpton's house on a very hot night
last week to attend a party for the new book *The Games We Played*,
to which both gentlemen contributed chapters. Clinton wrote
about playing a kind of bat-and-ball in Hot Springs, Arkansas, as
a kid, and Plimpton wrote about igniting cherry bombs to shoot
small rubber balls into the sky.

"I don't know how to introduce anybody, because I don't know
anybody here," Plimpton said in his genial, patrician manner, as
his Upper East Side home (which is also the headquarters of *The
Paris Review*) filled up with perspiring guests. They made twi-
light small talk, regularly casting casual but eager glances toward
the front door. Plimpton said, "I never had a President in the
house—just lots of senators and would-be's, like John Lindsay
and Bobby Kennedy and Ed Koch."

A red-haired young man approached. "I'm Steve Cohen, the
editor of the book," he said. "My red-haired baby, Abigail, is here,
and that's her mother holding her."

"I was just told the President likes to walk into a room with
hordes," Plimpton said. "He likes a sea of people around him." He
went outside to keep an eye out for Clinton.

"The President calls me Scoop," Cohen said. "I was just out of
college in the summer of 1991, and I heard a rumor about him, so
I jumped in my car and drove down to his campaign headquarters.
I just showed up. I told him about the rumor, and it turned out to
be false, but they've called me Scoop ever since. I was his press
aide until 1995, when I shifted over to Mrs. Clinton. I haven't
seen him since January. But he came through for the book."

. . . Plimpton dashed back into the room, sweating, and not his usual unflappable self. "I just met him out front!" he said. "Somebody handed him a child, and the child instantly began to cry. I then said something I'm sure he's heard a thousand times. I said, 'She must be a Republican.' Everything I said was out of order. But he's here!"

There he was, in a sea of sweating, shining faces, his own face cool and dry and cheerful, under a snowy thick mane of hair. His gray suit was uncreased, a yellow print Hermès necktie neatly done under his chin. When he walked in, the room seemed to tilt to one side, like a ship tossed by a wave, and suddenly all the party guests were pressed tightly into the spot where Clinton stood. He shook every extended hand with his right and signed autographs with his left. Everybody looked slaphappy to see him.

"Adoration!" someone said. "In 3-D!"

. . . "I'm Curtis Ellis," one middle-aged gentleman said. "How did you do at Belmont when you were last here?"

"I had a great time," Clinton said. "How 'bout you?"

"I did great. I picked the trifecta," Ellis said. "All three horses had about even money on them. The only way to make money was to bet the trifecta."

"What's the trifecta?" Clinton asked and listened carefully to the answer. "Thanks. I should have bet the trifecta," he said.

A couple of wineglasses were clinked for silence. Thanks were expressed by Steve Cohen's agent, at some length, to Plimpton and everybody who had come to the party. Then Clinton nodded to Scoop.

"You first?" Clinton asked. "After me? O.K."

So Clinton spoke first. "Scoop was virtually the first who came to work for me in the campaign," he said, and put his arm around him. "Now he has a wife and a beautiful child"—he paused— "with, I might add, a great grip."

Much laughter. Much applause. Cries of "We miss you!"

Then it was Scoop's turn to talk, which he did, at length, in detail, about everybody who had helped him with the book. Clinton listened with serious and patient attention, as though

he were being asked to consider a report on nuclear weapons.
Then, forty minutes after he'd arrived, he was hustled by his secu-
rity detail out the front door and into a black S.U.V. One guest
heard him say something about running late for another book
party, at Richard Holbrooke's house.

That was my idea of how to do a story, in the summer of 2001,
about President Clinton, about whom I had never tried to write any-
thing while he was running for, or in, office. I believe that every new
story a reporter takes on about any subject—especially about famous
world figures about whom millions of words of one kind or another
are published daily—should be fresh and alive and worth doing.

So what kind of story might possibly be written about President
John F. Kennedy, immediately following his assassination, on No-
vember 22, 1963?

Four days earlier, on the 18th, I happened to be in Miami work-
ing on another story, when I learned that President Kennedy was to
speak there to a crowd of voters, rounded up mostly by local
Democrats. After that, he was going to address a convention of the
Inter-American Press Association at the Americana Hotel, with
appearances at a couple of social-political gatherings squeezed
in between—all this after Saturday at Cape Canaveral, Sunday
in Palm Beach, and all day Monday in Tampa, there inspecting
McDill Air Force base, lunching at Army-Air Force Strike Com-
mand Headquarters, journeying by helicopter to Lopez Field, in
downtown Tampa, and speaking there on the fiftieth anniversary
of commercial aviation, addressing the Florida State Chamber of
Commerce, addressing a meeting of the Steelworkers' Union, and
riding around the Tampa streets, shaking hands through it all with
everybody he could reach.

That Monday afternoon, I went out with the press to the Miami
airport, still not knowing what kind of story I might get. I was
wondering vaguely about President Kennedy's physical stamina,
and I was thinking that his eagerness to make himself accessible to
the crowds was bringing him in contact with a million germs car-
ried by scores of people with colds.

I was also remembering that the then Florida Congressman
Claude Pepper had told me he was hoping that Kennedy would
carry the state of Florida in 1964, having lost it by only 46,776
votes in 1960. "Some Democrats didn't fight too hard for him in
1960," Congressman Pepper had told me. "I want to see the Dem-
ocratic Party fight harder in '64."

The President's plane was scheduled to land in the Delta Airlines
area, and a Delta hangar had been festooned with a red-and-white
banner reading "WELCOME MR. PRESIDENT." A Democratic State
Committeeman was passing out placards to the pubic, stationed
behind a wire fence. The signs read, "WELCOME PRESIDENT
KENNEDY BISCAYNE DEMOCRATIC CLUB" and "POLISH-AMERICAN
CLUB WELCOMES PRESIDENT KENNEDY," and "SENIOR CITIZENS'
COUNCIL WELCOMES PRESIDENT KENNEDY." Milling about in the
V.I.P. section were a number of V.I.P. children, wearing cardboard
buttons that proclaimed "My mom and dad are for you President
Kennedy." A hundred-and-forty-five member band—identified as
the "Band of the Hour" from the University of Miami—was play-
ing "March of the Mighty" and "God Bless America" and then
was instructed by an F.B.I. man to play ruffles and flourishes when
the president arrived, and then "Hail to the Chief."

Just behind the wire fence stood a pretty young black woman,
who was herding a small group of black children. She was Mrs.
Lillian Peterson, and the children were part of her fourth-grade
class at the Lillie C. Evans Elementary School. No one had invited
them to come to the airport; they had just come. I immediately
knew what my story should be. I talked to Mrs. Peterson and to
her students. I decided to write my story about them. I went back
to New York the next day and started writing it. It turned out that
the story would be one that William Shawn used in The New
Yorker's Notes and Comment right after the assassination.

Here are some parts of that story, using the old "we" device,
from the issue dated November 30, 1963:

The children looked at us solemnly and, at their teacher's
prompting, identified themselves as Barbara Laidler (wearing

a green ribbon bow in her hair), Anthony Shinhoster, Ietta
Odom, Gregory Gill and William Ingram. "We've just finished
studying the United States of America and our three chief execu-
tives," Mrs. Peterson told us. "I drew a diagram for the children
showing the mayor in a small circle on the bottom, the Governor
in a bigger circle over him, and the President in the biggest circle
on top. The fourth grade, you know, is really the foundation grade
for the rest of your life. These children have the responsibility of
sharing the President's visit with others in the class, who could
not come. They have the responsibility of writing a report about
what they see today. . . ."

President Kennedy emerged from the tail of the plane, looking
relaxed and good-humored, and got to work immediately, at what
he was expected to do, and more. With the Congressmen, the
Senator, and the Governor sticking close to him, he extended his
hand wherever he was directed to extend it, and he seemed to find
a number of hands to shake on his own, too. He varied his "Hello"
and "How are you?" and "Glad to see you" with an occasional
"Nice going, boy." When the President appeared on the platform,
there was a big cheer from the crowd (it numbered about eight
thousand), and though he had yet to be introduced, he came for-
ward eagerly to smile and wave and give a little bow. Pepper, on
the platform, introduced Governor Bryant, and the Governor, it
turned out, had the privilege of introducing the President. The
Governor said they were all proud of what President Kennedy
had done for Florida, and that he felt a special pride, and plea-
sure in presenting the President of the United States.

President Kennedy took it from there, in his own ebullient
way. "I've been making nonpartisan speeches all day, and I'm glad
to come here as a Democrat," he started off, in old-fashioned
campaign style. The crowd loved it. There were cheers from both
sides of the wire fence, and all the politicians on the platform
appeared happy and satisfied. The President went on to talk about
the national purpose—among other things, taking care of seven
or eight million boys and girls who will want to go to college in
the year 1970. The President said he was going to go on fighting

for congressional enactment of his program, even though certain
people "oppose what I am trying to do and everything Franklin
Roosevelt tried to do and everything Harry Truman tried to do."
The crowd cheered again. . . .

President Kennedy then left the platform and started walking
among the people, smiling, shaking hands, and saying hello. He
made a special point of going over to the conductor of the Band
of the Hour and thanking him. Behind the President, the politi-
cians piled up, greeting each other joyously with cries of "Hey,
Sheriff!" and "Hey, Judge!" and "Hey, Mayor!". . .

We noticed that Mrs. Peterson and her fourth-graders were
crowded against the wire fence, their hands outstretched, and
we noticed that the President kept trying to pull away from the
Secret Service men and head in the children's direction. A white
man was holding Barbara up high to get a better look (her green
hair ribbon was now untied and fluttering), so that she could give
a responsible report to the rest of her class and share with them
everything that she saw that day.

The next afternoon, we telephoned Mrs. Peterson to ask her
how the children had carried out their responsibilities. Barbara,
she told us, reading from their reports, wrote, "The first thing
we had was music. Then they took the President's picture many
times. The President has reddish hair and had on a suit. People
enjoyed seeing President Kennedy." Ietta wrote, "We waited and
waited and waited. At last we some airplanes and four helicopters.
We saw a lot of people. John F. Kennedy finally came. He said
a little speech." Gregory wrote, "I was glad to go and see our
President because this was my first time seeing him and I admire
him and his speeches. I think Mr. Kennedy is the greatest man in
the world." William wrote, "He went on the helicopter. Crowds
and crowds of people began to say goodbye as he flew away. The
crowd of people began to yell louder and louder and it sounded
like one thousand people saying goodbye."

ROBERT KENNEDY

IN LOOKING BACK at my reports on Robert Kennedy, and rereading, for instance, the way he talked about his son Bobby, I see again the kind of human being our country lost with his assassination. All of it is my way of trying to reveal the particular individuals in their incarnation as political leaders.

I wrote two stories about Robert Kennedy that utilized the traditional Talk "we," one about him as Attorney General, in June, 1961, and the other in 1963, after President Kennedy's assassination.

Although I was beginning to drop "we" as a literary device for telling stories, it still seemed appropriate to use it here. I didn't feel the Talk "we" was appropriate for some stories, stories I wanted to tell in the third person in order to give a story more immediacy, more action, more of a sense of a fiction story. Using the first person "we" was more personal. Actually, "we" for a long time, and still today, feels to me like "I." Perhaps, too, in this case, there was also a sense of "we the people." In the first story, I tried to give a sense of the man's character and personality. The later story reveals some alterations caused by the tragedy of his brother's death. The "we" in the writing came naturally; it wasn't even noticeable.

"ATTORNEY GENERAL"

Robert Kennedy came to town one hot morning last week to look
things over in the offices of the local United States District Attor-
neys and to make a speech at a State Attorneys General meeting,
and thanks to a long-distance chat the day before with his public
information aide, Edwin Guthman (a 1950 Pulitzer Prize reporter
on leave from the *Seattle Times*), we were on hand to greet the
Attorney General at La Guardia. He arrived at 8:30 A.M., at which
time, he told us, he already had behind him his usual tennis-before-
breakfast with his wife at their home, Hickory Hill, in McLean,
Virginia; a glass of orange juice with his seven children (ages one to
nine); blueberry pancakes and a glass of milk on the plane; work on
a written speech that he might discard in favor of talking impromp-
tu to the Attorneys General; and the reading, up to page 164, of
George F. Kennan's new book, *Russia and the West Under Lenin and
Stalin*. Taking long fast strides away from the plane . . . the
Attorney General was joined by a couple of equally fast-striding
local F.B.I. men, who informed him of their pleasure at being
assigned to accompany him, as a break in their regular work as bank
robbery agents. The Attorney General looked pleased and serious at
the same time. His face was freshly sunburned, and he had on a
navy-blue worsted suit, a white shirt with a button-down collar, and
a blue-and-silver striped necktie held by a brass pin, in the shape of
a PT boat, that was inscribed "Kennedy 60." In addition to the
Kennan book, he carried, in a transparent plastic wrapping, a white
Sulka shirt, 15½–33 (no button-down collar), with a blue paper
laundry band around it. As he walked along, he passed both book
and shirt back to Guthman for safekeeping.

"My wife handed me that shirt as I was leaving," the Attorney
General said. "I'll change into it just before the speech, I guess.
My wife hates to fly, but she would have come with me anyway,
only she had to go to the White House with Mrs. Johnson for a
reception, pinch-hitting for my brother's wife. My wife gave me
this tie to wear. I had another one on, but she said it didn't look
good. I don't have any other tie pins. I bought this one during the
campaign. We were selling them for fifteen cents.

"One thing I hope to do here before leaving on a six-thirty plane tonight is visit a toy store and find something for my son David. He's six tomorrow, and he's been talking about his birthday since the day after Christmas. He wants a billy goat, and my wife got him one, unfortunately. My second son, Bobby, collects animals. He's also a junior botanist. Bobby picks up bees with his fingers. I caught two turtles for him while riding last Sunday, to fill out the collection we've got at home—chicks, geese, horses, ponies, tadpoles, frogs, lizards, birds, cats, puppies, and dogs. I got a seal for the children for Christmas two years ago. He escaped once and was found by the milkman in the middle of town and had to be captured by the local police. This seal got to be real friendly, but when he found out food came from the kitchen, he was always trying to get into the kitchen, so we had to give him to the zoo. We had a deodorized skunk once, but it escaped while being transported from Hyannis Port to Washington and is still missing. A friend brought Bobby a toad the other day for his collection, half of which is kept in the house, the other half out. Bobby is really terrific with animals—has a wonderful way with them. I get to see more of my children now than I did during the campaign. At least, I see them Saturday night and part of Sunday and at breakfast. They're lucky in being aware of what is going on in the country and in the world, which I think is a great advantage. We do a lot of talking about what I do and what my brother does. We talk in the context of the history of the country—Lexington and Bunker Hill and the Boston Tea Party and the Civil War and so on. We talk about the kinds of things Jack does. The older children know all about Khrushchev and de Gaulle and Harold Macmillan—who they are and why Jack went to visit them. They're just regular children. The older ones wanted to know who the Freedom Riders are. That was a difficult one. Trying to explain to an eight- or nine-year-old that some people don't like Negroes. We have a Negro nurse who's been with us since my first child was born, so this doesn't make any sense to them."

"General, here's the car," one of the F.B.I. men said, opening the door of a Chevrolet sedan.

The Attorney General ushered us into the rear with him as Guthman got in beside the driver. A pink-faced and perspiring policeman in a short-sleeved shirt put his head in at the rear window on Mr. Kennedy's side.

"Well, well, glad to see you again, sir," the policeman said, and the Attorney General shook hands with him through the window. "Haven't seen you since the electioneering days. Remember those days? It's a long time ago."

"I certainly do," Mr. Kennedy said. "Nice to see you again."

"You've got good color. Keep it up," the policeman said.

"So have you," Mr. Kennedy said.

"Mine is high blood pressure," the policeman said. "Sorry we've got such terribly hot weather for you here. Hope it won't bother you."

"It won't. Thanks. Good luck," Mr. Kennedy said.

As we started off, Mr. Kennedy told us, "I went to South-Central Asia in 1955 with Justice Douglas, and the temperature there got over a hundred and thirty degrees—very dry heat, but even that didn't make me become accustomed to it. I don't like cities generally. The part of New York I like the best is Central Park—especially the zoo. If the election had turned out differently, and if Mr. Nixon hadn't made me Attorney General, I'd probably be making short trips to New York only to visit the zoo."

"Is your present job more difficult than being a campaign manager?" we asked.

"The hours are equally long," Mr. Kennedy said. "There was more real public pressure, actually, in the campaign, where one mistake could cost you a whole area. I was travelling continuously, speaking fifteen or twenty times in an eighteen- or nineteen-hour day. You're always open to pressure as a campaign manager. And when I worked with the Senate Rackets Investigating Committee, the public and the press were continuously interested. I think the decisions I make now have a more lasting effect and affect people more materially than anything I've done in any other job I've ever had."

. . . He was going to greet the staff of assistants to the United States Attorney. A few minutes later, he stood, hands in pockets,

below a photograph dated 1903 and showing the nine-man staff of the United States Attorney's office (we spotted a boyish-looking Felix Frankfurter and a young Henry Stimson), and greeted the thirty-odd members of [Robert] Morgenthau's staff who are in the criminal division.

"I'm delighted to be here," Mr. Kennedy said. "There's no question but that the Southern District of New York is the showcase for the Justice Department. . . . I wanted to come up and tell you how grateful we are to you for all the time and effort you give to the work, which I know is not for financial satisfaction. . . . We are always available to you and at your service. . . ."

A beaming gray-haired lady wearing spectacles said, "Ethel Backenroth. I'm the librarian. I have thirty-nine years of service to the United States Attorney for the Southern District."

"You were here before I was born," Mr. Kennedy said.

"I'm proud of my service," Miss Backenroth said.

"Five *years* before I was born," Mr. Kennedy said, looking slightly stunned.

The greeting-and-handshaking routine was repeated later on with another group of attorneys, in the anti-trust division, and then, with pauses to shake hands with guards, a shoeshine man, and other well-wishers, and to give a few autographs, Mr. Kennedy started out of the building.

We asked him whether he remembered the people he met in such long line-ups.

"I'm not too good at it," he said. "Jack is really good at it, and my wife is terrific."

In the year 2002, so many people have been batted over the head with gossip about Robert Francis Kennedy that it hangs like a shroud over the human being of that name. It was reassuring to me to find and reread that little story about him. By now, too, people have become familiar with his children as grownups. The name Robert Kennedy to millions of people means the environmentalist, the man who went to prison in 2001 for trespassing on the Vieques naval bombing site. It's especially interesting to read of the passion of Robert Kennedy, the father, for the outdoor life and animals, in

light of, among other things, the "Bobby" who "picks up bees with his fingers" and who grew up to become one of the nation's leading environmentalists. I like putting that story, from June, 1961, together with the following one about RFK from October, 1964, not quite a year after his brother was killed. Robert was campaigning for election to the U.S. Senate. I drove into the city with him one morning during the campaign from his home in Glen Cove, Long Island.

. . . His car, a rented white Chevrolet sedan, had a campaign-dented roof, a telephone, and a driver named Jim King, who informed Mr. Kennedy that his first appointment was a television interview. "You might want to put on your black shoes instead of those brown ones, as long as you're wearing the gray suit," Mr. King told Mr. Kennedy as we drove down Glen Cove Road toward the Long Island Expressway. "We've got the black shoes on the seat back there."

Mr. Kennedy said he'd change his shoes as soon as we reached the city.

"And change the cufflinks," Mr. King said.

Mr. Kennedy nodded, and showed us the cufflinks he was wearing—a handsome gold pair embossed with the Department of Justice seal. "People sometimes pull them off when I'm in crowds," he told us. "My brother and sister-in-law Jackie gave them to me about a year and a half ago. I lost one in Syracuse last week at the airport, but I found it a few seconds later myself, on the ground. A couple of weeks ago, I lost one in the ballroom of the Americana, and thought it was gone, but somebody picked it up and sent it back anonymously a couple of days later to my apartment at the Carlyle. The experience was very lifting. Now, just before I go into crowds, I put on substitutes—cloth ones. . . .

"I've been involved with a lot of campaigns, but this one is so different in so many ways. In previous campaigns, our family was so closely bound up together. There was one candidate, but we were all sort of involved, including my father, of course, who felt so strongly about it. Now my brother isn't here, and my father

can't speak, and my younger brother isn't around. . . . I like being
out of Washington. That's first. And I like seeing so many other
people. I like communicating again with that part of American
life. I like looking at people, in all the towns and all the cities all
over the state. They smile. They don't have an angle. It's very lift-
ing. They're just ordinary American citizens. . . . Here, the people
that come to an airport to meet you just seem to have sort of a
basic confidence that the country is in good hands. They repre-
sent the United States so much better than what we have in
Washington. They smile. The impression you have is that they
look happy, and yet serious at the same time. And they listen
to you. It's just nice, that's all. . . ."

"Any surprises?" we asked.

Mr. Kennedy considered the question for a while and then
said, "The intensity, I suppose, is greater than I would have antici-
pated. . . . I find I'm doing better in some places than in other
places. In my speeches, I haven't done as well as I should do, on
occasion. In Buffalo one night, I had to speak at a Democratic
dinner at eleven o'clock after a morning that started out at five-
thirty, and I know I may have made my points sharper in that
speech. I know when I make a good speech, just as I know when
I play a good game of tennis or swim well. You do the best you
can. I try to make an effort all the time. . . ."

We asked Mr. Kennedy whether he preferred one kind of
audience to another.

"College audiences usually," he said. "They usually ask the best
questions and when there's opposition in the audience, it's basi-
cally more stimulating. I'm always trying for communication.
Yesterday, I was supposed to make a speech before a group of
teachers—eleven hundred nuns. I was handed a speech written
for me at one in the morning and I was supposed to speak at ten.
I found I didn't like the speech. It was very pedantic and routine.
It just didn't have any idealism. It was just vaguely about youth.
So I spoke extemporaneously about some of the issues, and how
we needed intelligence to make the right decision. They listened."

"How's the campaign as a campaign?" we asked.

"I expected this campaign to be on a higher level," he said. "When you bring the campaign to that low level, it lowers the opinion of people about the people involved in politics. In a national campaign, you couldn't get away with it. If you made charges on that low level, they'd be answered immediately, but in the state campaign nobody bothers to answer, nobody gets very horrified at it. They print what somebody says, but nobody bothers to answer the false charges or writes what the facts are. On the other hand, in a campaign, people make such efforts for you. One young guy gave up his job in the Justice Department, in Washington, and came to New York with his wife. They have no money, and they're working as volunteers. There are a lot of people like that. They run out to a factory at five-thirty in the morning and open a door and take your coat, and you never see them again. That's inspiring. . . . There are terrific problems facing the country, including problems of whether people are going to live or die. I'd like to play a role in the future. I'd like to do something about it. If things work out, I'll be in the United States Senate. If they don't, I'll teach or something. Either way, I'll be glad I made the effort. It all pales in significance in the light of the events of the past year."

For this story, I dropped listening for any interchange with anybody else, and listened carefully to Robert Kennedy's words in response to my questions. To this day, I never heard a politician speak so openly and honestly about the way campaigning felt to him. In putting it together with the earlier story, one can see clearly, without his stating it explicitly, how John Kennedy's death was making him change and develop. One can see how hard he was trying, in his own terms, to be worthy of his brother's legacy. He was still being reminded to put on appropriate clothes, etc., and these humorous details make him all the more touching, in contrast to the solemnity of his efforts.

As the decades have gone by, some of the heroic martyrs in our history seem to have become buried under clouds of peripheral gossip. Journalistic stories have the capacity to keep these figures alive for us, to keep them from slipping away.

HUBERT HUMPHREY
AND RALPH BUNCHE

I N 1967, I WROTE a Talk piece about President Johnson's Vice-President, Hubert H. Humphrey, who had the misfortune of running against, and losing to, Richard Nixon in 1968 (popular vote: Nixon 43.4 percent, Humphrey 42.7 percent). The story demonstrates how it is possible, in reporting, to be sympathetic to a politician on a nonpolitical level. In writing this one, I used dramatic scenes. Humphrey had come to New York to meet with some anti-poverty Upward Bound participants in a program called Double Discovery and to appear on Johnny Carson's *Tonight* show. Humphrey was hustled into a small studio office that was smoky, windowless, airless, and crowded with Secret Service men, personal aides, and advance men. After his appearance with Carson, Humphrey would meet in the room with the anti-poverty people.

Johnny Carson came into the room.

Mr. Humphrey gave him a smile as they shook hands. "How are you, Johnny?" he asked.

"Great," Mr. Carson replied. "Just had three weeks in Las
Vegas. This is my first night back, after three weeks out there.
Phew! Was it hot out there!" Mr. Carson fingered the knot of
his tie, lifting his chin as he made adjustments in the area of his
Adam's apple, and, while everybody in the warm little office stood
around expectantly, he said, grinning and nodding and winking,
that Howard Hughes had just bought *another* hotel out there in
Las Vegas. "They wanted him out of the hotel he was in by New
Year's, and he didn't want to leave, so he bought it," Mr. Carson
went on, and looked around at everybody with an expression of
wide-eyed astonishment. "He just bought it. He *bought* the whole
hotel. . . " Mr. Carson grinned, nodded, and winked at the Vice-
President. "I'm delighted you're with us again. . . . I'm going on
now," Mr. Carson said, winking at everybody and at a television
monitor. To Mr. Humphrey, he said, "If they're no good out there
in the audience, you don't have to come *out*."

Mr. Humphrey laughed, and Mr. Carson left, followed by his
production men. There was a lull in the little office. On the TV
screen, a pineapple was doing the hula, and an announcer was
saying, "The best pineapple comes from Hawaii."

"I love that ad," Mr. Humphrey said, with a good-natured
laugh. "We have two senators, you know, from Hawaii."

When Humphrey walked out of the wings and took his chair
with Carson on the show, the audience applauded.

Mr. Carson looked wide-eyed at the audience and then at the
Vice-President. "I didn't get that much applause, and I was gone
three weeks," he said.

"I think I ought to quit while I'm ahead," Mr. Humphrey said,
holding in his grin like a pro. (Laughter.)

I deliberately set up the interchange between Humphrey and
Carson that would lead into showing what Humphrey the politi-
cian was willing to lend himself to. Carson's inimitable person-
ality and gestures and professional control over his manner
worked beautifully as counterpoint to revealing Humphrey the
politician. Also, it indicated how Carson was trying to help him.
On the show:

MR. CARSON: I understand you're here tonight with some of the youngsters in your Upward Bound anti-poverty project.

MR. HUMPHREY: Yes, and we've obtained a million jobs for needy youngsters. . . .

In the story, back in the airless little office after the broadcast, the Double Discovery people—about a dozen students, counsellors, directors, etc.—crowded in. Humphrey shook hands enthusiastically with everybody. I included an exchange between Humphrey and one of the students:

Humphrey said: "I hear awfully good reports about what you're doing. It proves what can be done if you make that extra effort. Juan, how long have you been in the program?"

"Three years," said Juan.

"How old are you, Juan?" Mr. Humphrey asked.

"Seventeen," Juan replied.

"Seventeen," Mr. Humphrey said, looking at the boy through weariness, strain, effort, good will, discouragement, and the confusion of sixteen minutes of televised talk on *Tonight*, and managing to come up with an impression of heartfelt enthusiasm. "And do you find the program a good one, Juan?"

"Yes," Juan said.

In the story, after the Double Discovery people left, and the *Tonight* show was over,

Mr. Carson came back to the little room and sat on the edge of the desk, facing Mr. and Mrs. Humphrey, on the sofa. He winked and blinked and nodded at them.

"The Vice-President got too many laughs," Mr. Carson said, and everybody laughed.

Each of these stories about politicians embodied a theme.

I've always been free, at *The New Yorker*, to find subjects that appealed to me. I don't think that I've ever had a negative response from an editor to anything I've wanted to write about. However, in the early Nixonian 1970's, I found that there weren't many heroic figures I wanted to write about. At that time, the most interesting

American heroes to me were black. I admired the blacks I wrote about, and I was drawn to what they represent. Of them, Ralph Johnson Bunche was one of the most quietly interesting. So I worked on reporting a story about him. It was published in 1972, after his death. Bunche was an Under-Secretary and an Under-Secretary General of the United Nations for sixteen years until his death in December, 1971. I wanted to tell his story, mostly by using his own voice. I didn't want to let anything get in the way of it.

The piece first established basic facts: Bunche was born in Detroit. His father, an itinerant barber, and his mother, an amateur pianist, both died in 1917, his father of influenza, his mother of tuberculosis. Bunche was raised in Los Angeles by his maternal grandmother, Mrs. Lucy Johnson, whose husband, the principal of a Negro elementary school in Waco, Texas, in the 1880's, had died of malaria, leaving his wife and five children penniless in Indian territory.

"My grandmother—I always called her 'Nana'—had ten children, but five died, and one of those who died was named Ralph," Mr. Bunche said. "Nana was a matriarch. She didn't take any foolishness from anybody. She had no education, but she had deep insights. She was very small but very strong, very wiry and very outspoken. She looked like a white, and was often mistaken for one. Once, in Los Angeles, where we lived in a mostly white neighborhood, a salesman for cemetery plots came by and gave my grandmother a sales pitch, one of his selling points being that they didn't allow Negroes or Jews in the cemetery. Well, she got a broom and chased him out of the house. Another time, the principal of my high school, when I was graduating, said to her, 'Mrs. Johnson, we're sorry to lose Ralph. We've never thought of him as a Negro.' My grandmother said to him, 'How dare you insult our race?' She always drilled into me, 'Do the best you can. Maintain your self-respect. Never let anybody detract from it.'"

Bunche went to U.C.L.A.

"In my senior year at college, I had the highest grades, and I was selected to be the commencement speaker," he said. "Dean

Charles Rieber took an interest in me. Although he was stiff
and formidable, his office was always open. He once said to me,
'You're going to be a lawyer.' Everybody just assumed I was going
to be a lawyer. If a Negro was going to be educated and a profes-
sional, he became either a doctor, a teacher, a minister, or a lawyer.
I walked into Dean Rieber's office and said I had no idea what my
commencement speech should be about. He handed me a book
of Edna St. Vincent Millay's poems and said, 'Here. Go to the
beach, and come back with a philosophical topic.' So I went and
came back with the topic 'The Fourth Dimension of Personality'
for my commencement address."

In his commencement address, Mr. Bunche said, in part:

"Humanity's problem today is how to be saved from itself. If
we are to develop our personalities to their fullest, we must add a
fourth dimension to this ordinary self—that we may expand up
and out from our narrow, immediate world.

"This fourth dimension—call it 'bigness,' soulfulness, spiritu-
ality, imagination, altruism, vision, or what you will—is that
quality which gives full meaning and true reality to others. In
identifying myself with my fellows and seeking to cooperate in
hearty good will and understanding with them, I find my life
in deed and in truth. My fellow graduates: We are youth, and
have the world yet to face. We are told that we have daring,
vigor, and resourcefulness. Then let us *dare* to live as *men* live!
Let us dedicate our vigor and our resourcefulness to the cause
of human fellowship! I commend to you the lines of Edna St.
Vincent Millay:

The world stands out on either side
No wider than the heart is wide . . . "

"I guess I was always hardheaded and independent," Mr.
Bunche said. "I always felt I wanted to do what I *wanted* to do.
I liked adventure, and I was willing to gamble, to take chances.
When I began teaching political science at Howard University,
in 1928, Mordecai Johnson, the president of the college, once
openly criticized me in a faculty meeting. 'Bunche is going all the

way to Africa to find a problem,' he said. Negro colleges are petty
places. The horizon is very limited, very narrow. They can be a
graveyard. They're diseased. They know they exist as expedients.
They're not in the free, competitive market. I had to get out. I've
always had faith in the essential goodness of people. I think that
basically man is good. He can be misled, but he's good. When you
believe that, there's a lot you can do in the world. The only limita-
tion in my job at the U.N. is that I can't participate in domestic
partisan politics. I draw the line at endorsing any candidate, and
I won't sign a petition on a piece of pending legislation. On the
other hand, I've never had trouble speaking my mind on the
race problem or poverty. At the beginning of the Montgomery,
Alabama, bus movement, led by Martin Luther King, I went
down there. I like to speak my mind. I've been asked to go into
politics, but to be a good politician you've got to tolerate idiots
as well as geniuses, and I'm a little impatient with idiocy. And I
could never go out and ask anybody to vote for me, and eat pizza
pie and bagels and lox, and all that. I've been asked what my main
drive has been, and I think one thing: competitiveness. I have the
pride of a competitor. I like to win. I think back on my school
days, when I was the only Negro in the class, and I was deter-
mined to show I was as good as the white kids. In later life, when
I worked for the O.S.S. and the State Department, I had the
pride in the fact that I was the first Negro to be given that kind
of job. And I was determined to show them."

KIDS

ABIES CAN'T REALLY talk for a story, but children can, and
I love watching them and listening to them. If I have any
special interest in reporting, it would be in children. For
one thing, they invariably offer material that is fresh and sur-
prising and very, very interesting. I often watch a baby sleep for
hours on end; actually I did exactly that with my son when he
was a baby.

One of my all-time favorite stories of any length is "The Shit-
Kickers of Madison Avenue," which I wrote for The Talk of the
Town in 1995 for the issue of *The New Yorker* celebrating its sev-
entieth anniversary:

> The tenth graders heading up Madison Avenue at 7:30 A.M. to
> the private high schools are freshly liberated from their dental
> braces, and their teeth look pearly and magnificent. They are fif-
> teen years old. During the week, they arrive, by bus or on foot,
> singly or in pairs or in clusters, and they make their way up the
> west side of Madison—they call it the "cool" side—toward their
> schools: Dalton, on East Eighty-ninth; Sacred Heart and Spence,

on East Ninety-first; Nightingale-Bamford, on East Ninety-
second; the Lycée Français, on East Ninety-fifth. Brearley and
Chapin are farther east; Collegiate, Columbia Prep, and Trinity
are in the west; Browning is south; Horace Mann, Riverdale, and
Fieldston are in the north. On the weekends, the tenth graders
from all points will find a way to get together. Today is only
Tuesday.

Boys and girls spill out of the Eighty-sixth Street crosstown
buses at Madison Avenue and join the flow of their counterparts
heading north. The walking tenth graders greet one another in
soft, kindly rhythms, in polite, gentle tones. The boys greet one
another with high fives. Girls with girls and girls with boys bestow
quick, sweet kisses on one another's cheeks—some cheeks still not
completely rid of hints of baby fat. No routine air kisses from these
kids. Their kisses are heartfelt, making their unity, their devotion
to and trust in one another, palpable. Kisses from their mouths are
like the little cool first nippy smacks of a very young baby.

Most of the tenth graders are in the habit of leaving home
without eating any breakfast. Still in clusters, with fifteen minutes
to get to school, they pause in doorways. One girl in a cluster of
five takes out a pack of Marlboro Lights—the brand favored at
the moment—and each member of the cluster participates in
lighting the cigarette, striking the match, guarding the flame,
offering a propane lighter. They share. The lighted cigarette is
passed from mouth to mouth. They all inhale, the girls twisting
their mouths like tough pros, exhaling the smoke from a tiny
corner opening on one side of the lips.

One angelic-looking blond beauty with raw, red nostrils takes
a puff, inhales deeply, and says wearily, "I've like got the fucking
flu or something."

"Fuck the you know fucking germs," another one says smoothly,
reassuringly, a positive reinforcer.

"I got home like three?" another member of the cluster says,
making her statement in the form of a question. "I sweat Henry?
Who you sweat? Anybody?"

The others regard her skeptically. "Nobody," one says.

"I sweat the shit out of Henry," the one who got home at three says mildly.

On the feet of all the members of this cluster are boots, not quite Timberland. The girls, some wearing black panty hose or black knee socks, have on chic, black laceups, all with Vibram soles, all with steel tips. One girl wearing laceups two feet high lifts a knee, turning the booted foot this way and that. "New shit-kickers!" she squeals, but in subdued ladylike tones.

"Cool," the angelic-looking one with the flu says. "Cool shit-kickers."

They crush out their shared cigarette with the heels of their shit-kickers, and they go to school.

Whenever the tenth graders have a break in their school program, and daily at 12:35 P.M., they head for one of their hangouts. The second floor of Jackson Hole, at the southwest corner of Ninety-first and Madison, is in at the moment. On this Tuesday, at 12:36 P.M., six four-place tables and a couple of two-place tables, accommodating twenty-eight customers, are filled. Ketchup bottles absolutely full are at the ready on every table. A teen-age Al Pacino–look-alike waiter serves them their first meal of the day: lone platters of ketchup-doused French fries or fried onion rings, or combo French fries and onion rings, and Cokes. A late arrival, dark-eyed, and smaller and chubbier than the ones settled in, turns up, and a place is found for her. Tearfully, she reports that her French teacher sprang a surprise test on her class, and she thinks she did badly on it.

"Don't like get fucking stressed out," a girl says, offering that same kindly positive reinforcement.

"Fucking teachers," a companion says, chewing on a fry and simultaneously taking a drag on a cigarette and passing it on. "I'm on my way you know to lunch, and the fucking teacher asks where I'm going?" The statements continue to sound as though they were questions. "I don't want teachers being like into my you know business?"

"I miss the teacher who used to be a model and then left the school and went to Africa to be a nun?" someone says. "She

would like talk you know about her experiences? She was very
like open to everybody?" The others at the table and the girls at
all the other tables agree that they miss the teacher who went to
Africa to be a nun.

One of the girls, very pretty, with long dark hair, is "present-
ing" a party and hands out invitations. She has dark glasses
pushed up on top of her hair. She wears silver loop earrings,
a double in the left ear, a single in the right. At her throat hangs
a large wooden cross. The invitation shows a picture of Stone-
henge on one side, and the other side has a long list of names of
people supporting the party, which has a title: "The Farside."

"I can't go to the party?" one of the fifteen-year-olds says. "My
father grounded me? Because I was smoking?"

"My mom is trying to like ship me off to a fucking school
in fucking Spain?" another girl says. "Unless I you know quit
smoking?"

"I want to quit, but I can't? I don't have a choice? It's too late?"
one fatalist says.

The party entrepreneur explains that she is working with six
other presenters to spread the invitations around, to telephone
friends at the schools to the east, west, north, and south, and to
obtain the services of a really topnotch d.j. They are working with a
well-to-do party producer, whose take of the proceeds will be forty
percent, the balance to be divided evenly among the seven pre-
senters. Admission to the party will be twelve dollars per person.

"This rich, older guy is like experienced you know?" she says.
"He's twenty-nine?"

The mention of the number draws forth gasps.

"Fucking twenty-nine," one of the girls says. "That's the age
of those actors in that mindless *90210* or that mindless *Melrose
Place*. They're twenty-nine, and they're like playing our age."

At any rate, there are plans to be made. The party is going to
start at 10 P.M. The girls will spend the afternoon before in
preparations.

"Here's what we'll do," the entrepreneur says. "We need five
hours. You three come to my house you know at five? You bring

all your clothes? I take everything out of my closet and spread everything out on the floor? We try on all the stuff? Depending on what kind of mood we're in, we make our selection?

"We have to be fucking blunt," one of the potential guests says. "About what looks good on us."

"Then we take showers? Half an hour? Then we like put cream on our legs? Half an hour? Then we call up everybody who's been like grounded? We talk to them for at least an hour? Maybe we give them an hour and a half? Then we go out and we buy a quart of vodka and some orange juice and cranberry juice? Then we go to somebody else's house and drink vodka with orange juice or vodka and cranberry juice? Then we get dressed? Then we get another quart of vodka and go to somebody else's house? We become like outgoing? And we make calls to friends and invite them over? By then, we'll be ready to go?"

On the first school day after the weekend, promptly at 12:36 P.M., the tenth graders are back in place at Jackson Hole, smoking, chewing gum, eating fries and onion rings, and reviewing the party. "I like feel real ripped off?" the young Farside presenter-entrepreneur is saying. "Too many people came to the party, which was at this nice club on West Forty-seventh Street. There were hundreds pushing and shoving and clogging the street, and the police came? And they said we had to be carded, because they had a bar. And we you know didn't like have cards, so this twenty-nine-year-old rich guy said the fee for getting the club had to be raised from three thousand dollars to eight thousand dollars, because they had to close the bar and were not allowed you know to sell us drinks? And everybody had to pay twenty dollars instead of twelve dollars just to get in? So, but even so, nobody like wanted to leave? And it was so crowded you couldn't even dance? And at the end of it the twenty-nine-year-old rich guy took forty percent, and all I got was about fifty fucking dollars, after I did all the fucking work and made a million phone calls?"

She chews on a French fry, accepts a glowing Marlboro Light from the girl beside her at the table, and takes a quick puff. The chubby, dark-eyed girl who was stressed out by her French

teacher comes over from another table and gives the entrepreneur
a soft, comforting kiss on the cheek, and one by one all the other
tenth graders in the area come over and do the same.

The story, when it was published, caused a bit of an uproar
among some parents and teachers, but very few of them said that
it was misrepresentative. A number of them told me, with wry
amusement, that the story was right on the button.

The key to being able to do this story was finding the charac-
ters. I've lived on the Upper East Side for many years, and for a
long time, I had watched these kids on their way to these schools.
When my son started first grade at a school in the neighborhood,
the dog and I would walk there with him. Later, a teacher I knew
at one of the schools mentioned to me that hanging out at
Jackson Hole was in at the moment. So I went there, and on my
second visit, I encountered all of the characters in the story. I was
immediately fond of them, in their honesty and in their straight-
forwardness. I was deeply touched by the way they accepted me,
strangely enough, as one of them. I told them I was doing some
reporting for *The New Yorker,* but they didn't seem impressed,
just vaguely interested. Not a single one of them—like, say, people
in the entertainment business—gave even a hint of wanting "pub-
licity." They were respectful and accepting and courteous. Fifteen
year-olds, I find, are sensitive and alert to hostility and criticism,
and they like to be taken on their own terms. They took me on
my terms. I loved the way they were. I admired them enormously,
and I still do.

The talk of these kids had to be absolutely true to the ear. Up to
then, I hadn't heard it accurately reproduced, in movies or on tele-
vision or in publications. I literally gloried in listening to it.

Here's a very short story from 1999 about a seventh-graders'
dance that demonstrates a different way of handling the subject. It
was entitled "Slow burn at a private school mixer."

Two hundred and fifty seventh-grade boys and girls from the
single-sex Independent schools came to the Goddard Gaieties
annual dance last month. It cost forty-five dollars a ticket and

was held in the basement of the Church of St. Ignatius Loyola, on upper Park Avenue.

The ritual, started by and for the benefit of the Goddard Riverside Community Center, has been going on since the mid-nineteen-forties. At that time, a live orchestra was engaged to play the traditional waltzes and foxtrots, and the children were required to "dress"—little suits and ties, little party dresses and gloves. In the nineteen-seventies, with the coming of rock and roll, the music became canned and amplified, and the dress code became "casual." Now the boys had on T-shirts, mightily over-sized jeans or khakis, and sneakers, and the girls had on tank tops or flimsy, tight cardigans, jeans, and thick-soled sneakers or platforms. The boys didn't have much in the way of muscles. The girls didn't have much in the way of breasts. The children, tense and anxious, were escorted to the entrance by tense and anxious parents, who clearly showed that they wanted to hang around. The boys and girls clearly showed that they wanted them to leave. The parents left.

Colored balloons hung from the ceiling. Off to one side, punch and cookies were at the ready on a table monitored by chaperons. At the far end, opposite the entrance, a young, single-earringed, goateed, and cheerful d. j., wearing blue jeans, was setting up his station, which came with a small stage platform emblazoned with the silver-lettered logo of the music providers, "EJM—The Life of the Party. . . " (EJM's fee for the party was five hundred and seventy-five dollars.) The m.c., a confident, muscular, young black man, in black pants and a black T-shirt, was testing a cordless mike.

The boys and girls waited, trying not to look around at each other. A group of boys who knew each other from Collegiate, Buckley, St. Bernard's, and Browning horsed around, pointedly ignoring a small group of girls waiting nearby who knew each other from Chapin, Brearley, Spence, Marymount, and Nightingale-Bamford. Some girls greeted each other with overjubilant, strained squeals of joy or simulated surprise. Boys played it cool and shook the hands of other boys lackadaisically. Everybody

I'm sorry, let me provide the actual content.

seemed to be mirrored in somebody else. Nobody was fat. The trousers of the boys sagged over their no-hips. The girls clumsily swung their pipestem arms around each other and then didn't seem to know how to unloosen them. So they shook them up and down purposelessly. They kicked their pipestem legs away from each other in awkward moves, anticipating the actual dancing. Their tiny, firm backsides revealed no gelatinous motion.

One tall-for-her-age girl wearing thick-soled Vans sneakers and a baby-blue hooded pullover offered me some dispassionate elucidation:

"I don't like tank tops? They're completely out of season? I think they're, like, silly? Some of these boys are, like, weird? One of them is mean to me. He says mean things about people with overbite? Not about my braces, about my friend's braces? He's got braces, too? Everybody has braces. He's mean about my friend? Because she chews gum? But she can chew gum, because there's this, like, special gum you buy for chewing gum with braces? So this boy is mean about the gum? Just because he doesn't like gum. See? He's over there with his clump. The schools, like, clump together? He says mean things about the way I sing along when they play 'Flagpole Sitta'?"

She sang, "I run it up the flagpole to see who salutes, but no one ever does." She had a good voice, "It's alternative rock?" she said. "It's a punk band but not, like, very punk? This is a two-hour party. I wish this was, like, a four-hour party?"

"Welcome, everybody!" the m.c. was saying into his mike at a decibel level that caused the punch to slosh on the table. "Let's start the party!"

The action was slow to get going. No wild party this. At the urging of the m.c., a few girls hesitantly stepped. They danced with each other. Then the boys did the same. The d.j. spun one song after another, so that "Pretty Fly (For a White Guy)" ran perilously close to Frank Sinatra singing "Come Fly With Me." . . . By the time "YMCA" came on, the dancers had loosened up. Boys and girls were mixed up on the floor. They took turns jumping onto the EJM platform and dancing on it. . . .

A quartet of girls in tanktops and platform shoes harmonized in a rendition of an Aaliyah ditty that went, "Are you that somebody boy I've been watchin' you like a hawk in the sky that fly and you were my prey boy I promise you if we keep bumpin' heads I know that one of these days we're gonna hook up probably talk on the phone but see I don't know if that's good I been holdin' back this secret from you."

Finally, at the end of the first hour of the Gaieties, the d.j. played a slow number: Aerosmith's "I Don't Want to Miss a Thing," from the soundtrack of the movie *Armageddon*. A few brave boy-with-girl couples held each other loosely—very, very loosely—heads not quite touching, the boys' hands splayed gingerly over the girls' backs. Looking dreamy, they moved slowly and rhythmically, in one-step, back and forth horizontally. The girl who had thought the anti-gum boy was mean stood on the sidelines, watching the couples and swaying empathetically. She looked charmed and forgiving.

There's hardly a moment ever, in my personal life, when I'm not automatically on the alert for a story. It's been a natural part of me. So, as my son grew up, I always found his school life of interest. I sent him to traditional, structured schools within walking distance of our home. I also paid attention to what he was learning, in high school, in college, and in graduate school. And I've been rather fascinated by his schoolmates and their parents. They provided me with splendid material for my stories. Here's one, written in 1980, called "Halloween Party," inspired by all of the above. It lent itself quite naturally to what *The New Yorker* used to run as a "Letter from. . . ."

A letter has arrived from a woman we know:

"My thirteen-year-old son gave a Halloween costume party for a bunch of boys and girls. I became his financier as he talked endlessly about his Count Dracula costume. Count Dracula seems to have been the most popular Halloween costume for the past ten years—a black satin Count Dracula cape ($18.95), Count Dracula fangs ($1.25), clown whiteface makeup($2), and Zauder's stage blood ($2). The menu for the part included fried

chicken, spaghetti, Cokes, salad, and cupcakes with orange or
chocolate icing (cost per guest $7). The candy, for visiting trick-
or-treaters as well as for the guests, was orange and black jelly
beans, sugar pumpkins, Candy Corn, Tootsie Rolls, Raisinets,
Almond Joys, Nestlé Crunch, Baby Ruths, Milky Ways, Heidi
Jujy-Fruits, Peanut Chews, and Cracker Jacks (total $38.65). My
son also had eight cookies, six inches in diameter and decorated
with black cats ($1.25 each); eight little plastic pumpkins full of
hard candies, each with a trembly plastic spider on top ($2.50 each);
eight orange-colored balloons that blew up to resemble cats
(eighty-five cents each); eight orange-colored lollipops with jack-
o'-lantern faces (seventy cents each); a large paper tablecloth
showing a black witch standing over a black caldron with spiders
popping off the caldron ($2.25); matching napkins ($1.10); match-
ing paper cups ($2); matching paper plates ($1.75); a "HAPPY
HALLOWEEN" sign ($1.25); a dancing skeleton ($3.99); some-
thing called a Happy Spider ($4); a classic jack-o'-lantern, made
of a real pumpkin ($4, plus labor). Total investment in props:
$181.59. Total investment of labor in jack-o'-lantern, kitchen
cleanup, and laundry: $35. Total investment in emotion and puz-
zlement indeterminable.

"I watch the guests arrive. The first one, A, comes as Darth
Vader, of *Star Wars*. B comes as Luke Skywalker, of *Star Wars*. C
comes as The Incredible Hulk. D comes as a tramp. E comes as a
ghost. F comes as a ballerina. G comes, in one of her mother's old
evening gowns, as Bette Midler. All are in an advanced stage of hys-
teria. A pulls at C's costume. G immediately starts throwing sugar
pumpkins at E. . . . They tear into the fried chicken, most of them
eating three bites and wasting the rest. They sprinkle jelly beans on
the chicken and on the spaghetti. They pick at the spaghetti, which
is on the menu because my son said that everybody likes spaghetti.
They eat it one strand at a time, dropping a strand on the floor for
each strand they consume. They gulp down the Cokes, another
'must'—their appetite for the caffeine insatiable.

"And what are they talking about, these eighth graders who
are eyeing each other fishily? They are talking about their *careers*.

They are talking about getting into Exeter. They are talking about
Yale and Yale Law School. They are talking about how to get in
here and how to get in there. They are talking about who makes
more money, the president of Chase Manhattan or the president
of General Motors. Nobody is talking kid talk. Nobody is talking
about the present time and what to do with it. Nobody is talking
about learning. Nobody sounds *young*. A, a pudgy boy who tries
to find out the grade marks of every other child in his class, wants
to be 'a successful corporation lawyer.' He doesn't say just 'corpo-
ration lawyer.' It's success that he's bent on. . . . Next, A tells my
son that he wants to go to Exeter. Why? 'Because Exeter is a step-
ping stone to Harvard,' he says. Not Exeter for the wonders of
Exeter but Exeter because it will be useful *after* he leaves it.

"B, with his mouth full of Almond Joy, is asking the others a
question: 'Do you want to be a little fish in a big pond or a big fish
in a little pond?'

"Now A is talking. His mother, he is saying, has taken him
rock climbing, because rock climbing is an impressive activity to
put down as his 'interest' on the application to Exeter.

"'But you *hate* rock climbing!' says D, who is a mischief-maker
with the face of an angel under his tramp makeup. 'You hate to
move your *ass*,' D adds.

"All right, who else is here? C, who is wearing a mask of The
Incredible Hulk. C is the jock of the group. He has been in training
since the age of two in the craft of giving nothing away. He's wary
and tight and already immunized to the teeth against charity for its
own sake. H, too, wants to be a corporation lawyer; so do B and D.
The girls, though—the ballerina and Bette Midler—both want to
be big-corporation presidents. They are both relaxed, being well
aware of what women's lib has done for them. E, the ghost, is the
only one with a simple costume, made of a sheet. A, talking to B,
points out that E doesn't have to bother about a costume, because
he's rich, very rich. His grandfather lives in Texas and owns oil
wells—not new ones but very old and very productive oil wells. . . .

"D squirts a little Coke at A, and the future lawyers get up and
make for the door. They cram their loot bags with the orange-

and-black jelly beans, the Candy Corn, the cookies, the trembly
spiders, the balloons, the jack-o'-lantern lollipops, and the rest.
They make a big point of thanking me loudly. The girls amble
out, smiling knowledgeably at each other. E and my son run to
catch up to them. They, too, thank me extravagantly. And they all
go off, in their disguises, to do their tricks and get their treats. I
am left wondering what it's all about."

Writing about children—of almost any age—offers a reporter
endlessly challenging ways of subtly revealing, with facts, his own
point of view. The children at the Halloween party wore costumes,
but unlike their elders, they were—as children usually seem to me
to be—without camouflage. I enjoy finding the humor and the
charm and the meaning in the way children are uncamouflaged, as
well as revealing, perhaps, what they might be fated to become. A
toy store is a splendid setting to cut them loose in and to report,
not only on them, but on their mothers.

Here's a Talk story, December 10, 2001:

"Toy Dept.: Girls and Dolls"

Reassuring signs lately—on the streets and in the parks—of little
girls dramatically mothering baby dolls in their arms or pushing
them in tiny strollers were somewhat diffused by what some little
girls were doing in toy stores last week. The brand-new Toys R Us
in Times Square—Store No. 1595 in the chain—had, on four
levels, a sixty-foot indoor Ferris wheel with toy-themed cars (Mr.
And Mrs. Potato Head, Tonka Truck, Pokémon, and eleven oth-
ers); a five-ton, thirty-four-foot-long animatronic *Jurassic Park*
Tyrannosaurus rex, and a four-thousand-square-foot, two-story
Barbie Dollhouse. Nearby shelves were stocked with boxes of My
Real Life Baby ($59.99)—she sleeps, cries, laughs, and burps.
Each box bore the line "Learn what it's like to be a little mommy."
Little girls looked blankly at them.

Across the aisle, a Babyland General Hospital/Cabbage Patch
Kids and Babies shop featured a seventeen-foot-high tree and large
plastic heads of cabbage in a patch staffed by white-clad multilin-
gual "nurses," looking as though they were just out of their teens.

Each nurse had a toy stethoscope around her neck and a nameplate on her lab coat. A few hopeful, chattering little girls, shepherded by a Spanish-speaking woman, gathered around.

"We do not sell them. These are real babies," Nurse Michelle said emphatically to the little girls, who looked respectful and paid attention.

"Do they grow?" one of the little girls asked.

"It's a toy," the tallest of the girls said. "You buy it."

"You don't *buy* your baby here," Nurse Michelle said, looking stern. "You adopt. This is an adoption center."

"All our babies are born from a cabbage," Nurse Jo-Ann said. "This cabbage patch is exclusive to our store here. Mother Cabbage is about to give birth. I'm dilating Mother Cabbage now, and she'll be dilated for ten full cabbage leaves. Push, Mother Cabbage, push!"

Nurse Tracey said, "Mother Cabbage is nervous. Calm her down."

Everybody around the cabbage patch looked anxious.

"This is creepy," one of the little girls said. Their shepherd gave a deep sigh.

"Cabbage Patch Kids are about to have their twentieth anniversary, so Head Nurse Linda came all the way from head-quarters, in Cleveland, Georgia, to train us in the birthing," Nurse Jo-Anne said. "I never had to do a C-section, though. I just give the babies T.L.C. in this bottle—it's like an I.V.—and some imagicillin. Push, Mother Cabbage, push!" She reached into a hole among the cabbage leaves and pulled out a naked doll about fourteen inches long.

"It's a boy," Nurse Tracey said. "Say hello to John Adam." She gave the doll a spank. "Bunnybees, who fly like bees and hop like bunnies, sprinkle magical crystals on the babies—blue Bunnybees for boys and pink Bunnybees for girls."

The woman who was with the little girls said, *"Cuanto cuestan los bebés?"*

"Los chiquitos son $64.99," Nurse Michelle said. "The old Mattel Cabbage Patch Babies are $14.99. But these are exclusive

Toys R Us Cabbage Patch Babies. When you adopt ours, you get
to choose your own name and can change the birth date.
Remember, you adopt. Remember, we never sell."

"I don't want it. I want Barbie," one of the little girls said.

"Donde están las cosas de Barbie?" the woman asked. *"En la casa
de Barbie?"*

"Barbie! Barbie!" the little girls cried, and they deserted the
Cabbage Patch for Barbie's walk-in Dollhouse. At the entrance, a
beautiful young woman dressed as a fairy held a wand and, with
it, touched the little girls and the Spanish-speaking woman on
the shoulder, smiling and murmuring to them. Along with hordes
of other little girls and their mothers, they jammed hysterically
into the Dollhouse. The air smelled of bubble gum. Barbie was
starring in her first movie, *The Nutcracker*, with Ken as Prince
Eric, Little Sister Kelly as the Snow Fairy, Friend Jenny as the
Flower Fairy, and the hell with Tchaikovsky. White "Nutcracker"
Barbie had blond hair; black "Nutcracker" Barbie had black hair.
Both wore ballet slippers, an organdy dress with sparkles, a golden
necklace, and a crown.

The little girls tried on Barbie-brand clothes for Barbie owners
—furry or shiny or denim jackets with flowers and sparkles. Their
baby-sitter picked up a pink Barbie telephone set. On the box, it
read *"Intercomunicadores—¡Hola, say Barbie!"*

"Do we adopt Barbie, too?" one of the little girls asked. Her
guardian answered breathlessly in Spanish: "The pretty fairy
touched me with her wand and told me that we would have
everything we wanted."

This story required specific indications of how merchants count
on the real yearnings transmitted by grown women to little girls.

CINDERELLAS

IT'S COMPLETELY UP to the writer to find the "story" in whatever he sets out to report. At a newspaper, a city editor may send a reporter out to cover what is called a story, and the reporter follows a fairly well-established pattern of gathering facts and writing them coherently in a fairly well-established form. In my kind of journalism, the reporter sees into the facts and recognizes what is to him, and perhaps only to him, "the story." One delightful aspect of reporting for *The New Yorker* is one's freedom to recognize the story embedded in the facts and to find a special way of telling it.

For example, several months into the year 2001, Susan Morrison, the editor of The Talk of the Town, asked me to do a story about Jamie-Lynn Sigler, the nineteen-year-old actress in the HBO series *The Sopranos,* who was opening in the title role of *Cinderella* in the latest version of the Rodgers and Hammerstein musical. I went to the opening, wondering what the story might be. Sitting behind me in the audience, I saw a pretty little girl, about eleven, who had black hair worn down to her shoulder blades. She had on a stiff, full-skirted, long white organdie dress, white stockings,

white patent-leather slippers, a diamond necklace, a gold bracelet, a gold Mickey Mouse wristwatch, and a sparkling silvery tiara. She was holding a souvenir "Cinderella" wand. Her name was Bianca Bethune. Sitting next to her was her mother. They told me that Bianca was in the fifth grade at a private school in a small town in New Jersey. They had been driven into New York by the show's producers in a limo, and they had been invited to the cast party after the show, because Bianca had won a dance contest at which Jamie-Lynn Sigler was the judge. Bianca had won the tiara in a "Sunburst Beauty Pageant" when she was about seven or eight. After chatting with Bianca, I knew immediately what my story should be. I stayed with Bianca and her mother, went to the party after the show with them, and wrote the story in the form of a short piece of fiction. The editor entitled it "A Cinderella Story." In part:

> Bianca was expressionless. Her mother did the talking.
> "Bianca is in school from eight o'clock to two-fifteen," Mrs. Bethune said cheerfully. "After school, my aunt or I pick her up and take her to New York, where she attends Broadway Dance Center, Monday through Sunday. She does ballet, tap, jazz, hip-hop, point, theatre dance. She goes Saturdays nine to three and six to eight. She has a piano lesson once a week. She gets weekly private lessons with a voice teacher and an acting coach. When we get home, we always read the Bible before bed. We pray and don't ever forget to thank God for getting us to where we are. All this started when I took Bianca at eighteen months to Mommy and Me classes. As they say, you do what you got to do."

From the story:

> At the party, at the restaurant One51, Bianca ran into a girl her age, named Allison Flood, with whom she had appeared in a Burger King commercial.
> "We jumped up and down together in a crowd and screamed and hollered," Bianca said. For the first time that evening, she smiled.

The ending to the story:

> It was almost midnight. Bianca was finally getting photographed
> with Cinderella. Someone asked Bianca's mother if she was ready
> to take the limo with Bianca and go home.
> "No way," Bianca's mother said. "We've got to work the room."

This little piece is an example of how a reporter can express an
opinion, clearly, strongly, and with humor, without saying literally
what that opinion is.

An element of "newsiness" is in many of the stories in The Talk
of the Town, but it's different from what is found in newspapers
and other branches of the media. I'm not drawn to doing a "news"
story head-on. For instance, the twin daughters of George W. Bush
were the subjects of "news" stories when they were found to be
carrying on illegally in bars or parties. That kind of gossip doesn't
interest me. But there was validity for my kind of journalistic focus
in Lauren Bush, the sixteen-year-old niece of the 43rd President,
when she came to town in the spring of 2001, and, aided by her
mother, welcomed some public attention brought to her modelling
career. This branch of the Bush family getting into the act was
worth taking a look at. So I did the following Talk story, "First
Niece Steps Out":

> Sixteen year-old Lauren Bush came to town from Houston last
> Monday with her mother, Sharon, her twelve-year-old sister,
> Ashley, and her father, Neil (President Bush's younger brother), to
> find a new dress for a party that night celebrating her appearance
> on the cover of a special edition of *Tatler*. In the cover photograph,
> Lauren is wrapped in an American flag, with her face frozen in the
> standard fashion-photographer-directed expression of *sultry*.
>
> The first stop for mother and daughter was the Celine-by-
> Michael-Kors showroom, in the LMVH Building, on West
> Fifty-seventh Street, where a trio from the E! *Fashion Television*
> program awaited them.
>
> "Get the arrival!" the E! producer, Mimi Tompkins, said to her
> camera crew.

Lauren was cute and more self-confident than her *Tatler* photo revealed—her blond hair pulled into a ponytail, her mouth engaged in chewing a wad of Extra ("The green kind," she said happily). She was wearing a black ribbed sweater, tight bluejeans, and flip-flops. Her mother was more artfully arranged—Christian Dior sunglasses pushed on top of her blond hair, a gray pantsuit, Manolos, heavy turquoise beads holding a matching cross, and a wide Elsa Peretti silver cuff on her wrist.

The Bush ladies and a couple of aides were greeted by Celine's vice-president in charge of communications, Lisa Pomerantz, who quickly determined that Lauren was a size 4. She then asked Mrs. Bush what she was interested in trying on.

"I want to have her taken care of first," Lauren's mother said, fingering her cross.

Some of the goodies were brought out, and Lauren slid behind a curtain to try one on.

"How does Lauren feel about the speed with which all this fame has happened to her?" Mimi Tomkins, the TV producer, asked Mrs. Bush.

"Well, she's got a lot on her plate," Mrs. Bush replied. "She's the captain of her high school tennis team, and she's just coming off her finals and S.A.T.s. Modelling is just a hobby for her."

Lauren reappeared in a gray stretch tank dress that was quickly nixed for being uncomfortable. It was replaced by a bronze honeycombed beaded shift dress, to be accessorized with a bullet belt and Jimmy Choo bronze shoes with four-inch spike heels. This outfit was determined to be just right for the party.

Tomkins asked her cameraman to zoom in on the belt.

"Impressive," Tomkins said. "All those places for big bullets."

"How much?" the cameraman asked.

"Approximately five thousand," Lisa Pomerantz said coolly. "We like to say they borrow the dress. Then, if they like it, they come back to us as buyers."

"Tomorrow night, you'll need something for giving out the scholar-athlete awards," Mrs. Bush said to her daughter. "That's the one sponsored by the European-American Bank and New York 1."

"Then I don't need to dress up," Lauren said.

"Oh, yes, you do," her mother said. "The photographers will be there." Tomkins had her camera turned on Mrs. Bush. "Lauren and I have had great bonding trips these past three years," she said. "Ever since she was thirteen and started modelling shorts and stuff for Abercrombie & Fitch and for Tommy Hilfiger. But it's always been just a hobby."

For the scholar-athlete awards, they chose a gray wool pullover, encrusted with Swarovski crystals, to be worn with gray tropical-wool hip-huggers, along with silver leather sandals and a silver clutch bag.

Back at her hotel, Lauren had her hair done by Lorenzo Micciche. "Very *Charlie's Angels,*" an aide said. At the party that night, at the Globe, on lower Park Avenue, Lauren looked smashing in the five-thousand-dollar bronze honeycombed beaded shift dress with the bullet belt. Admiring guests included the Hilton sisters (Paris, twenty, and Nicky, seventeen), who told Lauren that she looked beautiful and volunteered that Paris was wearing an Ungaro top with a Dolce & Gabbana belt, and that Nicky had on a Diane Von Furstenberg wrap dress. Another guest, Candace Bushnell, came over and told Lauren that her *Charlie's Angels* hair looked spectacularly fresh and clean and beautiful. "When I was sixteen, my hair was never like that," she said, looking wistful.

Neil Bush stood to one side hugging his twelve-year-old daughter, Ashley, who wore a little pale-blue suit. She watched her sister with considerable amusement. "All this is just Lauren's hobby," Neil Bush said. "All my kids are great, because of my mother. Every Sunday, we're over there at my parents' place for lunch."

"I don't care about my clothes," he said. "I'm wearing this old hand-me-down jacket. Look." He pulled up the collar and pointed to the name tag sewn on the frayed inside and read it aloud: "George H. W. Bush."

The Talk of the Town has always had an eye on fashion. But my interest for a story was in the kind of creative force behind the

fashion. Here is the first "fashion" story I wrote, in 1957, about Mlle. Gabrielle Chanel, who had recently come out of retirement and who had presented a collection of dress and suit designs that had got a response from buyers that was every bit as powerful as her designs of thirty years earlier. She was fresh from three strenuous weeks in New York and in Dallas, where she had received an award as the most significant designer of the last fifty years.

Here is the story entitled "The Strong Ones," written forty-five years ago, about Chanel in New York.

At seventy-four, Mlle. Chanel is sensationally good-looking, with dark brown eyes, a brilliant smile, and the unquenchable vitality of a twenty-year-old, and when, giving us a firm handshake, she said, "I am *très, très fatiguée*," it was with the assurance of a woman who knows she can afford to say it. Since the Chanel look is causing such a stir these days, we took particular note of what its begetter was wearing: a natural-colored straw sailor hat; a natural-colored silk suit, with box jacket and straight skirt; a white silk blouse, with gold cufflinks; low-heeled brown-and-white shoes; and plenty of jewelry—a pearl hatpin, pearls and diamonds in her ears, ropes of pearls about her neck, and, on her jacket, an enormous brooch of antique gold studded with rubies, emeralds, and diamonds.

"The brooch is of my design, and the dress is nothing, *très simple*," she said when we congratulated her on her appearance. "The cuff links were given to me by Stravinsky, thirty years ago. The occasion? Admiration, of course—the admiration *I* bore *him!* You see this ring?" She extended the little finger of her left hand, and a topaz suddenly blazed in the light. "I would trade all my other jewels for this. It was given to me when I was sixteen, in my home province of Auvergne, by an old woman who liked me. She handed me the ring and said, 'Here, *petit Coco*'—let me explain that all my life I have been called Coco; when I was born, my father was away and I was named Gabrielle, which he didn't like, and he made me promise that if anyone called me by that name, I wouldn't answer, and I never have—'*petit Coco*,' she said,

'wear this ring always. Never, never let it leave your finger. It will
bring you luck, your life will be magnificent.' What she said then,
so long ago, has proved true—my life is magnificent."

Mlle. Chanel said that she had been too busy in Texas to do
any shopping but had managed to buy a lot of Texas shirts and
hats right here in New York, which she was carrying back to
Paris to give friends. "In America, it seems to me that people
look at me in such a nice way," she said. "In Europe today, it is
as if people had no more time to be nice. I liked very much
Texas. The people of Dallas, *ah, je les aime beaucoup! Très gentils,
très charmants, très simples.* Never in the least haughty." Mlle.
Chanel did a skillful and funny pantomime of a haughty per-
son. "I had the stage fright when I went to Dallas, and no won-
der, for in truth I was afraid it would be a huge movie stage, but
I found everything real and the people real, like a big family,
and the fright went away."

We lighted a cigarette for Mlle. Chanel and asked her how
she had happened to be in retirement so long. Her brown eyes
flashed. "Never was I really in retirement in my heart," she said.
"During the war, nobody thought anymore of making beautiful
clothes, and after the war I watched the couturiers, the young
men, to see what they were doing. I travelled. I enjoyed life at
my country place in Switzerland. But I was bored not having
anything real to do. Always, I observed the new clothes. At last,
quietly, calmly, with great determination, I began working on
une belle collection. When I showed it in Paris, I had many critics.
They said that I was old-fashioned, that I was no longer of the
age. Always, I was smiling inside my head, and I thought, I will
show them. In America, there was great enthusiasm. In France,
I had to fight. But I did not mind. I love very much to battle. Now,
in France, they are trying to adapt my ideas. So much the better!
But when I see some things they call 'after *la mode Chanel,*' I
protest vigorously. There are no potato sacks among my dresses!

"I must tell you something of significance. Fashion is always of
the time in which you live. It is not something standing alone.
The problem of fashion in 1925 was different. Women were

just beginning to go to work in offices. I inspired the cutting of
the hair short because it goes with the modern woman. To the
woman going to work, I said to take off the bone corset, because
women cannot work while they are imprisoned in a corset. I
invented the tweed for sports and the loose-fitting sweater and
blouse. I encouraged women to be well groomed and to like per-
fume—a woman who is badly perfumed is not a woman! The
problem today is *très différent*. Nearly all women work, and if they
don't work, they want to work. So many women in France have a
little car. They find it difficult to get in and out of the little car.
This you cannot do with a crinoline skirt. Many of the big for-
tunes today have crumbled. In former years, rich women did not
go shopping themselves. Now they do. They have to be practical.
Today people travel a lot. The clothes must be light in weight for
the flying. But the grand problem, the most important problem,
is to rejuvenate women. To make women look young. Then their
outlook on life changes. They feel more joyous."

Mlle. Chanel flicked the ash off the last inch of her cigarette,
which she held pinched between the thumb and forefinger of her
left hand. "As for myself," she said, "I am not interested anymore
in 1957. It is gone for me. I am more interested in 1958, 1959,
1960. Women have always been the strong ones of the world. The
men are always seeking from women a little pillow to put their
heads down on. They are always longing for the mother who held
them as infants. Women must tell them always that *they* are the
ones. They are the big, the strong, the wonderful. In truth, women
are the strong ones. It is just my opinion. I am not a professor. I
am not a preacher. I speak my opinions gently. It is the truth for
me. I am not young, but I feel young. The day I feel old, I will go
to bed and stay there. *J'aime la vie!* I feel that to live is a wonder-
ful thing."

How is that for a woman who was ahead of her time? It was an
extraordinary experience for me during the interview to listen to
Chanel. All these years later—knowing what we all know about
women today—I still find her extraordinary. I'm proud, early in

this twenty-first century, of having been able to capture her mid-twentieth-century extraordinariness.

A year or so before the end of the last century, The Talk of the Town gave me the opportunity to observe a certain difference in the complexities involving fashion: Title: "Mario Testino's Steamy Evening":

Mario Testino, "the world's hottest fashion photographer," according to proclaimers at the opening, last week, of his Mary Boone gallery exhibition, was literally steaming under a barrage of warmer and moister than usual air kisses. The white-walled gallery looked cool and elegant, but it seemed to be getting warmer by the second as guests advanced on Testinos priced from twenty-five hundred to five thousand dollars a pop. The opening reception was packed with fashion editors, a few models, and a mixture of young, cute, eye-contact-making, spiky-haired boys and not quite mirror copies of Kate Moss. A vague eroticism floated unrestrained over the bodies in the room.

Testino is forty-four, a good-natured, fleshy, large-faced, loosely-put-together six-plus-two-inch-footer, who was hand-somely attired in a Bergére dark-green coat, a Charvet painterly-green shirt open at the collar, and black English brogues. He carried a couple of small Contax cameras and took photographs of his own photographs and of people looking at them. Sweating, and wiping his face with a damp handkerchief, he went from Testino to Testino offering comments. "I love being a voyeur," he said. "The whole life. The people. The clothes. The girls. The travel. I visit my mother at least twice a year in Peru. We are a close family. My brother is my business manager. I love my three sisters. I adore my mother.

"I am so lucky to do what I do," he went on, patting his face with the handkerchief and looking lovingly at a picture called *Roving Finger,* which showed a forefinger curled into a woman's cleavage. He spoke in a mysteriously pleasing and undefinable accent, derived over time from his Peruvian birthplace, American schools, and London waiter jobs. "As a boy in Lima, when we vis-

ited museums I was always told, 'Do not touch,' so I wanted to
touch. Now I touch."

On to *Carolyn Murphy. Georgina Grenville, Kylie Bax and Carla
Bruni at Dior,* all partly or completely nude in dressing quarters.
Testino took a picture of his picture and said, "Very sexy, these
girls. They are very young, about eighteen. I'm fascinated by youth.
Young people have this big freedom with their bodies. I like to
push them when they start. Then I drop them. There always have
to be new ones. It's life. Life is about shedding certain things."

Sheet Marks. On a man's chest, sheet marks indeed. "I'm fasci-
nated by sheet marks," Testino said, dabbing sweat from his face.
"I'm often the first one awake in a house full of people, and I see
the sheet marks. It's a part of life."

Extrovert, a shot, taken from behind, of a man in a Brazil hotel
room exposing the better part of his buttocks. "Brazil is desperate
for the perfect behind, perfect roundness—like sculpture," Testino
explained, pinching and shaking the shoulders of his Bergére
jacket for a breeze.

"He's the best, the sexiest of all the fashion photographers,"
one pretty young fashion editor said. "And he really loves his
mother."

Another fashion editor, one with gray hair, and identified by
Testino as "a legend," gave him a longer than usual air kiss and a
big, knowing hug. "There's smoke coming out of the front door,"
she said to him with a loudly confident, born-to-the-old-New
York guffaw. "You're so hot you're burning."

The fun for me, in reporting, is not to chase the latest thing in
the news, but to find some related aspect to what's in the news. So
it was—with the announcement that Oprah Winfrey was planning
to bring out a new magazine called *O* named for herself—that my
editor, Susan Morrison, suggested I have a talk with Oprah's old
friend, Gayle King. Here is "Oprah's Understudy":

No need to worry about Oprah Winfrey, founder and editorial
director of the new magazine *O,* who is staying put in Chicago
while her fifty-odd underlings hole up in the Hearst Magazines

headquarters, on Broadway. Gayle King, the editor-at-large and the boss's forty-five-year-old best friend, has the job as staff liaison to Oprah. Miss King is a statuesque, super-confident, cheery former news anchor, with a perfect face and perfect teeth, auburn hair worn straight to the collar, and the immediately chummy, quick-talking, eager, breathy rhythms of the Rosie-Barbara-Katie sisterhood.

"Make no mistake, O is Oprah's magazine, and it's going to have the stamp and spirit of Oprah all over it. She wants themes of self-improvement and self-empowerment. As Oprah's oldest and closest friend, I know what Oprah likes and what Oprah wants, and I'm here to see that she gets it," Miss King said last week, sitting in a large conference room at the Hearst corporate offices, on Eighth Avenue (carpeted corridors and Robert Motherwell paintings on the walls) a block away from where the O staff works.

Miss King had on a navy tailored suit with light-blue pinstripes and wore navy silk Donna Karan slides. As she talked, she wiggled a pinkie with a diamond ring on it. "Oprah gave me this—it's actually a toe ring," she said. "Oprah had two very, very large diamond earrings, and she had them made into several toe rings. She gave another one to Steadman's daughter, Wendy. Steadman, as you know, is Oprah's longtime beau."

Miss King talked about how she came to work at O. "I told the Hearst people that I didn't want a made-up job, in case they were saying, 'Let's get her something; she's Oprah's friend.' I don't have a magazine background. Oprah doesn't have a magazine background. But we have others for that. My dad was an electrical engineer, and we lived in Turkey and travelled all over Europe. Much different background from Oprah's. She was molested as a child, raped at fourteen, gave birth to a baby who died after ten days. But everybody knows Oprah is tops.

"Oprah and I have been friends since 1977. I was twenty-one and she was twenty-two. She was the anchorwoman at WJZ-TV in Baltimore, and I was a lowly production assistant. I barely knew her. I had an Oldsmobile Cutlass, a much better car than

her Chevy Chevette. Even so, one night there was a bad snow-storm, and she said—typical of her—"Why don't you stay over at my place? I said, 'I have no clothes.' She said, 'We're the same size. I'll give you clothes.' I said, 'I have no underwear.' She said, 'I'll give you underwear.' So we stayed up all night talking. We told each other all the gossip, who was going out with whom. Some people just click. We clicked. We haven't stopped talking since. Oprah knows all the dirt. We never run out of things to talk about. We have so much in common. Our shoe size is the same, ten. Our contact lenses have the same prescription. Our phone numbers—it just happened—are the same, backward.

"Why me in this job? A: I can get to Oprah quickly, late at night, early in the morning, whenever. B: I make a contribution. I know a good story. I'm smart. Oprah really works as the editorial director harder than she ever thought. She's putting in five hours a day after she does both of her TV shows. She comes up with all the creative ideas, like the 'Something to Think About' page, where we ask questions like 'How would I change my life if I only had a year to live? One month? One day?' and leave space for the reader to write things down. Or 'The O List,' the list of things she likes: for instance, a particular Burberry dog collar, because she's nuts about her dogs—two cocker spaniels. Another one of Oprah's ideas is the 'Who Knew?' department, stuff like 'Did you know that Tina Turner likes scary stories?' On that one, I said no to a particular celebrity, because I know that this celebrity is not a good person.

"Now I'll tell you something that we were arguing about for days, about the cover: whether to put the O on top and 'The Oprah Magazine' under it, or leave it 'The Oprah Magazine' on top and the O underneath." Miss King drew a sketch of the choices on a scrap of paper. "Which do you prefer?" she asked.

"O on top."

Miss King gave a squeal of delight. "That's what I said! And everybody else was against it. But that's what I told Oprah, and that's what she chose.

"I work with the others at the magazine as an ensemble. If I disagree with them about sending something on to Oprah, I say,

'Go ahead, send it to her.' But *I* know what Oprah thinks. I even
sound like her. It's funny. When my three sisters hear Oprah on
her show, they can't tell who's talking. They think it's me."

After hearing all that from Miss King, I felt confident that O
would be a success. Oprah seems to demonstrate, in everything she
undertakes to do, that she knows exactly what she is doing and is
perfectly capable of doing it all on her own. She's absolute proof of
what Buddy Hackett says later on in this book (p. 230) about him-
self: " . . . gotta be honest, true to myself" and to be "making it out
of your own self."

MISS AMERICAS

I N SEPTEMBER of 1999, I decided to do a story about the Miss
America contest. I wanted to see exactly what I wanted to see
fifty years before, in 1949, when *The New Yorker* published
one of my early long pieces. It was entitled "Symbol of All We
Possess," about the Miss America contest in Atlantic City. In doing
the earlier piece, I had a close look at what impelled a pretty young
woman to compete for that title. I also wanted to find out what the
title *was,* actually. There were moments, fifty years later, in revisit-
ing the scene of the event, when I felt as though I had fallen through
a time warp. Then it turned out that there was a story beyond that
warp, and it was an element that might not have been possible fifty
years earlier.

"There are thirteen million women in the United Sates between
the ages of eighteen and twenty-eight," is the way I started my
story in 1949. "All of them were eligible to compete for the title of
Miss America in the annual contest staged in Atlantic City last
month if they were high school graduates, were not and had never
been married, and were not Negroes."

I thought it was important to point out the prejudice right off
the bat, in the lead, and then let it go. Before the Miss America

REPORTING BACK wait, let me transcribe properly.

story went to press, Ross sent Shawn six and a half single-spaced pages of typewritten notes (his customary procedure with long pieces) questioning my pointing up the fact that "Negroes" were prohibited from participating in the contest. Ross wrote: "I am rather strongly of the opinion that in these days of unrest it would be better not to inject the race problem into this as Miss R. has done—positively instead of negatively. Moreover, this provocative wording is downright misleading—makes reader believe that the point is made here for development later (which it isn't) and is therefore misleading. Could deduct the number of colored maidens and fix unobtrusively as marked." Bill Shawn told me about Mr. Ross's query and gave me his notes. Even though I knew Ross had a point about the writing, I said the lead should stay as written. I was repelled by the discrimination in the Miss America business, and I felt strongly that I should emphasize it. I understood what Ross meant about the writing, but I cared more about the issue; it was the only time in reporting I ever found necessary to set up that priority in a deliberate way. Bill agreed with me; the story was published with my lead intact. And Ross did not object.

At any rate, I set out to do my story by following the adventures of Miss New York State in the contest. I wrote that she was a twenty-two-year-old registered nurse named Wanda Nalepa who lived in the Bronx. "She has honey blond hair, green eyes, and a light complexion and is five feet three."

This was her family's adieu to her as she left for the contest:

"Well, goodbye," said Miss Nalepa.

"Don't forget to stand up straight," her sister said.

"What about breakfast?" her mother asked mildly.

"I don't feel like eating," Miss Nalepa said.

"Good luck, Wanda," said Teddy.

"Well, goodbye," Miss Nalepa said again, looking at her father.

"All right, all right, goodbye," her father said.

Miss Nalepa was about to walk out the door when her mother stepped up timidly and gave her a peck on the cheek. As we were going downstairs together, Miss Nalepa clutched at my wrist. Her hand was cold.

"That's the second time I ever remember my mother kissed me," she said, with a nervous laugh. "The first time was when I graduated from high school. I looked around to see if anybody was watching us, I was so embarrassed."

She was wondering what she might do at the Pageant to demonstrate her talent. "All I know how to do is give a good back rub," she said.

In Atlantic City, her boyfriend said to me: "She's not going to win. I told her she's not going to win. That nursing isn't the right kind of talent. They'll want singing or dancing or something like that."

Miss New York State met Be Be Shopp, Miss America of 1948. "She made fifty thousand dollars in her year as Miss America," said Miss New York State, without much enthusiasm. . . . She looked at the other contestants and remarked, with surprise, that there were a lot of short ones. She said this made her feel better. Miss Arizona, she pointed out, was about her height. Miss Arizona looked worried. Her chaperone, a freckle-faced woman, touched her arm, and Miss Arizona tried to smile. Miss New York State thought Miss Arizona was sort of pretty. The reason *she* gave the Pageant for entering the contest: "Because it would be a great honor to be Miss America."

"The kid looks so strained," said Miss New York State, finally. Be Be Shopp, Miss America of 1948, welcomed the contestants.

She smiled and told the contestants to keep smiling from the moment they woke up every day to the moment they fell asleep.

One of the Pageant officials told them: "Always have that smile on your face. Your smiles make people feel happy, and that's what we need—happier people in the world."

Be Be Shopp's talent in the contest she won to become Miss America 1948 was playing the vibraharp. She told Miss New York State that she was going to play the vibraharp every night at the Pageant. "I play my vibraharp everyplace I go. I've made two hundred and sixty-one appearances with it, opening stores and things. The vibraharp weighs a hundred and fifty pounds, and a man usually carries it for me. They were the only men I got close

to all year. I worked so hard I didn't have a chance to have any real dates."

Miss Florida, who was standing nearby, shook her head sadly. "Mah goodness, no dates!" she said.

Miss Florida's mother said to her, "Don't forget to smile, honey."

"Ah don't have any trouble smilin', Mama," said Miss Florida.

"That's a good girl, honey," her mother said.

The statistics on Miss Florida showed that at eighteen she was already a veteran beauty. She was Citrus Queen of Florida in 1947, Railroad Exposition Queen in Chicago in 1948, Miss Holiday of Florida of 1949, and Miss Tampa of 1949. Her reason for entering the contest: "Because the Chamber of Commerce of Tampa asked me to compete."

The Miss America Pageant song in 1949:

Let's drink a toast to Miss America,
Let's raise our glasses on high
From Coast to Coast in this America,
As the Sweetheart of the U.S.A. is passing by
To a girl, to a girl,
To a symbol of happiness.
To the one, to the one
Who's the symbol of all we possess.

Miss New York State's picture was in the New York, Philadelphia, and Atlantic City newspapers. She was shown at the Atlantic City Hospital wearing her uniform and holding a two-year-old girl who had just had her tonsils out.

At Pageant-Talent time, Miss Arizona, who had played Juliet at Phoenix Junior College, showed her talent at the Pageant by coming out in a wispy white nightgown and, in the auditorium that could be transformed in a few hours into a full-size football field, called up the faint, cold fear thrilling through her veins that almost freezes up the heat of life. The audience was restless and noisy as she expressed her fear that she would die ere her Romeo came.

Miss New York State, wearing her ice-blue evening gown, gave a short talk on nursing: "Ever since I was a little girl, I was taught that people are here for the purpose of serving others," she said. Later, she told me that she had enjoyed standing before all those people and telling them about nursing, and she had enjoyed watching the talent of others. "Wasn't Miss Arizona good?" she said. "She got hysterical so easily."

At the grand finale, Eddie Cantor, who was in the audience, was asked to come up on stage, and he said: "Communism hasn't got a chance when twenty thousand people gather to applaud culture and beauty." Then the winner was announced and crowned—Miss Arizona.

Miss New York State offered the new Miss America her solemn congratulations. "I'm glad you won, kid," she said. "I was rooting for you.". . . The two of us walked back to the dressing room, where we found Miss Missouri tearfully folding up her Catalina swimsuit. Miss New York State looked puzzled at her tears and said that she hadn't cried, because when you don't expect very much, you're never disappointed. She was returning to New York the next morning with her boyfriend. She had the name of a photographer who wanted to take a lot of pictures of her to sell to magazines, and another man wanted to talk to her about becoming a model. She was not going back to nursing if she could help it. "You get more when you're a model," she said.

That last line is the key to the story, and it's also the key to the story I wrote about the pageant in 1999. "More" is also what Brandi Burkhardt, the blond, even-featured, green-eyed twenty-one-year-old Miss New York State in the 1999 Pageant seemed to be seeking in Atlantic City. What she got was indeed more, making the story surprisingly dramatic.

"Even if I don't win," she said to me on the eve of that Pageant. "I don't come away with nothing."

Be Be Shopp, Miss America of 1948, put in an appearance, offering bits of wisdom such as "Classy ladies do not bump or grind"; advising the girls to "always have that smile on your face"; and

reminding the candidates that her scholarship money was five
thousand dollars, one-tenth of the prize today. She used her
money to go to the Manhattan School of Music. "Miss America
gave me my life," she said.

Brandi was a singer. She was going to sing "Take Me As I
Am" in the competition.

At the beginning, Brandi was at one with her fellow contes-
tants, bolstered by her own "support team," and also, like many of
them, by her Christian faith. Her pocket New Testament, well
worn and with passages marked throughout in pen and pencil,
was constantly at hand. She even found time, during the competi-
tion to inaugurate and lead a regular Bible-study class.

Her support team included Paul Brown, a fitness fanatic and
nonpracticing radiologist, who has been volunteering his time to
pageants for twenty years. He accompanied Brandi to her local
competitions, along with her boyfriend Randy Clifford, a pre-law
student from Maryland, where Brandi, attending New York
University, still had her home with her mother.

"I'm the kind of person who likes to oblige others. I like mak-
ing other people happy. Once I got into it, though, I think I want-
ed to do it. I wanted to be Miss America," she said in my story.

She also said: "It's not just the money. It's all so fulfilling. For
the first time, people were asking me for my ideas. I liked the
attention."

Brandi did not win. Heather French, also a singer, "a chesty
brunette—who, since the age of nine, had been in at least forty
beauty pageants—became Miss America 2000.

"All I wanted to do was sleep," Brandi told me, a few weeks
later, when she was back in New York. "But I went to church with
Randy, and we talked. I felt bad for my mom and for Paul. My
mom took what happened to me very hard. But I didn't cry. It
wasn't the end of my life. And my grandmother is still wearing
my Miss America T-shirt whenever she goes to the mall.". . .

Brandi tried to get work as a singer, alternating in New York
between living in Paul Brown's apartment and with relatives
on Staten Island. Then she was invited by Kate Shindle, Miss

America 1998, to share her apartment on the Upper West Side.
Kate had an understudy job in *Jekyll & Hyde*.

Soon Brandi was telling me about "an incredible point in my
life. I've got an agent! He's sending me out on auditions." She
looked calm and untroubled. With hardly a pause or a change
in tone, she added, "And Randy and I have separated. It became
clear to me that Randy and I are now in two separate worlds."

The next time we met, she was telling me about her auditions
for various soap operas. She sounded happy and relaxed.

"I'm going to a Club Med in the British West Indies with
Michael," she said casually. "My whole life is changing. I don't
know if it's a test or a blessing. I'll call you when I get back."

Michael? About ten days later, she was telling me about
Michael—Michael Russek. "I've had such an interesting jour-
ney," she said. "Michael has changed me completely. He is a
take-charge man. When we enter a room, he says where we'll
sit and he holds the chair for me. I never had anybody that sin-
cere. Michael is Jewish. I'm in love with him, and he's in love
with me. It happened quickly, and it happened. He's a jeweler,
and he's twenty-nine, dark, with curly hair. The opposite of me,"
she said with a laugh.

I had never heard that tone from her in all the time since her
embarkation on the path to Miss America, through the aftermath
of auditioning for shows.

"I love going to Hineni. That's Hebrew for 'Here I am,'" she
said, and she said it in the way some people—usually people under
the age of seven—make an assumption that everybody in the
world is familiar with what they are talking about. "Michael and
I go to Hineni twice a week at Congregation Kehilath Jeshurun
to listen to Esther Jungreis, the rebbetzin," Brandi said. Then
Brandi said. "I've been thinking about becoming Jewish."

I met Michael very soon, over supper with Brandi. "I knew I
was going to marry this girl the moment I saw her," he said, hold-
ing Brandi's hand with both of his. He was just as Brandi had
described him—dark and handsome and personable. He exuded

energy and warmth and entrepreneurialism. It wasn't long before
he had me trotting along after Brandi and him to the synagogue
for Hineni.

The next time I talked to Brandi, she had moved out of Kate
Schindle's apartment and into Michael's. They were busy meeting
with people in the music industry. "Michael knows how to create
deals," she told me. Then she called one day and told me that
Michael had taken her to Washington, D.C. to visit his brother
and the Holocaust Museum. Michael's brother had introduced
her to a rabbi, who gave her books to read entitled *To Pray as a
Jew* and *The Kosher Kitchen.*

My story went on:

When she and Michael returned, they worked with writers on
songs for her to sing and made plans. "We're establishing ground
rules," she told me. "Everybody gets a fair share. It's all done on a
handshake."

"Has anything actually happened?" I asked.

"Not production-wise, but relationship-wise," she said.

Next, Brandi told me that Michael thought they needed a
vacation, and he was going to take her on a four-week cruise to
Israel, among other stops. "Michael says we've been working so
hard," she said.

Brandi called before leaving on her cruise. "Everything will
have to wait until we get back," she said. "But we'll be working
on the ship. We're taking a CD player, a mini tape recorder, and
a CD with songs on it. . . . We're taking our copy of *All You Need
to Know About the Music Business.* The ship has a computer room,
and we'll be reading torah-dot-org every day on the Internet."

The name of their cruise line was, fittingly, Renaissance.

Neither of these stories, both starring a Miss New York State
aiming for the Miss America title, requires the author's stepping
in and making a judgement, moral or otherwise. Everything is
implied in the facts. The young women were separated by fifty

years in their character and personalities, and also in their quest. The challenge was to let the story demonstrate, without moralizing, that the beauty contest is—now as it was in the past—the same desperate path to finding "more."

You Dig It, Sir?

L ONG OR SHORT, a story that defines a situation or an individual often gives me the opportunity to use dialogue between one or more people, together with single quotes, in a way that brings the story to life with both a quality of immediacy and timelessness. Also, it's usually very funny. "You Dig It, Sir?," about the first Newport Jazz Festival, ran in *The New Yorker* under the heading of "Our Footloose Correspondents" in 1954. The piece is of historic interest almost half a century later because so many of the musicians at the festival are now famous. Most of them are now dead, but they are very much alive in the story. Jazz to Newport, at that time, was still not a respectable, familiar cultural phenomenon, so it was great fun to show the jazz artists and the classic wealthy people being drawn to them as potential patrons. An introduction to the situation was called for, so the story began:

"You Dig It, Sir?"
When, earlier this summer, Mr. and Mrs. Louis Livingston
Lorillard, a young and adventurous couple who spend their

winters in Capri and the warm weather months in Newport, Rhode Island, decided to put on an American Jazz Festival at the Newport Casino, they invited sixty-five of their neighbors at the famous old resort to join them in sponsoring it. They received only two acceptances—and only one from a long-established member of the community; that was Mr. George Henry Warren, of New York, who has summered in Newport practically all his life. Undismayed, the Lorillards went ahead with their project. As a token of good faith and to help ease the rest of the summer colonists into the spirit of the occasion, Mr. Warren and his wife decided to give a dinner party on the Friday of the weekend the Festival was scheduled to be held and invite the sixty-three reluctant neighbors. The invitations, which were sent out a fortnight or so before the party, were unanimously accepted. Suddenly, the prevailingly chilly mood changed, with the result that more than fourteen thousand people turned out for the brassy, four-hour concerts that were held on Saturday and Sunday nights on the neat, spacious grass courts of the nineteenth-century gabled Casino, perhaps best known as the birthplace of lawn tennis in this country, and another thousand attended a Sunday afternoon forum on the subject of "The Place of Jazz in American Culture."

To promote the affair, the Lorillards and some jazz-loving friends set themselves up as Newport Jazz Festival, Inc. (Official purpose: "To encourage America's enjoyment of jazz and to sponsor the study of our country's only original art form.") They got permission to use the Casino for the nominal fee—approved without dissent by the Casino's board of governors—of three hundred and fifty dollars. They also found a producer for the Festival—a Boston jazz impresario named George Wein. . . . Much to the surprise of the sponsors, after two nights of good, solid jazz, ranging from Dixieland to very modern and played by sixty-five musicians, a number of whom had never before seen the surf beating against the rocky shores of old New England, they emerged with the sure and not inconsiderable profit of more than eleven thousand dollars. . . .

The Warrens' dinner party was held in the garden of their house, which is near the Old Stoner Mill, known to local historians as the most controversial building in America because it has never been determined who built it or when. I was fortunate enough to be invited to the party, and a few minutes after I checked in at the Hotel Viking on Friday evening, Mrs. Lorillard telephoned to see if I had arrived. "Everybody's here, and they're all talking about the Festival!" she said, in a tone of wonder. "They're warming up!"

When I got to the party, I found the guests in the garden, casually grouped around a singer named Lee Wiley, a pretty blonde in a shell pink decolleté gown, who was being accompanied by Teddy Wilson on an upright piano. Miss Wiley is a specialist in singing songs by George Gershwin, Rodgers and Hart, and Cole Porter; Wilson is one of the nation's leading jazz pianists. Miss Wiley was singing "We'll go to Yonkers, where true love conquers. . . . We'll go to Coney and eat bologny. . ." in a soft, low voice, and her audience, finely tanned and formally dressed, looked rapt. They applauded vigorously when she finished, and there were many cries of "Bravo!"

Mr. Warren, a gracious, jolly, pink-cheeked man wearing tortoise-shell glasses and a tuxedo, who used to be a financier and now devotes most of his time to philanthropic activities, led me to a chair next to Mrs. Lorillard. "Newport is not on the skids, no matter what anybody says," he assured me. "Have you ever seen anybody more alive than this crowd?"

"I'm still uneasy," said Mrs. Lorillard, an attractive, titian-haired woman in a sapphire-blue satin gown. "It could be Guy Lombardo, and they'd act just as enthusiastic."

"Thank heavens it *isn't* Guy Lombardo!" said a woman who had on an evening wrap of white ostrich feathers.

"Thank heavens it isn't *Meyer Davis!*" said a third woman, who, somewhat older than the others, was wearing a black lace dress with a high collar. "I've been getting Meyer Davis for nineteen years, and now I'm enjoying that nice Mr. Wilson at the piano. George, I must say it's a change. Mr. Wilson is musically somehow or other more frolicsome.". . .

Miss Wiley started singing "I've Got a Crush on You." A tall,
ruddy-faced man moved forward, sat down on a gravel walk beside
her, and, hugging his knees, looked up at her.

"Oh, my!" said Mrs. Lorillard to me. "That's Barclay Douglas.
You know—the stockbroker. He's president of the Clambake Club.
The most exclusive private club in Newport.". . .

Mr. Lorillard, a serious-looking man with a round face, whose
great-grandfather, Pierre Lorillard, helped found the Casino in
1879 and built The Breakers, one of Newport's earliest mansions,
made his way over to his wife and said out of the corner of his
mouth, "Just heard that the Carl Haffenreffers bought *two* boxes."

Mrs. Lorillard gave me a significant look. "You know—beer,"
she said.

This piece made the most of the contrast between the elegant
Newporters and the scruffy jazz players.

A few exchanges at the after-party:

Senator Green was pumping Mr. Lorillard's hand. "Enthusiastic
congratulations!" he said. "Magnificent success! Bold, bold enter-
prise!"

Cleveland Amory congratulated the host and hostess.
"Tonight Newport went back to its beginnings," he said. "Back
to the time when it hummed with artists, writers, schoolteachers,
ministers, and freedom."

A scholarly-looking young man in the doorway said, "Jazz has
made the grade—from Storyville to Newport in fifty years."

The Lorillards thanked everybody and looked happy.

Mrs. Amory was saying to Wild Bill Davison, "My husband
used to play the trumpet. How do you get that sound?"

"All you got to do is feel good," Davison told her.

Nearby, Pee Wee Russell was being presented by Mrs. Taylor
Chewning, a vivacious, deeply tanned woman with long blond
hair, to another guest—the Argentine Ambassador, Hipolito J.
Paz. "I've been told that Mr. Russell has played with the greatest
jazz musicians," Mrs. Chewning said. "He played with Mr. Bix
Beiderbecke."

Russell and the Ambassador shook hands.

"Chum, I don't boast, you know," Russell said, with a self-deprecating gesture. "But a couple of times tonight I played all right."

"Superb," said the Ambassador.

In another corner, Eddie Condon (guitar, Dixieland) was carrying on a friendly conversation with Gerry Mulligan (baritone saxophone, very modern). Between them stood the jazz buff Professor Stearns, who said: "Never thought I'd see the day come when you two would be playing together."

"Well, I'm not exactly hysterical about kids playing saxophones bigger than they are," said Condon.

"Anybody who still chooses to play a four-stringed instrument is practically prehistoric," said Mulligan.

"We're all one big happy family," said Stearns.

James H. Van Alen, president of the Casino, came up and announced the he was something of a songwriter himself. He produced a piece of sheet music entitled "Good evening, Mr. President," and handed it to Condon. Below the title was the inscription, "Respectfully Dedicated to Dwight D. Eisenhower. Words and Music by J. H. Van Alen (Rhode Island)."

"It was played at the inaugural ball," Mr. Van Alen said.

Condon started reading the words of the song aloud:

Believe us, Mr. President,
We're glad it's you, not we,
Who have got the job of keeping
Our great country safe and free . . .

Condon looked up from the music. "What did you say you played there at the Casino?" he asked.

"Tennis," said Mr. Van Alen.

Condon shook his head sadly. "After what they heard at the Casino tonight, tennis will never be played there again," he said.

"You fellows certainly had the crowd giving our lawn a workout," Mr. Van Alen said. "All that steady undulating motion."

Maxim Karolik—a Bostonian and patron of the arts who has
spent the last twenty-five summers in Newport and who with
his late wife donated collections of eighteenth- and nineteenth-
century furniture and paintings to the Museum of Fine Arts—
was sitting with Gerry Mulligan.

"Jazz is no longer for cabarets," Karolik said. "No question
about it."

"You dig it, sir?" Mulligan asked.

"It's something to ponder," said Karolik. "Rachmaninoff spoke
about it. It is an established fact. Jazz is America's contribution to
music."

Wein joined the group, his energy and enthusiasm undimin-
ished. "Wait till tomorrow," he said. "We'll have Billie Holiday.
One of the greatest. Billie is a real queen."

"Pres will be here," the trombone man said to Wein. "Billie
doesn't talk to Pres. Pres," he went on for the information of
the Newporters, "is Lester Young. He's president of all the saxo-
phone players, and that's why we call him Pres. Pres and Billie are
bugged with each other. They haven't spoken for five years."

"Oh, do try to get them to make up," a lady in the group said.

Last paragraph of the story:

After the final number. Tony Corey, the head greenskeeper at the
Casino, waited until most of the audience had left, and then sig-
naled for the removal of the folding chairs from his lawn. He said
he would soak his grass with water continuously for three days.
"Got to keep the alcohol from eating away at it," he explained.
"I'll take it slow and bring it back gradually. We've done a lot of
suffering, but I guess it was worth it."

If journalism does indeed contribute somewhat to our social
and cultural history, "You Dig It, Sir?" might serve as an example.
Essentially, I've used the same reportorial approach in other stories
to reveal various aspects—both major and minor—of cultural pre-
occupations in our nation. For instance, in the matter of women of
privilege and wealth indulging their bodies and extending their life

spans at luxury spas, there's the story entitled "The Golden Ladies of the Golden Door." How to do that one? Easy. In 1995, I attended one. I hadn't intended to write about it, but when David Kuhn, then my editor at The Talk of the Town, was alerted to my being at the Golden Door, he asked me to write about it. It was important to tell all of the parties involved that I was writing a story about our adventures, but that I wasn't interested in using any of their names. Their identity was irrelevant. Gossip wasn't the point of the story. Besides, people who spend a lot of money going to spas are mainly interested in themselves and not in what anybody else is doing.

I happen to enjoy the spa life, so this experience was fine with me. Also, even when I'm not reporting on this kind of phenomenon, out of long habit, I'm usually, in my mind, outside of it. Most people who participate in any kind of group activity, naturally lend themselves to it. I always feel outside of it, an observer. Even as a child, in kindergarten, say, when we were asked to sit or skip in a circle and hold hands or sing, I never understood it; I would wonder why. As I explained at the start of this book, as a reporter, I seem always to have operated on what I've thought of as "a borrowed sensibility." I've always enjoyed and appreciated having that. It's my sister Helen or Bill Shawn, or both simultaneously, guiding me, listening and seeing for me, laughing with me at what is funny—or at what I am making funny. I am never alone. Helen or Bill is always with me.

Here's the story about the spa:

The ladies, traditionally limited to a quota of thirty-nine, arrive on a Sunday at the Golden Door, a spa situated on a hundred-and-seventy-seven-acre tract of land in the Peninsula Range, about an hour's drive north of San Diego. Mostly, they come wearing designer jeans and designer blazers and carrying small bags containing their bathing suits (near-bikinis) and their sneakers (aerobic and running) and their underwear and socks and nighties. Everything else they will need for their four-thousand-two-hundred-and-fifty-dollar week is provided by the spa—

shorts, warmups, T-shirts, terry robes, sun hats, and assorted
creams and potions and pastes and a fresh toothbrush. They go
quickly to their rooms, each with private bath, a perfectly mat-
tressed queen-size bed, good lamps, a radio, stationery inscribed
with the guest's name in gold letters, and reading material ("Chop
Wood, Carry Water," "Fifty Simple Things You Can Do to Save
the Earth"). All the guests receive, on request, bottles of Evian
and the daily newspapers of their choice. They never refer to
what, if anything, they have read in the news.

The ladies emerge quickly, uniformly democratized in aqua-
marine-colored warmups and gray T-shirts. They are mostly
fortyish and fiftyish, with husbands and children, but there are
also a few nervous singles and hopeful fatties, and a scattering of
heavy oldies (thigh-covering bathing suits), hoarse-voiced, with
Barbara Bush hair, icy blue eyes, false teeth, and scads of grand-
children. Children—anybody under the age of sixteen, in fact—
are banned from the premises. "We don't want to remind anybody
of what she left behind," one of the spa's supervisors explains.

Most of the guests have heard that exercise increases sexuality,
and they think a lot about sex and youth and health. They are
immediately eager to mention their husbands, quite a number
of whom are power figures in the entertainment business. The
Hollywood wives have Vogue-cover faces and, as revealed in the
Jacuzzi, large and mathematically correct breasts. The New York
power wives are often good-egg types, sort of old-fashioned
tomboys. There are many wealthy Eastern do-gooders with, or
married to, a lot of money, and they quickly bring up their good
works as a counterbalance to other revelations—about the coun-
try house, the tennis court, the horse that jumps, brilliant children
who are going off to do admirable and hazardous work in devel-
oping countries. (The West Coasters don't bother counterbalanc-
ing anything.) As the ladies hungrily register with one another
what they have in common, they still seem to be searching wist-
fully for something indefinable, perhaps a surprise.

The visual backdrop is inspired by Japanese culture—koi pool,
rain chains, stone lanterns, sand gardens, a wooden bridge that

juts crookedly because "evil spirits go in a straight line." The over-
all ambience reflects the passions and the interests of Deborah
Szekely, a cherubic, pink-cheeked, Brooklyn-born dynamo, and
the widow of an ahead-of-his-time Hungarian philosopher and
nature lover, Edmond Szekely. In 1939, the couple settled in the
tiny village of Tecate, in Baja, California, and started a health
camp. People brought their own tents and paid seventeen dollars
and fifty cents a week for the privilege of chopping firewood and
helping to milk goats for cheese. Professor Szekely gave radical
lectures lambasting cholesterol. The popularity of the camp grew,
especially with people from Hollywood, who then wanted a
retreat with more privacy. So, in 1958, the Szekelys founded the
Golden Door, with weeks limited to men only, women only, and
couples only. Today, most of the weeks are for women only.

At the first dinner, the ladies introduce themselves and state
why they've come to the Golden Door. "I came because I couldn't
get into my bras." "I came to get away from my four children." "I
came because my husband gave me this for my birthday." "I came
to bond with my sister." They leave the first dinner feeling high
on one another, high to be with women only, high to be away
from their men, high to boast about those men. They learn an
amazing lot about one another's husbands in only minutes, and
then at 9:30 P.M. each goes to her room and to sleep.

The next day, reporting for the daily hike at dawn, the ladies
are drinking mugs of freshly brewed coffee (black) and gulping
Vitamin C tablets. They talk briefly about the howling coyotes
heard in the mountains. Their talk has the semblance of dialogue,
but there is no back-and-forth. "Did everybody sleep through the
coyotes?" one lady asks a companion, and the companion says,
"I've got to call my husband's office, but it's too early in New
York." "Nothing bothers me when I sleep," the first one says.

Their preoccupation with "I" and "me" seems to rule out any
interest in hearing answers to questions. In pairs, as they do their
hamstring and quadriceps stretches, arms around each other's
shoulders, one lady says to her partner, "I was going to do the
five-mile hike, but now I think I'll do the three." "I never have jet

lag," the partner replies. The warmup exercises end with an ever cheery, seemingly euphoric fitness guide reading one of Deborah Szekely's favorite Japanese-flavored aphorisms: "Success is not an end; it is a journey," or "The intellect is always fooled by the heart." The ladies listen blankly to the aphorisms, make no comment, and turn quickly to the business at hand.

As they head up the mountain, they pay little attention to the surrounding purple daylilies, the orange poppies, the baby daisies. They walk fast, seriously heel to toe, and they continue talking, still adhering to the first person singular. They identify further aspects of themselves. They talk more about their husbands. They outline for one another their husbands' routines—getting up early, being driven to work, outmaneuvering the other guy, obtaining courtside seats at basketball and hockey games, flying here and flying there, and running offices that efficiently deliver plane tickets and chauffeured cars to the ladies on request. Confidences abound. A West Coast lady tells an East Coast lady that her husband is Jewish and that being married to him is nice, because she's Irish and German and Irish-and-German husbands are not as kind or as warmhearted as her Jewish husband. The East Coast lady responds by telling a long story about how *her* husband is afraid of cats, but she *understands* his fear of cats. Both ladies look as though they are communicating. Talking all the way up the mountain (one-and-a-half miles) seems to take no toll on the ladies' wind or stamina. At the top of the trail, high-spirited fitness guides offer water and slices of oranges from the Golden Door's own trees. On the way back down, the ladies talk about food, about the breakfast that awaits them in their rooms on their return, at seven-thirty—today it is Baked Apple with Seven Grains, Raisins, Cinnamon, and Honey served with Orange Slices. . . . "I miss chewing," one of the bonding sisters, both Golden Door repeaters, says to the other.

By Wednesday, the ladies are demonstrating much affection for and pride in one another. In fact, quite a lot of bonding is going on. Everybody seems to share in the general exhilaration; even the oldies and the fatties are getting in on it. Nobody has

worn any makeup for three days. Everybody respects potassium. Everybody looks cleaner. Everybody has had a daily herbal wrap, a daily facial, and a daily body massage. Everybody will do more country line-dancing, yoga, ballet, slide aerobics, tap dancing, self-defense, wreathmaking with herbs and flowers, nutrition lectures, and a tour of the herb garden. Digestive systems are working splendidly. Adrenaline is flowing. The atmosphere is bursting with good will. Both Easterners and Westerners express pride and joy in the oldie giving her Ruby Keeler all in aerobic renditions of "There's No Business Like Show Business" and "Give My Regards to Broadway." Nobody has as much as mentioned a husband all day.

By Thursday, though, the ladies are letting go with some negative remarks about men in general and husbands in particular. They are saying things like "Some men think that having a baby is very glamorous. Hah. Hah." They are saying things like "Men are from Mars; we are from Venus." Quite a few ladies are saying yoga things to one another, like "The light in me sees the light in you." Some of the powerhouse husbands on the West Coast and on the East Coast are coming in for complaints from their wives. An oldie who is also a fatty as well as a toughie, says at the dinner table, "At home, we have a condo. We have a big pool. Everything. Does my husband use it? No!" "The light in me sees the light in you," one of the fortyish ladies says. "You'd better believe it," the old toughie says.

On Friday, however, everybody is all business re the body. The talkers on the morning hike are muted. The bonding has become visibly loosened as each lady tends to herself. Saturday night, the ladies, manicured, pedicured, hairdressed, tighter, lighter, firmer, are having their farewell dinner of California Gold Salad with Grapefruit, Avocado, Edible Flowers, and Garden Greens and Grilled Prawns with Garlic and Ginger on Portobello Mushrooms, Wilted Spinach, and Couscous. Prizes are given out— for Hiking Maniac, for Pumping Iron Icon, for Most Active Newcomer, for Ms. Fred Astaire. There is a lot of laughter. The ladies hug, kiss, go through motions of exchanging addresses and

telephone numbers. But they are retreating from one another.
Almost every lady makes a point of saying loudly that waiting
impatiently at home is her husband.

For myself, I've loved doing various sports as well as enjoying
spas, but to write a valid story about something the writer personally
loves to do requires a detachment. Also, I believe that every story,
whatever the subject, usually should have humor for the simple rea-
son that humor enables the writer to find a workable point of view.
Hitting the reader over the head with a point of view—no matter
how reasonable or worthy—weakens a story or invalidates it entirely.

David Remnick happened to know that I've spent a lot of time in
Central Park going around the reservoir. So he asked me to con-
tribute a piece on "Jogging" for the "Sports Edition" in the summer
of 2000.

This is the way I worked it out:

For thousands of Manhattan apartment dwellers, including me,
the running track around the Central Park reservoir is a lifesaver.
It's our compulsion, our obsession, our drug. It gives us our daily
doses of light-headedness, firm-footedness, and delusions of
immortality. Some of us break out of our caves at dawn. Others
hold off until midday or twilight or midnight, undeterred by rain
or snow or any other stuff on the postal boast. Everybody goes at
his or her democratically individual pace.

The 1.57-mile track marks out an urban comfort zone that's
ours to ogle: seagulls lined up on the jetty that once divided the
reservoir in half; the lake-smelling water licking at the shore. In
the spring, we glory in the Yoshino cherry blossoms on the east
side, and in the new leaves on the oaks and cedars on the west.
We bask in the changing light over the Carlyle or the Citicorp
or the Chrysler or the Guggenheim or Mount Sinai Hospital
or the old twin-towered apartment buildings on the West Side.
We breeze past water fountains, benches, escape ramps, the
three nineteenth-century cast-iron rail bridges.

The 1.57-mile says hello to Alberto Arroyo, the muscular, eighty-
five-year-old who was proclaimed "Mayor of Central Park" by

Rudolph Giuliani. Arroyo makes his all-day headquarters on a bench near the South Gate House—the set for the demise of Laurence Olivier in *Marathon Man*—at the edge of which he's often doing headstands, bare-chested. He converses while upside down. . . .

Our feet pound the recently refurbished surface of crushed bluestone and erosion-fighting stabilizer, for which the Central Park Conservancy managed to raise half a million dollars. The very occasional no-goods and criminals don't stop us. We've got police call boxes, even though they are sometimes, when you need them, non-operative. We fly past the lamps circling the track, which come on automatically when darkness falls. They glow with an eerie green light, reflected from the leaves of the trees.

Now and then we would have a glimpse of Madonna in tank top and very short shorts, jogging around the track with her trainer. For years, we would see Jacqueline Onassis running alone, wearing a brimmed white hat and white gloves on hot days and a black knit cap and black gloves in the cold. When she died, in 1994, the track was supposed to be named for her. A sign went up on the reservoir fence, but "Onassis" was misspelled and after a few days it was taken down, never to reappear.

Henry Stern, the city's Parks Commissioner, says he doesn't run on the track or anywhere else. "I'm a swimmer," he says. "But I like to see all the people in the parks running around in their underwear."

Jazz, spas, and running have yielded valid stories, and so has tennis, another interest of mine. One's own interests, if mined alertly, can be productive. The trick is to put the subject in the clear by holding to an unsticky, uninvolved approach. I'm often carried away by my enthusiasms, but I try to watch myself carefully when I'm writing about one of them. For The Talk of the Town at the 1997 U.S. Open, I was relieved to have the title composed by my editor Susan Morrison: "John McEnroe's serve may have slowed down, but his mouth keeps on going." For this little story, I didn't want to conceal my admiration, as well as

my affection, for John McEnroe, because he had brought so much
freshness and spirit, as well as his genius, to the game of tennis, a
sport that I revere. And the same goes for what he's done as a
broadcaster.

If, during these Sampras–Hingis U.S. Open days, you're missing
the tennis playing of good old (thirty-eight-year-old) John
McEnroe (four singles championships and four men's doubles
championships), console yourself: he's missing himself. In his
current incarnation, as an announcer-commentator on the USA
Network and CBS, he not only describes the action; he can tell
you, with a lot of instructive discourse, what the players are think-
ing and feeling before and after each shot.

Last week, on the Open's Day Three, McEnroe arrived,
a huge, black Nike carrying bag slung over a shoulder, at the
USA broadcast booth in the Arthur Ashe Stadium a few min-
utes before airtime. He grabbed a hot dog, took a couple of big
bites, and called for makeup to powder his face, especially the
sunburned and peeling top of his nose. He looked like the early,
puckish, vigilant McEnroe—the one with the audible mouth,
ready to wake up myopic umpires—but with modestly graying
and thinning hair. He wore a slate-blue silk designer suit, a navy
shirt, an elegant gray-print necktie, shiny black shoes, and white
tennis socks. He had an exceptionally handsome gold loop
attached to his left ear.

"Six years ago, I was having difficulty going to a tennis match,"
he told me. "I wanted to be there, but I had no reason to be there.
I have to give credit to Vitas Gerulaitis. He was here." McEnroe
put on his headphones with mouthpiece and took his position,
facing several TV monitors, alongside Ted Robinson, his co-
announcer. "Vitas got me doing this. The producer Gordon
Beck said, 'Hey, you guys are great together.' So I started doing
it with Vitas. Lately, I've been doing Wimbledon, the French
open, and this. It's been good for me. I feel comfortable now at
tennis matches. I hang out with the guys in the locker room. It's
an opportunity for me to get the feel for the way the intensity is

affecting them. I sort of try to be there for them. I know what it
is. I've been there." . . .

 During a commercial, Robinson had a hot dog. McEnroe
turned down a second hot dog. He said, "Vitas didn't digest hot
dogs; he just ate them, four or five at a time." . . .

 Another commercial break. McEnroe said, "I could always tell
what my opponents were thinking; then I'd be imposing my will
on them. That's how I got to be No. 1."

 Former Mets first baseman Keith Hernandez, a McEnroe pal,
entered the booth grinning. No. 17. Also missed.

The little story above comes close to expressing affection for
McEnroe, but backs off quickly by putting the emphasis on
Hernandez.

 Two years later, André Agassi was the subject. Again, the story
had to avoid sounding like it was written by a doting Jewish moth-
er. It was entitled "The Man Who Keeps André Agassi from
Getting Dehydrated":

> On the third day of the U.S. Open last week, with both the
> injured Pete Sampras (ranked No. 1) and the injured Patrick
> Rafter (last year's winner) withdrawing, people started telling
> André Agassi (No. 2), "Now you're going to win!"
>
> So, with that unwelcome pressure, Gil Reyes, Agassi's personal
> trainer and security manager, and Brad Gilbert, his coach, tried to
> keep their cool as they quickly hustled Agassi—trailing a horde
> of eager fans—to an available court for their between-matches
> routine of practice hitting. It was a hot, sunny, high noon. Agassi,
> unsmiling and with his head shaved, was bare to the waist and
> was wearing black shorts and white, endorsed Nikes. He took
> two bottles of custom-blended vitamin-and-mineral-spiked
> electrolyte liquid from Reyes and sampled it. Gilbert, a some-
> what rumpled thirty-eight-year-old veteran of the Lendl-
> Becker-Edberg eighties, who had a No. 4 ranking in 1990,
> gave the drinks a disdainful smirk. Agassi got down to business,
> sending his impressive line drives, crosscuts, forehands, and
> backhands aggressively at Gilbert.

On the court, Agassi took a short break and sipped his sports drink. "Every day, we try to assess the elements, and we determine what he needs," Reyes said. "You can't hold back on liquids. Every day, I pray for his safety. . . ."

Reyes is a serious, soft-spoken forty-eight-year-old man with a mustache and a Mr. T-like body. Clutching a large bag that contained electrolytes, vitamins, and minerals, he settled in at a far corner of a court. Around his neck he wore a heavy gold chain with a gold pennant, an abstract rendering of the Holy Trinity given to him by Agassi. "I never take it off; it's a symbol of our unyielding friendship and faith. André made a smaller copy of it for his earring," Reyes told me. "He's my closest friend. He's now the most physically fit he's ever been in his life. He's five-eleven. He weighed one hundred and forty-six pounds when he was eighteen. Now we got him up to one hundred and seventy-two pounds. This past year, he's demonstrated the enormous capacity of the human heart and the human will. . . ."

On the court, Agassi came to the net and tried to drop-shot Gilbert, but the ball was stopped at the top of the net. Gilbert grinned. . . . After the session, Gilbert tossed used tennis balls to the fans as gifts. Agassi, now all easy smiles, his bald dome sparkling with sweat, polished off a bottle of electrolytes. Then he hit a ball upward with his racquet, and quickly hit a second ball to bounce off the first one, still in the air. The fans applauded mightily.

BENNY, YEHUDI, AND GLENN

▬▬ ▬▬ ▬▬ ▬▬ ▬▬ ▬▬ ▬▬ ▬▬ ▬▬ ▬▬ ▬▬ ▬▬ ▬▬

THREE OF MY Talk stories about the clarinetist Benny
Goodman—appearing in *The New Yorker*'s The Talk of the
Town in 1950, 1956, and 1981—demonstrate how report-
ing pieces, each separated from the others by a number of years,
can build on each other to reveal a special theme—in this instance,
a famous jazz artist's devoted, modest, and stubborn pursuit of the
mastery of classical clarinet music.

The Talk story has always been my favorite form for reporting.
I've never been bored by anybody I've written about in a story of
any length, but the Talk story form gives me an opportunity to sat-
isfy my interest quickly and immediately; it tells me everything I
want to know about the subject, no more and no less. If I find it
interesting to write, I naturally assume the reader will find it inter-
esting to read.

The Talk story places no restrictions on the writing; in fact
it opens it up to all kinds of experimentation. The form it takes

grows directly out of the material. It depends on what I find to report. That is why it is always different, always changing from week to week. Implicit in the facts usually is a theme. The theme is subtle; but it's always there. In the recently published book *The Fun of It,* a collection of Talk stories by the best writers of the magazine from 1925 to 2000, I called these stories "gems" that ". . . now bear out the ultimate refinement of what Harold Ross wanted his magazine to be," and I quoted Bill Shawn, who succeeded Harold Ross as editor in 1952, as saying that the Talk story is *sui generis* and that it imposes ". . . certain demands on the writer, among them discipline, technical agility, swift movement, the power to make every word and every touch count, a feeling for facts, a warm response to people, and a sensitiveness to the particulars of place, situation, and event."

The story I wrote in 1950 told about Benny Goodman, the "old jazz man," taking a lesson in his New York apartment with Reginald Kell, an "old classics man" and "considered by many to be the greatest living master of the clarinet." Kell had just arrived in this country from his native England, with the intention of settling down here to play and teach. The story described Goodman in his bedroom,

. . . seated in a straight-backed chair facing a music stand, which stood before a mirrored dressing table; and Kell, seated in an armchair behind Goodman. The score on the stand was the Clarinet Concerto No. 1 in F minor, by Weber. Goodman, in shirtsleeves and bedroom slippers, was working away at an arpeggio. His face was flushed, his hair tousled. Kell, in heavy tweeds, with his clarinet tucked under one arm, had his hair neatly slicked back and looked as fresh as a daisy.

After worrying the arpeggio, Goodman broke into despairing laughter. "I'm getting winded," he complained to Kell.

"The best place for a breath, Benny, is between the two E's," Kell said mildly. "You haven't got that part in focus at all."

"Yeah, yeah," Goodman said. "You do it for me, Reggie."

Kell obligingly ran through the arpeggio, not turning a hair.

"The trouble with you is that you fly all over the place," said Kell. "You skid over the top. I have every note under control. You try to play them in lots. Have another quick bash at it, will you, Benny?" Goodman had a quick bash at it.

"Not bad," Kell said. "Keep playing. And look out for that B natural. That's the weakest note in your run, Benny—B natural."

"Yeah, yeah," Goodman said. "Little on the soft side, my reed."

In the ending of the story, after they had tackled a Hindemith Concerto for Clarinet and Orchestra, a piece Goodman had commissioned Paul Hindemith to write, Goodman said he was going up to New Haven the next day to play it, with the composer at the piano, for the first time.

"Reggie's going to New Haven with me," Goodman said. "That's not to help me, though. It'll be too late for that. It's so I can teach him jazz on the way up."

Six years later, I drove out to Commack, Long Island, with Goodman to call on his old friend Gustave Langenus, a clarinet teacher who had written "all the best books on the subject." "Gus is seventy-two and knows more about the clarinet than any other man alive," Goodman said in the Talk story. Langenus, he said, had coached him in playing the Mozart Clarinet Concerto. "Made me realize that the only way to deal with that music is to *sing* it with the clarinet, as if it were an aria in a Mozart opera."

We found Langenus at his house, a trim white cottage in a clearing in the woods. He was sitting under a hickory tree, a "good-looking man in blue slacks, a cream-colored corduroy shirt, and crepe-soled shoes." His yard had half a dozen bird-houses fixed on trees and posts, one of which was decorated with a clef and notes in black wire. He suggested going inside for a little clarinet playing. "After all, we're in the country and the clarinet is *the* pastoral instrument," he said. He suggested they play some Bach duets.

"Then let's go, Gus," Goodman said, in my story. "I'll play the first part."

Langenus gave him an indulgent smile. "No hurry," he said.
"These Bach duets are like a walk through the woods. With every
measure, it's as if a new view came up. The clarinet is the most
beautiful instrument that has ever been made, because it comes
closest to the human voice, which is the most beautiful instru-
ment of all."

"Come *on*, Gus!" Goodman pleaded, and they started to play.

Bill Shawn's emphasis on "every touch" and a "warm response
to people" and "sensitiveness to the particulars of place, situation,
and events" was always with me, even before he put those ideas
into words. I might even have absorbed them by a kind of osmosis.
By now, of course, it seems to me that they represent everything I
care about, and perhaps have always cared about, in life.

In 1955, I caught up with Goodman again, when he went back
to playing his own kind of jazz at Basin Street, an underground
nightclub, where he was packing them in nightly, the biggest
crowds since the late thirties, and playing with Teddy Wilson, Milt
Hinton, and others. He invited me to a rehearsal. "We don't know
what the hell we're doing," he said. "You might say we're having
an old-fashioned jam session here, only better." He told me:

> "I've never had a trombone and a saxophone in a small group
> before. Maybe they're what give us some of that fresh sound we
> have. Not that I really know how we get it. If you enjoy yourself—
> why, it sounds fresh, that's all. The most important thing is that I
> got myself kids with talent. Ruby Braff doesn't read much music,
> but who cares? He's warm, he feels the way the rest of us feel, and
> he's having fun. There was a time, a few years back, when all the
> kids were playing on this bop kick, but they ran up a dead end and
> now they're coming around to swing. There's a terrific trend to
> what they call rock and roll, and to race music. As for me, maybe
> I've been rejuvenated. What I play is still swing, but as a group I
> guess we have a different sound. When I was playing here last
> summer, I was just trying to get *back* to something I used to do,
> but now it's a new thing that grows right out of the past but is
> new and alive."

The next year, I caught up with Benny Goodman again, when he returned to play in the Empire Room of the Waldorf about twenty years after his first appearance there as the "King of Swing." He said to me:

"We'll use the full band for dancing, and between sets, I'll come on with a trio or quartet. Playing is easy enough with three or four, because you just spiel, but with the whole band, you got to work. It's been a real hassle digging up new talent, but you have to find it. We got Hank Jones on piano and Urbie Green on trombone, and some boys who don't read so good—they call it 'seeing the paper'—but who sure know how to play. They got their hearts in it. A man who doesn't think this is important music, he'd better not fool with it, that's all."

Goodman also said:

"When you stay out of the band business as long as I have, a lot of phony ideas turn up that are hard not to fall for. Like giving concerts and working up phony nostalgia for the thirties, which is a lot of baloney. Once I decided to put a band together again, I said to myself, 'What the hell we doing playing *shows?* Why not play for *dancing?* It's more in keeping with the music. Oh, we might play 'Mr. Bach Goes to Town' with the quartet, but I get a kick out of playing for dancing. It's more *fun*."

Fifteen years later, I had for the most part abandoned the "we" in reporting Talk stories. My story about Benny Goodman—in his apartment rehearsing, with the violinist Yehudi Menuhin and the pianist Paul Coker, to play a Bela Bartók work written for and dedicated to Benny Goodman and Joseph Szigeti—began as follows:

One rainy midmorning last week Benny Goodman arranged a couple of antique music stands alongside the Mason & Hamlin baby-grand piano in the large living room of his apartment high up in Manhattan House. Mr. Goodman, at seventy-one, was suntanned and looked almost exactly as he has looked for decades— the same lip, the same quick grin, the same just about everything, except for a bit of grayness and wispiness of hair. He was wearing

a light-blue worsted suit over a khaki safari shirt open at the collar.
He cleared the top of the piano, scooping up a half-dozen framed
pictures of his family—his late wife, Alice; his daughters, Rachel
and Benjie, both now in their early thirties and married, and living
in Florence, Italy, and East Deerfield, Massachusetts, respectively;
Rachel's daughter, Naomi, one and a half—and put them all on the
coffee table, next to a battered and peeling brown leather-covered
clarinet case. He lifted the lid of the piano and fixed it open. One of
the music stands, which he had placed close to the piano bench,
was a double one of oak, early-nineteenth-century French, with
candelabra, and with an inlaid edging of birch. The other stand,
near the tail of the piano, was of indeterminate age, was painted
mostly black, and was inlaid with mother-of-pearl. Mr. Goodman
set chairs, taken from around his dining-room table, in front of the
stands. Then he tossed worn-looking sets of sheet music onto each
of the music stands and onto the piano rack.

The piece gives a quick picture of Yehudi Menuhin as he arrived
and,

> . . . holding a brown canvas-covered violin case under one arm
> and supporting the case with the other hand, greeted Mr. Good-
> man, introduced Mr. Coker, and made a beeline for the piano.
> "Oh, a Mason & Hamlin!" he said happily, in a light British
> accent. "Such a good firm, isn't it, Benny?"
> "Yeah," Mr. Goodman said. He spoke in his familiar hoarse,
> drawling voice and added his characteristic hoarse laugh.
> "They gave three pianos to my sister and me," Mr. Menuhin
> said, with a beatific smile.

The characterization of Goodman is consistent with that of him
in the previous stories, but I think it becomes even deeper in this
one. Later on, he says:

> "I even got you Szigeti's music stand," Mr. Goodman said, indi-
> cating to Mr. Menuhin that he was to take the stand with the
> candelabra. "I bought it from his wife about thirty years ago,
> when they had to move away."

"It's a beautiful stand, Benny," Mr. Menuhin said. "Very pretty."

"I use it as an end table," Mr. Goodman said, with his laugh. He took off his jacket and put it around the back of a chair.

"Are we going to sit or stand?" Mr. Menuhin asked.

"I like to stand," Mr. Goodman said.

"So do I, Benny," Mr. Menuhin said. "Do you find you have more breath when you stand?"

"Yeah," Mr. Goodman said.

This kind of dialogue was not only true to the way they talked, but it was important, in offering the reader an almost tactile sense of being with the characters, to select the appropriate words and to get them right, as, for example, in the use of Goodman's "Yeahs"— which is the way he spoke in the other two stories. Also, Menuhin's generosity and gentleness are revealed in the way he defers graciously to Goodman.

The story goes on:

Mr. Goodman made most of his remarks by singing. "Dee-da-da-dee," he would sing to Mr. Menuhin. Mr. Menuhin would respond by playing the passage that way and then saying, "Oh, that's very nice. That's so nice. I like the fingering." He would play it again and then say, "Do you like it, Benny? Or would it be cleaner—" And he would play it another way.

"Daddle, deedle, daddle, da da," Mr. Goodman would sing to him.

"Wonderful!" Mr. Menuhin would say, and he would play it that way.

The ending of this story:

They started from the beginning and played the piece all the way through.

"Lovely," Mr. Menuhin said at the end.

"Yeah, better, wasn't it?" Mr. Goodman said.

"You play Bartók with such feeling," Mr. Menuhin said.

"The cadenza you played," Mr. Goodman said. "Beautiful."

This was a very important "short story" touch—the demonstrable effect on Goodman and the way he reacted with generous praise for the other artist.

Then:

> No one said anything for a moment.
> Mr. Menuhin slowly put down his violin, and then he said, "The piece is so full of life and humor."

What I intended, of course, was to show, in addition to the effect of Menuhin on Goodman, that these two musicians were themselves full of life and humor. I deliberately pointed up the contrast between them, in order to reveal their happy respect for each other and their joint reverence for what they were able to create. I loved watching them and listening to them. I have always been aware of my good fortune, in the role of a reporter, to have the special blessing of simply being there.

When the humor is subtle, it takes time to build gradually, and the impact, ideally, is very strong. Here's an example from The Talk of the Town in 1963. It was with this piece that I dropped the "we" and cast the story entirely in the third person. I felt that "we" would just get in the way.

There are quiet little events, unheralded, that go on all over that reflect our humanity and culture. Glenn Gould, the late pianist, was a genius, and he wanted desperately to go his own way with his music. He didn't like following the conventional patterns of giving public concerts. I respected and admired his remarkable independence. When he invited me to the event described below, I loved being able to show something, in the story, of the purity of these two musical artists in a very unusual get-together.

> Mr. Glenn Gould, the pianist, held a private showing one recent morning, for Mr. Yehudi Menuhin, the violinist, of a movie starring himself. The movie, which had been made from an hour-long video-tape recording, was entitled *The Anatomy of Fugue*. It was projected on a screen the size of a pillow case, in a room the size of an average closet, in the local office of the Canadian

Broadcasting Corporation, which had broadcast the tape. Mr. Gould, unslept and unbarbered, was in town for a couple of days from his home, in Toronto. He had on his usual baggy dark-blue suit with outmoded overpadded shoulders, a raggedy brown sweater, and a worn-out bluish necktie. A yellow pencil protruded, eraser end up, from his coat pocket. He was burdened with a baggy brown overcoat, a brown wool muffler, and a navy-blue cap.

Mr. Menuhin, pink-cheeked, chubby, trim, and serene, had come to town from *his* home, in London, to start on a three-month, twenty-eight-city recital tour that would include several benefit performances and one appearance on the *Bell Telephone Hour*. He was neatly encased in well-tailored pin stripes and well-laundered supplementation. Mr. Gould sat on a straight-backed office chair, with his coat, cap, and muffler on his lap, and with his arms crossed and his hands tucked under his arms. Mr. Menuhin sat on a straight-backed office chair right behind him, his fingers entwined over his midriff.

"I'm so glad you could come. I'm so glad you could really make it," Mr. Gould said, turning around, to Mr. Menuhin. "I want you to see this one. This one is a special pet."

"Such a nice thing to do in New York," Mr. Menuhin said, in a light, warm voice. And gave Mr. Gould a gentle, warm smile. "Seeing a movie at eleven o'clock in the morning. I'm so glad you suggested it."

"I like making these films," Mr. Gould said. "I've always felt this terrible frustration in concerts—you do it and it's gone. Why not put it on film and have it? So that it will *be* there."

"Wonderful idea. Wonderful," Mr. Menuhin said, his smile broadening and a look of appreciation coming into his eyes.

Mr. Gould grinned.

"I did a television film on Bartók, covering the musical influences in his life, and playing some of his arrangements of Hungarian folk tunes and excerpts from the solo violin sonata he wrote for me, and speaking in between, and I did another one about Yoga," Mr. Menuhin said. "I find it rather difficult when they put you in front of the camera and say '*Do* something.'"

Mr. Gould bobbed his head in agreement. "We had a very good director for this one, and we even built a set, as you'll see," he said. "We shot the whole thing in two days. After two months of conferences, of course."

"Was it dreadfully expensive?" Mr. Menuhin asked. "These things do cost so much."

"Thirty thousand dollars, about," Mr. Gould said. "But I wanted to do it right. There's no point in doing it at all if you can't get what you want." He waved a hand at the projectionist, who was peeking out of a square hole in the back wall. "We're ready any time you want to start," Mr. Gould said.

Mr. Menuhin gave a little sigh and tightened his hands around his middle. "I hope this will be made available to television in this country," he said.

Mr. Gould grinned again. "Well, *they've* got Leonard Bernstein," he said. "I don't do it the way he does it. Not that I don't admire the way he does it. He has the ability to communicate on a great many levels at once. My way is different." He bobbed his head vigorously. "I don't know if my film is for the mass public. Sometimes I think they don't know what the hell I've said, but they feel elevated."

Mr. Menuhin's eyes twinkled.

"Roll it," Mr. Gould said to the projectionist behind the wall. He turned back to the screen, and tossed his coat, muffler, and cap on the floor. The lights went out, and the movie started showing Mr. Gould at the piano playing an improvisation based on "Do Re Mi," from Richard Rodgers' score for *The Sound of Music*. When he had finished it, he looked up, on the screen, and said to the camera, "For hundreds of years, musicians have been doing the sort of things that I was attempting just now. They have been taking little bits of musical trivia like that theme from *The Sound of Music* and trying to find complicated equations into which, like a common denominator, these tidbits will fit. In fact, there is some part of almost every musician that longs to experiment with the mathematical quantities of music and to find forms in which these quantities can function most

successfully... And perhaps the long-time favorite of such forms is that special musical mix we call the fugue. . . ."

Both men settled back more easily in their chairs. Mr. Gould crossed his legs. He hunched forward as he heard himself say, on the screen, that he was now going to play a much more intense fugue from Volume II of *The Well-Tempered Clavier*—the B Flat Minor, "one of the finest of Bach's fugues."

"Wonderful," Mr. Menuhin said at the end of the fugue.

"It's a great piece," Mr. Gould said. . . .

The movie ended. The lights came on.

"Wonderful program!" Mr. Menuhin said. "Beautifully done!"

Mr. Gould suddenly looked shy. "Thank you," he said. "It was really quite fun to do. But it took a hell of a lot of work."

"I love your approach to the music and the completely unmechanical way you play," Mr. Menuhin said, beaming at Mr. Gould with admiration. "And you spoke throughout so smoothly. Was it impromptu?"

"I had it on the TelePrompter," Mr. Gould said. "I looked at it often enough to pick up all the cues, but I forced myself to invent phrases as I went along, to keep it sounding natural and not too formal."

"Yes, wonderful," Mr. Menuhin said. "Especially if the words are your own."

Mr. Gould laughed shyly.

"For the one I did on Bartók, I had quite good dialogue, but not quite as good as yours," Mr. Menuhin said. He gave a little sigh. "Most enjoyable," he said.

"Next year, if you're going to have some time, we might do one together," Mr. Gould said. "You ever done the Schoenberg *Fantasia?*"

"Yes!" Mr. Menuhin gave a little gasp. "What a splendid idea! I must look at the music."

"It's a dry work—one of his last things," Mr. Gould said.

"I have the music," Mr. Menuhin said. "You're not coming to England next summer? We might do it there."

"I'd love to come and visit you," Mr. Gould said. "But I'm finished with concerts. You know my feeling about concerts. I'm bored with them."

Mr. Menuhin smiled wistfully. "On the screen, it does gain dimensions," he said.

"Some people say that every performance is an experience, but it's not that for me in concerts," Mr. Gould said. "It's animal. It's all a circus. It's immoral."

"Yes, I do know what you mean," Mr. Menuhin said mildly. . . . "Would you come to England in July?" he asked. "To make the film?"

Mr. Gould bobbed his head and grinned. "The Schoenberg," he said. "In July."

Mr. Menuhin got up to go, smiling and looking utterly at peace. He gave Mr. Gould his hand. "It will be lovely," he said. "We will do it, and then it will be there."

I've kept this piece in mind—after its writing thirty-eight years ago—as a kind of model reportorial story. Time does not diminish it or change it. I loved observing these two men, these two keenly individual musical artists. They openly and honestly permitted me to show their respect and admiration for each other, and the integrity of their different professional yearnings and prejudices. The humor is of the subtlest and quietest kind, based on their two unique personalities and their joint love of their work. It reveals quite a bit about the timeless classical music world, with a couple of geniuses working in it. (If you look back at the excerpt from the 1981 story about Yehudi Menuhin, eighteen years later, practicing for a concert with Benny Goodman, you can see exactly the same characteristics of Menuhin—modest, loving, pure, and deferential to his fellow musician.) The story moves along as they warm up to each other. And then, to top it off, it also yields an extra bonus, because something happens at the end: they make plans to make a film of their playing a modern composition together.

Hemingway

━━ ━━ ━━ ━━ ━━ ━━ ━━ ━━ ━━ ━━ ━━ ━━ ━━

"Come In, Lassie!"—written in the late 1940's, a few years after I'd joined the staff of *The New Yorker*—was the first long piece in which I discovered a way of using dialogue to establish the characters, to reveal their interrelationships, and to move the action of the story along. It was a fun way, and always a factual way, of characterizing people. The subjects themselves usually loved it. From that point on in reporting, I found the dialogue, at the exact moment of hearing it, that would become an integral part of each story.

Dialogue for me is the most effective and most interesting way of defining a character, making it unnecessary for the writer to intrude with any song-and-dance routine of his own. Moreover, as in a play or in a movie, dialogue moves the action along. That is why so many readers write to me and say that they felt, while reading a piece, that they were right there, with me. I am most comfortable having my characters talk for themselves. I set them up, get out of their way, and let them go. Now and then, I might interject a question or two, or even a comment, to help them along. Staying out of their way, however, is essential. A tape recorder gets in the

way, too. I, not the machine, must do the listening. And you must
be selective in listening to the characters. If I edit the dialogue a bit
to make it more truly theirs, I do it in a way that is not noticeable
to the talker or to anyone else. Not once, in my half-century of
reporting, has any of my subjects ever claimed that their talk is not
theirs. And I've been most fortunate in having run into some splen-
did talkers.

The Profile of Ernest Hemingway, which was published in *The
New Yorker* on May 13, 1950, with the title "How Do You Like It
Now, Gentlemen?" received an enormous response and considcr-
able attention that year and in the years since. In 1961, the year of
Hemingway's death, it was published as a book, *Portrait of Hem-
ingway,* and has gone through many subsequent editions and been
translated into various languages. *Portrait of Hemingway* includes
an Afterword about the many letters Hemingway and his wife,
Mary, wrote to me during the eleven-year period after the Profile
was published. The most recent edition was published by Modern
Library in 1999. Ernest Hemingway and I were friends before I
wrote the Profile, and we remained friends for the rest of his life.
I've used common sense in choosing my subjects. I've chosen sub-
jects I'd be able to write comfortably and freely about.

Here is an example of the dialogue in the Hemingway Profile. I
accompanied Hemingway and his wife to the hotel suite they set-
tled into after arriving in New York en route to Europe. They had
invited their old friend Marlene Dietrich, whom they affectionate-
ly called "the Kraut" over to dinner. There was a knock at the door,
and Hemingway got up quickly and opened it. It was "the Kraut."

> Their reunion was a happy one. Mrs. Hemingway came out of the
> bedroom and greeted the guest enthusiastically. Miss Dietrich
> stood back from Hemingway and looked at him with approval.
> "Papa, you look wonderful," she said slowly.
> "I sure missed you, daughter," said Hemingway. He raised his
> fist to his face, and his shoulders shook as he laughed silently.
> Miss Dietrich was wearing a mink coat. She sighed loudly, took
> off the coat, and handed it to Mrs. Hemingway. Then she sighed

again and sat down in an overstuffed chair. Hemingway poured a
glass of champagne, took it to her, and refilled the other glasses.

"The Kraut's the best that ever came into the ring," he said, as
he handed me my glass. Then he pulled a chair up beside Miss
Dietrich's, and they compared notes on friends and on them-
selves. They talked about theatre and motion-picture people,
one of whom, a man, Hemingway referred to as a "sea heel."

Miss Dietrich wanted to know what a sea heel was.

"The sea is bigger than the land," he told her.

Mrs. Hemingway went into the serving pantry and came out
in a few minutes with caviar spread on toast.

"Mary, I am telling Papa how I have to behave because I am a
grandmother," Miss Dietrich said, taking a piece of toast. "I have
to think always of the children. You know, Papa?"

Hemingway gave a sympathetic grunt, and Miss Dietrich took
from her purse some snapshots of her grandson and passed them
around. He was eighteen months old, she told us. Hemingway
said that he looked like a winner, and that he would be proud
to own a piece of him if he ever got into the ring.

Miss Dietrich said that her daughter was going to have another
child soon. "I'll be a grandmother again, Papa," she said.

Hemingway gave her a bleak look. "I'm going to be a grand-
father in a few months," he said. "My son Bumby's wife."

". . . Everything you do, you do for the sake of the children,"
Miss Dietrich said.

"Everything for the children," Hemingway said. He refilled
Miss Dietrich's glass.

"Thank you, Papa," she said, and sighed. She lived at the
Plaza, she told him, but spent a good deal of her time at the
apartment of her daughter, who lived on Third Avenue. "Papa,
you should see me when they go out," she said, and took a sip of
champagne. "I'm the baby-sitter. As soon as they leave the house,
I go around and look in all the corners and straighten the drawers
and clean up. I can't stand a house that isn't neat and clean. I go
around in all the corners with towels I bring with me from the
Plaza, and I clean up the whole house. Then they come home at

one or two in the morning, and I take the dirty towels and some
of the baby's things that need washing, and, with my bundle over
my shoulder, I go out and get a taxi, and the driver, he thinks I am
this old washerwoman from Third Avenue, and he takes me in
the taxi and talks to me with sympathy, so I am afraid to let him
take me to the Plaza. I get out a block away from the Plaza, and
I walk home with my bundle and I wash the baby's things, and
then I go to sleep."

"Daughter, you're hitting them with the bases loaded,"
Hemingway said earnestly.

There was no need, in this scene, to write any exposition. The
dialogue did it all.

Here's a bit from the Profile about Hemingway going to Aber-
crombie & Fitch to buy a coat.

The doors opened at our floor, and we got out and headed
for a rack of topcoats. A tall, dapper clerk approached us, and
Hemingway shoved his hands into his pants pockets and
crouched forward. "I think I still have credit in this joint," he
said to the clerk.

The clerk cleared his throat. "Yes, sir," he said.

"Want to see coat," Hemingway said menacingly.

"Yes, sir," said the clerk. "What kind of coat did you wish to
see, sir?"

"That one." He pointed to a straight-hanging, beltless tan
gabardine coat on the rack. The clerk helped him into it and
gently drew him over to a full-length mirror. "Hangs like a
shroud," Hemingway said, tearing the coat off. "I'm tall on top.
Got any other coat?" he asked, as though he expected the answer
to be no. He edged impatiently toward the elevators.

"How about this one, sir. With a removable lining, sir?" the
clerk said. This one had a belt. Hemingway tried it on, studied
himself in the mirror, and then raised his arms as though he were
aiming a rifle. "You going to use it for *shooting,* sir?" the clerk
asked. Hemingway grunted, and said he would take the coat. He
gave the clerk his name, and the clerk snapped his fingers. "Of

course!" he said. "There was *something*. . . " Hemingway looked
embarrassed and said to send the coat to him at the Sherry-
Netherland, and then said he'd like to look at a belt.

"What kind of belt, Mr. Hemingway?" the clerk asked.

"Guess a brown one," Hemingway said.

We moved over to the belt counter, and another clerk
appeared.

"Will you show Mr. Hemingway a belt?" the first clerk said,
and stepped back and thoughtfully watched Hemingway.

The second clerk took a tape measure from his pocket, saying
he thought Hemingway was a size 44 or 46.

"Wanta bet?" Hemingway asked. He took the clerk's hand and
punched himself in the stomach with it.

"Gee, he's got a hard tummy," the belt clerk said. He measured
Hemingway's waistline. "Thirty-eight!" he reported. "Small waist
for your size. What do you do—a lot of exercise?"

Hemingway hunched his shoulders, feinted, laughed, and
looked happy for the first time since we'd left the hotel. He
punched himself in the stomach with his own fist.

"Where you going—to Spain again?" the belt clerk asked.

"To Italy," Hemingway said, and punched himself in the
stomach again.

Scenes of this kind, showing Hemingway having a good time,
apparently bothered some critics. Hemingway wrote to me after
the Profile appeared and said he had found it "funny" and "good."
I wrote the following in a Preface to it when it was republished as a
book:

> To the complete surprise of Hemingway and the editors of *The
> New Yorker* and myself, it turned out, when the profile appeared,
> that what I had written was extremely controversial. Most readers
> took the piece for just what it was, and I trust that they enjoyed it
> in an uncomplicated fashion. However, a certain number of read-
> ers reacted violently, and in a very complicated fashion. Among
> these were people who objected strongly to Hemingway's person-
> ality, assumed I did the same, and admired the piece for the

wrong reasons; that is, they thought that in describing that personality accurately I was ridiculing or attacking it. Other people simply didn't like the way Hemingway talked (they even objected to the playful way he sometimes dropped his articles and spoke a kind of joke Indian language); they didn't like his freedom; they didn't like his not taking himself seriously; they didn't like his going to boxing matches, going to the zoo, talking to friends, going fishing, enjoying people, celebrating his approach to the finish of a book by splurging on caviar and champagne; they didn't like this and they didn't like that. In fact, they didn't like Hemingway to be Hemingway. They wanted him to be somebody else—probably themselves. . . . Either they had dreary, small-minded preconceptions about how a great writer should behave and preferred their preconceptions to the facts or they attributed to me their own pious disapproval of Hemingway and then berated me for it. Some of the more devastation-minded among them called the profile "devastating." When Hemingway heard about all this, he wrote to reassure me. On June 16, 1950 [a month after the profile appeared], he wrote, "Don't worry about the piece, it is just that people got things all mixed up." Some people, he said, couldn't understand his enjoying himself and his not being "really spooky"; they couldn't understand his being a serious writer without being pompous.

Here's one more scene: Hemingway at the Metropolitan Museum of Art.

As we walked along, Hemingway said to me, "I can make a landscape like Mr. Paul Cézanne. I learned how to make a landscape like Mr. Paul Cézanne by walking through the Luxembourg Museum a thousand times with an empty gut, and I am pretty sure that if Mr. Paul was around, he would like the way I make them and be happy that I learned it from him." He had learned a lot from Mr. Johann Sebastian Bach, too. "In the first paragraph of *Farewell*, I used the word 'and' consciously over and over the way Mr. Johann Sebastian Bach used a note in music when he was emitting counterpoint. I can almost write like Mr. Johann

sometimes—or, anyway, so he would like it. All such people are easy to deal with, because we all know you have to learn."

About five decades after I heard this from Hemingway about the first paragraph of *A Farewell to Arms,* it was interesting to read a piece about Hemingway written for *The New Yorker* by Joan Didion. She began by quoting that very same first paragraph, published in 1929, and then saying it "bears examination: four deceptively simple sentences, one hundred and twenty-six words, the arrangement of which remains as mysterious and thrilling to me now as it did when I first read them, at twelve or thirteen, and imagined that if I studied them closely enough and practiced hard enough I might one day arrange one hundred and twenty-six such words myself." She referred to "the liturgical cadence of the paragraph." If Hemingway had lived, he would have been able to tell her that *he* knew that he could almost write like Mr. Johann Sebastian Bach sometimes—or, anyway, so he would like it.

MAILER

_____ _____ _____ _____ _____ _____ _____ _____ _____ _____ _____ _____ _____

Norman Mailer is one of the people I wrote a piece
about who then became a friend; I liked his writing; I liked
talking to—and occasionally arguing with—him; I liked
his second wife, Adele, and his sixth and present wife, Norris
Church, and although I lost track of most of his life in between
those two wives, I never lost track of his writing; I liked hearing
him talk about his kids; I very much liked his mother, Minnie
Mailer, and it was a treat to go to their home in Brooklyn; I partic-
ularly loved his mother's cooking, especially her pot roast with
potato pancakes (as good as my own mother's, maybe better); I
was appalled when he invited me to join him and others, on glori-
ously sunny Sunday afternoons, in some smoky bar to drink and
smoke and talk, talk, talk, because I wanted to be outdoors play-
ing tennis or immersing myself in the ocean. I enjoyed seeing him
in Hollywood in the early 1950's and thoroughly appreciated
going with him to visit Robert Mitchum. I always felt he had so
much, in so many different ways, to offer in writing. I even got a
kick out of his resistance when I told him that I didn't believe in
putting myself personally as a character in my factual stories, and

REPORTING BACK

R E P O R T I N G B A C K

going to be an alcoholic," he said, "I'll be one by November 2nd, thanks to the rigors of the political campaign. I've been making speeches for Wallace. I've made eighteen so far and have another dozen ahead of me. I'm not doing this because I like it. All last year, I kept saying that the intellectuals had to immerse themselves in political movements or else they were only shooting their mouths off. Now I am in this spot as a result of shooting my mouth off."

In general, Mailer told us, the success of his novel has caused him to feel uncomfortably like a movie queen. "Whenever I make an appearance," he said, "I have thirty little girls crowding around asking for my autograph. I think it's much better when people who read your book don't know anything about you, even what you look like. I have refused to let *Life* photograph me. Getting your mug in the papers is one of the shameful ways of making a living, but there aren't many ways of making a living that aren't shameful. Everyone keeps asking me if I've ever been psychoanalyzed. The answer is no, but maybe I'll have to be by the end of another five years. These are rough times for little Normie."

Mailer's royalties will net him around thirty thousand this year, after taxes, and he plans to bank most of it. He finds apartments depressing and has a suspicion of possessions, so he and his wife live in a thirty-dollar-a-month furnished room in Brooklyn Heights. He figures that his thirty thousand will last at least five years, giving him plenty of time in which to write another book. He was born in Long Branch, New Jersey, but his family moved to Brooklyn when he was one, and that has since been his home. He attended P.S. 161 and Boys High and entered Harvard at sixteen, intending to study aeronautical engineering. He took only one course in engineering, however, and spent most of his time reading or in bull sessions. In his sophomore year, he won first prize in *Story*'s college contest with a story entitled "The Greatest Thing in the World." "About a bum," he told us. "In the beginning, there's a whole *tzimes* about how he's very hungry and all he's eating is ketchup. It will probably make a wonderful movie someday." In the Army, Mailer served as a surveyor in the field

artillery, an intelligence clerk in the cavalry, a wireman in a com-
munications platoon, a cook, and a baker, and volunteered suc-
cessfully for action with a reconnaissance platoon on Luzon. He
started writing *The Naked and the Dead* in the summer of 1946, in
a cottage outside Provincetown, and took sixteen months to finish
it. "I'm slowing down," he said. "When I was eighteen, I wrote a
novel in two or three months. At twenty-one, I wrote another
novel, in seven months. Neither of them ever got published."

After turning in the manuscript of *The Naked and the Dead*, he
and his wife went off to Paris. "It was wonderful there," he said.
"In Paris, you can just lay down your load and look out at the
gray sky. Back here, the crowd is always yelling. It's like a Roman
arena. You have a headache, and you scurry around like a rat, like
a character in a Kafka nightmare, eating scallops with last year's
grease on them."

Mailer has an uneasy feeling that Dostoevsky and Tolstoy,
between them, have written everything worth writing, but he
nevertheless means to go on turning out novels. He thinks *The
Naked and the Dead* must be a failure, because of the number of
misinterpretations of it that he has read. "People say that it is a
novel without hope," he told us. "Actually, it offers a good deal
of hope. I intended it to be a parable about the movement of man
through history. I tried to explore that outrageous proposition of
cause and effect, of effort and recompense, in a sick society. The
book finds man corrupted, confused to the point of helplessness,
but it also finds that there are limits beyond which he cannot be
pushed, and it finds that even in his corruption and sickness there
are yearnings for a better world."

In my pattern in reporting on certain individuals, I followed
up—twelve years later—on what Mailer was doing in keeping up
with the times in his particular way. This story, in 1960, was called
"Movement."

Fawcett Publications invited us to a party last week to celebrate
the publication of a paperback anthology entitled *The Beats* and
containing poems, essays, and stories by a couple of dozen writers

who are now leading (according to Fawcett) the Beat (with, according to Fawcett, a capital B) movement. The party was held in the lobby of the Living Theatre, a second-floor walkup at Fourteenth Street and Sixth Avenue, a couple of hours before curtain time of that conspicuously living play called *The Connection*, which is housed there. As we climbed the stairs, we found copies of *The Beats* pasted to the walls. Some displayed the front cover, which has on it a photograph of a pretty young girl and a bearded young man wearing shell-rimmed eyeglasses, plus warnings that read, "Here are the most vital and controversial writers on the American scene," and "Raw, penetrating stories, poems and social criticism by JACK KEROUAC, NORMAN MAILER, ALLEN GINSBERG, LAWRENCE FER-LINGHETTI, and many others. Edited by Seymour Krim." Other copies of the book showed the back cover, which added, "The drive, the fury, the frankness they bring to their writing has made the Beat Generation the most hotly discussed literary movement of this century."

Upstairs, the party seemed slow in getting started. Several lovely young ladies, all of them wearing conservative black dresses, were putting up more copies of *The Beats* at the corners of a square bar in the middle of the lobby and helping bartenders open bottles of whiskey. We approached a young man, impeccable in Ivy League oxford gray and a knitted black tie, who was putting up still more copies of *The Beats* on the walls. "Nobody here yet who's authentic Beat," he told us. "All of us are from Fawcett. We're here to inspire confidence. How do you like the girl on the cover? She's an associate editor on our books. She's not Beat at all. We put her on because she looked so typical." He paused. "Ah, at last! Seymour Krim!"

With this, the Fawcett man turned us over to Mr. Krim, a tall, skinny young man, friendly and wide-eyed, who was sporting a dark maroon shirt, a black four-in-hand, a brown V-necked pullover, dark gray trousers, and a silvery coat.

"I'm so nervous," Mr. Krim told us. "I never presided over a cocktail party before. What am I supposed to do? Introduce

people? Mix drinks? Offer them cheese crackers? I wish I didn't
feel so nervous. Would you like some Scotch? I think it's real."

We moved over to the bar, and the bartender poured Krim and
us some Scotch. "Tell me something, will you, kid?" the bartender
said to Krim. "What are you kids calling this a movement for?
You make it sound like the Communists, when all you are, you're
a bunch of not too brainy, warmhearted kids."

"*Fawcett* calls it a movement," Krim said. "Actually, it's sort of
a wave. Actually, it's sort of an *attitude* in anybody who's young or
young in heart. It's a posture of rebellion. It's for anybody unwill-
ing to put up with older compromises."

"O.K., O.K., kid," said the bartender. "I only thought any
writer worth his salt, he stuck to his attic all by himself and
wrote."

"We're like the French Impressionist painters, that whole
group, although the analogy is a little square," Krim said.
"Actually, there's less competitiveness among us than you find
among most other writers. The wave brings ideas useful to all
of us interchangeably. We turn each other on."

"A writer should be like an island," the bartender said. "Alone."

The party was warming up, with a number of informally
attired youthful guests arriving in twos and threes. We were
joined by a young man wearing chino trousers, a wrinkled khaki
shirt open at the collar, and brand-new white sneakers, who had a
small, childlike face and shining eyes. "Where's Norman Mailer?"
he asked Krim. "I want to meet Norman Mailer. He's the only
really good writer in the whole room."

"He's not here yet," said Krim.

"He's the only writer here with major talent,'" the young man
said.

"What about yourself?" Krim asked, plucking a copy of *The
Beats* from the wall, introducing the young man to us as Dan
Propper, and opening the book to a page headed "Dan Propper—
The Fable of the Final Hour."

"I don't regard myself as a great writer," said Propper. "Norman
Mailer has made it. He's there. This is my wife, Eunice," he

added, introducing a little, round-faced, black-haired girl wearing
a black shirt, black pants, and white sneakers as clean as her hus-
band's.

"Where's Norman Mailer?" Eunice asked.

Another young man, handsome and confident, came by and
waved a manuscript packed between black hard covers at us.

"Got a carbon copy?" Krim asked.

"I never make carbons," said the young man.

"You'll regret it someday," said Krim

"I don't even belong here," said the young man. "I'm a senior at
Harvard. This party looks like any old party at Harvard."

"Where's Jack Kerouac?" a chic, attractive lady asked. "My son
told me if I came to this party I'd see Jack Kerouac."

"He plays hard to get," said Krim. "Too bad Ginsberg is in
Chile. Or we'd have had ten good arguments already. Nobody has
opened up yet. The party's tame. Anyway, here's Ted Joans."

We shook hands with a bearded young Negro who had a Mid-
western accent and was wearing a heavy sweater with brown and
gray horizontal stripes. "I'm splitting Friday," Joans told us. "That
means leaving town. Going on a trip around the world. Getting
on a boat. Going to read my poems in the middle of the Atlantic.
Going to read all over the world—in Liverpool, London, and
Brussels. No matter where I am, I always find a place to read."

"You make a lot of money getting rented?" Krim asked him.

"Enough to get me on that boat to Liverpool," Joans said, and
held us by the sleeve. "My friend put this ad in the *Village Voice*
offering to rent Beatniks for your party," he said. "I'm the one
got rented. People always ask me don't I feel commercial letting
myself get rented? What I always reply is 'There's nothing wrong
with a Cadillac if you don't let it drive you.' I tell them it's the
same as renting yourself out as a capitalist. Nothing wrong with
that, long as you get paid."

As we made our way back to the bar, we ran into Mr. and
Mrs. Propper. "Norman Mailer is here!" they said happily. Sure
enough, in a few seconds we came upon Norman Mailer, looking
very conservative in a business suit and very much the elder

segment...stopokLet me transcribe properly.

statesman. We introduced him to the Proppers, whose beaming faces were a joy to see.

"Boy!" said Propper. "I read the scenes from your play! It's a groovy play."

"I read your fable," Mailer said, a fatherly twinkle in his eye. "I liked your fable."

"I was young, rebellious and adolescent when I wrote that fable," said Propper.

"His current stuff is much better," said Eunice.

Mailer gave them a fatherly nod. "It's a good fable," he said.

"Your play is a groovy play," said Eunice. "That part where the atom bomb goes off."

"That part's all right," said Mailer. "Then I've got two more scenes after that, they're even better."

Ted Joans joined us. "Norman Mailer!" he said. "In one of my poems, I tell them to buy your book."

"Say, thanks," Mailer said, looking bashful.

"I'm splitting Friday," said Joans. "Leaving on a trip around the world. Going to tell everybody, all over, to buy your book."

"I've never heard so many non sequiturs in my life," the bartender told us when we got back to him. "What kind of writers are they, they all talk the same? These kids, they are not Tolstoy."

"Kerouac isn't here yet," the chic, attractive lady said to us. "But I met this cute little Dan Propper. He gave me a copy of the book. I asked him for his autograph. I told him, 'I'm going to take it home, where I can read it *properly*.' He didn't get it."

We came upon Propper and Eunice a few minutes later.

"Nobody asked Norman Mailer for his autograph," Eunice said.

"That's a mark of his skill," said Propper.

We started to shove off, and, on our way to the door, passed Krim. "Fawcett is putting water in the drinks," he told us. "But the party is opening up."

The story above about *The Beats* may well be regarded as social history, after all. Mailer, at this point in 1960, was practically considered to be a "father figure" at the age of thirty-seven.

Thirty-eight years later, in 1998, as my ending to this sort of "three-part factual short story," I caught up with Mailer again in a story entitled "Two fighting legends reminisce and ruminate over the cheese puffs":

Norman Mailer, his eyes sparkling and his laughter bubbling up as usual, was in top form, generous and gracious, last week, at his Random House party celebrating the publication of *The Time of Our Time,* an astonishing, three-and-three-quarters-pound literary retrospective spanning his career since the publication, fifty years ago, of his first novel, *The Naked and the Dead.* Present and accounted for at the Rainbow Room were Mailer's family, including Norris Church, the tall, handsome, red-haired painter who is his sixth wife, most of his nine children, from his eldest, Susan (married to an economics minister in the Chilean government), to his youngest, John (a student at Wesleyan); and a friendly assortment of luminaries from literature, television, academia, entertainment, sports, politics, and the underworld.

So what did Mailer busy himself with at his party, where all his guests were given a copy of his new book, in addition to excellent champagne, a lot of superior cheese puffs, chicken satay, grilled-tuna toasts, coconut shrimp, ravioli, roast beef, and the offerings of a well-stocked bar? This: Mailer brought his guests over to his friends Muhammad Ali and Ali's wife, Lonnie, and introduced the guests by name one at a time. He looked on happily as dozens of people said to Ali, "Muhammad, you will always be the greatest!" and shook his large paw. Some said, "I saw you fight in '64!" or "It's an honor to meet you," or "It's a great honor to meet you," or "I saw you fight Sonny Liston, the Big Ugly Bear," and bowed their heads in wonder. Muhammad Ali looked each guest in the eye and smiled gently. José Torres, another boxer, came over and said, "You're still the greatest." Ali raised a clenched fist at him kiddingly, and Torres said, "Not me. All I can do is run away from you." Ali gave him a bigger smile, and Mailer was joyful.

Mailer told Muhammad Ali a little bit about how things were going with his television appearances to promote his book. "Katie Couric reminded me of your style, Muhammad, in the way she hit at me," he said at one point. "You know, the way you move, sweetly, and then—ow!—punch sharply. With her sweet little voice, she called me a 'male chauvinist pig.'" Mailer's laughter bubbled up, and Muhammad Ali smiled.

A lot of photographers were at the party, and they took a lot of photographs of Mailer with Ali. George Plimpton came over, and the photographers took pictures of the trio as they made rabbit ears over each other's heads. Thus stimulated, other guests stood with Ali to be photographed. Most of the Rainbow Room waiters rushed over and put their heads into the frame with Ali, and they also got photographed, Mailer looked on and beamed. After that Muhammad Ali did some magic tricks, including one involving a fake thumb that made a crinkly piece of tissue paper disappear in his hand. Then Muhammad Ali signed his own name to a number of copies of *The Time of Our Time*. And the guests at Norman Mailer's book party left smiling and satisfied.

That is the kind of thing that only journalism can do, especially with several stories that fit together. It may be attributed to the fact that one lucky reporter wrote all the stories from a single point of view.

JOHN HUSTON

THE RESPONSE TO the Hemingway Profile—from Harold Ross and Bill Shawn, and from my colleagues and the public—was heartening. I now knew that I loved to create my stories as much as possible in the form of scenes and dialogue. About a year later, when I accepted John Huston's invitation to come out to Hollywood to watch him direct the filming of Stephen Crane's *The Red Badge of Courage,* I saw immediately that I would be able to write this new story using a novelistic form. When Bill Shawn telephoned me out there, I told him, in great excitement, about my discovery. I also wrote him a letter about it, which turned up in *The New Yorker Records* at the New York Public Library Rare Books and Manuscripts Division. It was dated August 12, 1950. I quoted from it in my 1998 book *Here But Not Here:*

> . . . Huston as a person is almost too interesting to be true—he's complicated, funny, colorful, lonely, generous, crazy, driven, talented and outside of the conventional pattern of Hollywood, yet drawn and held by it, and the people in the business are attracted

to and held by him. I actually feel at times that I'm not awake. In
addition to all this, there is the picture he is making and the way
he works, the kind of cast he has assembled for this most-roman-
tic-of-wars war picture—almost all baby faces—and the way he
works with them. Now I could limit myself there to the story as a
profile, but I am beginning to think there is more in it than that,
because there will be the actual making of the picture. It is going
to involve so many of the elements of Hollywod that it is too
good to let go by. . . . You see, if the story turns out to be what
I think it is, it's really almost a book, a kind of novel-like book
because of the way the characters may develop and the variety of
relationships that exist among them. I don't know whether this
sort of thing has ever been done before, but I don't see why I
shouldn't try to do a fact piece in a novel form, or maybe a novel
in fact form. It's an exciting thing to think about. It's almost as
though the subject material calls for that kind of form."

My discovery of using this untried new form in my reporting
was electrifying. When I was around my principal characters in the
unfolding drama, I would hear their interchanges as the dialogue I
planned to use in my evolving scenes. I was already in the habit of
listening in that way to people I was writing about, but not on such
a large scale. In another letter to Bill, dated September 3, 1950,
which I came upon in the New York Public Library, I told him: "If
things work out the way I want them to, I will take four charac-
ters, Huston, first, then Schary, Reinhardt and Mayer, and tell my
story about Hollywood through them, against the background of
the industry and in relation to each other. It is the most exciting
story to think about that I have ever known."

In *The New Yorker*, the story was entitled "Production Number
1512," and it was published in five consecutive weekly install-
ments (5/24/52 to 6/21/52). Bill Shawn and I heard that the maga-
zine sold out on the newsstands in Hollywood as soon as it
appeared. Then the series was published as the book *Picture* (Bill's
title), which garnered widespread praise. Hemingway wrote to me,
saying he had sent my publisher a quote for the dust jacket: "Much

better than most novels." *Newsweek* wrote, "It is the best book on
Hollywood ever published." Today, I'm especially proud when I
hear praise for *Picture* from talented young movie directors,
including Joel Coen and Wes Anderson, whose work I admire so
much; they weren't even *born* yet when the book was first pub-
lished. What meant most to me, of course, was Bill Shawn's origi-
nal jacket copy for *Picture,* in which he defined, for the first time,
the factual story in the form of a novel.

Here are some elements from *Picture* that show how this form,
with dialogue, can bring a story to life, provide drama and action
and humor and move the story along. At the outset, I established
my main characters—John Huston, Gottfried Reinhardt, Dore
Schary, and Louis B. Mayer—as I had told Bill Shawn I would.
Huston, son of the legendary actor Walter Huston, was the classic,
wild, free artist, and Reinhardt, son of the legendary theatrical pro-
ducer Max Reinhardt, longed to be classic, wild, and free, but was
pressed by his role to be commercially—as well as artistically—
responsible for the production. Schary was the young, ambitious,
wise-cracking, successful-for-the-moment vice-president of M-G-
M production. L. B. Mayer, the willful and shrewd head of the stu-
dio, had opposed making *The Red Badge of Courage;* he liked
money-making Andy Hardy–type movies. Mayer predicted that
Huston's movie would fail, but Schary came aboard in favor of
making it, and so the film went into production. The power strug-
gle that would unfold over the picture took place over a period of
several months, while I watched and listened. All of the principal
characters in the drama, including Mayer, cooperated with me
fully, making it possible for me to report and write my story.

This scene in the book is my favorite:

The maze of paths followed by all the individuals at M-G-M
who work together to make a motion picture led inexorably to the
office of Louis B. Mayer, and I found him there one day, behind
a series of doors, talking to Arthur Freed, a producer of musicals
for the studio. Mayer's office was about half as large as the lounge

of the Radio City Music Hall, and he sat behind a huge cream-colored desk overlooking a vast expanse of peach-colored carpet. The walls of the office were panelled in cream-colored leather, and there was a cream-colored bar, a cream-colored fireplace with cream-colored fire irons, cream-colored leather chairs and couches, and a cream-colored grand piano. Behind Mayer's desk stood an American flag and a marble statue of the M-G-M lion. The desk was covered with four cream-colored telephones, a prayer book, several photographs of lions, a tintype of Mayer's mother, and a statuette of the Republican Party's elephant. The big desk hid most of Mayer, but I could see his powerful shoulders, decked in navy blue, and a gay, polka-dot bow tie that almost touched his chin. His large head seemed set upon the shoulders, without an intervening neck. His hair is thick and snow-white, his face is ruddy, and his eyes, behind glasses with amber-colored frames, stared with a sort of fierce blankness at Freed, who was showing him a report on the box-office receipts of his latest musical, then playing at the Radio City Music Hall.

"Great! I saw it!" Mayer said, sweeping Freed back with his arm. "I said to you the picture would be a wonderful hit. In here!" he cried, poking his index finger at his chest. "It wins the audience in here!" He lifted his snowy head and looked at the cream-colored wall before him as though he were watching the Music Hall screen. "Entertainment!" he cried, transfixed by what he seemed to see on that screen, and he made the face of a man who was emotionally stirred by what he was watching. "It's good enough for you and I and the box office," he said, turning back to Freed. "Not for the smart alecks. It's not good enough anymore," he went on, whining coyly, in imitation of someone saying that winning the heart of the audience was not good enough. He pounded a commanding fist on his desk and looked at me. "Let me tell you something!" he said. "Prizes! Awards! Ribbons! We had two pictures here. An Andy Hardy picture, with little Mickey Rooney, and *Ninotchka*, with Greta Garbo. *Ninotchka* got the prizes. Blue ribbons! Purple ribbons! Nine bells and seven stars! Which picture

made the money? *Andy Hardy* made the money. Why? Because it
won praise from the heart. No ribbons!"

"Hah!" Mr. Freed said.

"Twenty-six years with the studio!" Mayer went on. "They
used to listen to me. Never would Irving Thalberg make a picture
I was opposed to. I had a worship for that boy. He worked. Now
they want cocktail parties and their names in the papers. Irving
listened to me. Never satisfied with his own work. That was
Irving. Years later, after Irving passed away, they still listened.
They make an Andy Hardy picture." He turned his powerful
shoulders toward me. "Andy's mother is dying, and they make the
picture showing Andy standing outside the door. *Standing*. I told
them, 'Don't you know that an American boy like that will get
down on his hands and knees and *pray?*' They listened. They
brought Mickey Rooney down on his hands and knees." Mayer
leaped from his chair and crouched on the peach-colored carpet
and showed how Andy Hardy had prayed. "The biggest thing in
the picture!" He got up and returned to his chair. "Not good
enough," he said, whining coyly again. "Don't show the good,
wholesome, American mother in the home. Kind. Sweet.
Sacrifices. Love." Mayer paused and by his expression demon-
strated, in turn, maternal kindness, sweetness, sacrifice, and love,
and then glared at Freed and me. "No!" he cried. "Knock the
mother on the jaw!" He gave himself an uppercut to the chin.
"Throw the little old lady down the stairs!" He threw himself in
the direction of the American flag. "Throw the mother's good,
home-made chicken soup in the mother's face!" He threw an
imaginary plate of soup in Freed's face. "Step on the mother!
Kick her! That is *art*, they say. Art!!" he repeated, and gave an
angry growl.

"You said it," said Freed.

"*Andy Hardy!* I saw the picture, and the tears were in my
eyes," Mayer said. "I'm not ashamed. I'll see it again. Every
time, I'll cry."

"In musicals, we don't have any of those phony artistic preten-
sions," Freed said.

Mayer gave no sign that he had heard Freed. "Between you and I and the lamppost," he said, straightening his bow tie, "the smart alecks around here don't know the difference between the heart and the gutter. They don't want to listen to you. . . ."

"Thoreau said most of us lead lives of quiet desperation," Freed said quickly. "Pictures should make you feel better, not worse."

Again Mayer did not seem to hear, "*The Red Badge of Courage,*" he said. "A million and a half. Maybe more. What for? There's no story. I was against it. They wanted to make it. I don't say no. John Huston. He was going to do *Quo Vadis*. What he wanted to do to the picture! No heart. His idea was he'd throw the Christians to the lions. That's all. I begged him to change his ideas. I got down on my hands and knees to him. I sang 'Mammy' to him. I showed him the meaning of heart. I crawled to him on hands and knees. 'Ma-a-ammy!' With tears. No! No heart! He thanked me for taking him off the picture. Now he wants *The Red Badge of Courage*. Dore Schary wants it. All right. I'll watch. I don't say no, but I wouldn't make that picture with Sam *Gold*wyn's money!"

Here is John Huston celebrating his forty-fourth birthday at a formal dinner party in Hollywood attended by a couple of dozen of his closest friends and associates:

The party was given by Reinhardt, in the private dining room of Chasen's Restaurant. The host stood near the door. He looked cynical, and scornful of everything about him as he pumped the hand of each arriving guest, but he managed, with a half-smoked cigar fixed firmly in a corner of his mouth, to beam with delight. The guests all exuded an atmosphere of exclusiveness and intimacy. It seemed to have nothing to do with Huston's birthday. The birthday, apparently, was merely the occasion, not the cause, of the guests' effusions. Good will was stamped on the faces of all, but there was no indication as to whom or what it was directed toward. As they entered, the guests exchanged quick glances, as though they were assuring each other and themselves that they were there.

Some bits:

Reinhardt's wife, Silvia, asked Huston's agent, Paul Kohner, and the movie stars Edward G. Robinson and John Garfield, both smiling broadly at her, whether it was true that the men were going to play poker after dinner, while the ladies would be "given the brush."

Robinson smiled even more broadly.

Garfield said, "The girls can go to a movie or something. Eddie, you buy any paintings in Europe?"

"Julie, you are not playing poker," said Mrs. Reinhardt to Garfield.

"I have news for you," said Garfield, "I am. Eddie?"

"Not this trip," Robinson said, without ceasing to grin at Mrs. Reinhardt. "In New York, a Rouault. The time before in Europe, a Soutine."

"Last night, I met somebody owned a Degas," said a tall and glamorous-looking but nervous girl with red hair, who had detached herself from a group of ladies and was now at Robinson's elbow. Mrs. Reinhardt and the three men did not bother to acknowledge her remark.

"This Degas," the red-haired girl said miserably, "it's getting out of the bathtub, for a change, not in."

Here is Reinhardt explaining why he was giving the party at Chasen's:

"We entertain each other because we never know how to enjoy ourselves with other people," Reinhardt said to the guests at his table. "Hollywood people are afraid to leave Hollywood. Out in the world, they are frightened. They are unsure of themselves. They never enjoy themselves out of Hollywood. Sam Hoffenstein used to say we are the croupiers in a crooked gambling house. And it's true. Every one of us thinks, You know, I really don't deserve a swimming pool."

The guests did not seem to mind what he had said, but, on the other hand, there was no indication that anyone had listened to him.

Here is John Huston with the writer James Agee and the producer Sam Spiegel, with whom he was intending to make his next film, *The African Queen,* in Africa.

"So," said Spiegel. "How are things on the script?"

Huston said things were fine. "Only trouble is. Sam, we just demolished two weeks' work. Threw out every bit of it," he added lightly.

Spiegel swallowed hard. "When?" he asked.

"Just now," Huston said, with a forced grin.

"My ulcers are being formed," Spiegel said, and gave Agee an appealing look.

Agee seemed bewildered.

"We leave [for Africa] in four weeks," Spiegel said to Huston. "We must have the script before we leave."

"Don't worry, Sam'l," Huston said, in the reassuring tone he had used in talking with Reinhardt about the script for *The Red Badge of Courage.*

Spiegel said, "Beneath this façade of worry is worry. Did you get anything done today?"

"Don't worry," said Huston. "There's nothing to worry about."

"I like to *know* what I'm worrying about," said Spiegel. "Now it's that I worry and I don't know why."

"John," Agee said, "when are you going to do the retakes for David Selznick?"

Spiegel wet his lips. "You expect to do retakes for Selznick?"

Huston nodded. "David is in a jam," he said.

"You can't. You have no time," Spiegel said. "Why? Is he offering you a fortune?"

"I'm doing it for nothing," Huston said.

Spiegel shook his head. "You can't do it," he said.

"When a pal of mine is in a jam, I do what I can to help," Huston said.

"You can't do it," said Spiegel.

"Like hell I can't," Huston said.

"No," Spiegel said.

Huston gave a choked laugh. "Your ulcers, Sam'l," he said softly.

For almost four decades following *Picture,* Huston and his family continued as my reportorial subjects and friends. (In fact, John's wife, Ricki, whom I had first met when she was carrying Anjelica,

was instrumental in helping me find a newborn baby for adoption, my son Erik.) I continued writing about Huston because the stories were too good to resist. I wrote my last Talk of the Town story about John in 1984, when he was seventy-eight and afflicted with emphysema. Tethered to an oxygen tank, and asking no quarter, he directed his fortieth movie, *Prizzi's Honor,* starring Anjelica, Jack Nicholson, and Kathleen Turner. Huston, now white-haired with a matching moustache and beard, was working sixteen hours a day and filming on cold, damp October mornings and nights in Brooklyn.

A director's traditional canvas chair, with "JOHN HUSTON" stencilled in large letters on the back, had been placed before the remote control unit. Mr. Huston sat down in his chair. The Director of Photography, Mr. Bartkowiak—a handsome young man with long hair—came over. Speaking very softly, Mr. Huston said he wanted to do some tricks. "We'll do lap dissolves," he almost whispered, conspiratorially. "While pulling back from the shot of the big stained-glass window, we'll dissolve to close-ups of the main characters." The younger man nodded appreciatively, his eyes literally gleaming in anticipation.

John died in 1987, at the age of eighty-one. His last picture, based on the James Joyce story *The Dead*—with a screenplay written by John's son Tony and starring Anjelica—is considered by many people, including myself, to be his best—a powerful, beautiful masterpiece.

In 1996, I had the pleasure of writing about Anjelica Huston directing her first movie, *Bastard out of Carolina,* based on the Dorothy Allison novel:

"It's scary as hell," Anjelica told me on her set, looking confident and energetic and happy as hell. She was directorially clad in an oversized parka and bluejeans and twenty-year-old cowboy boots. Her good-natured husband, the artist Robert Graham—gray-bearded and sleepy, eyes closed, side of face resting on the palm of one hand (they get up at four A.M. in this business)—sat on a canvas folding chair that said:

ANJELICA HUSTON
DIRECTOR

". . . This certainly beats doing a prequel or a sequel to *Prizzi's Honor*, which they wanted me to do," she said. "I didn't want to do more *Prizzi's Honor, Prizzi's Honor* belongs to Dad. I want to do something of my own."

CHAPLIN

F IFTY YEARS AGO, I would often take for granted stories that
I now realize I was privileged to do. For instance, I wrote a
Talk of the Town story about Charlie Chaplin visiting New
York in 1950. It was called "Feeling Lost" and was written in the
then traditional voice of "we" before I abandoned it.

This story cleared the way for me to establish a genuine friend-
ship with the Chaplins that I would write about years later, and
that continues through following generations to this day.

Charlie Chaplin has been spending a few days at the Plaza, and
we found him in his suite there, handing soiled laundry to a maid.
The first words we heard him speak were *"Here's* a very dirty
shirt." He looked in fine shape—pink-cheeked, with pure white
hair, bristling white eyebrows, and freckled hands. The problem
of the laundry left him slightly distraught, and as soon as the
maid departed, he turned around once or twice, in a sort of dance,
then motioned us to a chair and lighted on the edge of a couch.
Mrs. Chaplin came in from the next room to say that she was
going shopping, and Chaplin asked her to pick up a couple of

hundred dollars for him. "I don't like to cash checks at the desk in the lobby," he told us, after Mrs. Chaplin left. "At the same time, I hate to slash into a place with no money at all. It makes me feel lost." He gazed thoughtfully at a toy on a nearby table. "There's something I got for the kids," he said. "I have three from the age of four down, besides the two grown boys, Charles, Jr., and Sydney. They're both actors. Sydney is a good comedian, whimsical, with an excellent lilt, and he has size and stature. For one thing, he's over six feet. But I'm not sending *him* the toy. You put in a penny . . ." Chaplin searched his pockets. "There's me— haven't a cent," he said. "Anyhow, you put in a penny, and out comes a colored ball of chewing gum. My kids love chewing gum. This toy will be wonderful for them. I found it yesterday, along Forty-second Street. There was this little squashed-in place, with the toy in the window. There was a toy for chocolates, too, but I wasn't sure about giving the kids chocolate."

Chaplin told us he has been walking around town a lot, to take the place of tennis, which is how he gets his exercise at home. "The other day, I walked all up and down Tenth Avenue, and I loved it," he said. "But, oh, the dirt and the ash cans!" He sat silent for a moment, and then suggested that we go downstairs and have lunch. The two of us adjourned to the restaurant, where, walking just like Charlie Chaplin, Chaplin led the way to a table by a window. He sat down and looked out at Central Park. It was snowing. "What beautiful snow!" Chaplin said. "I remember sitting here in this room, just like this, in the winter of 1916, after my first success. I registered as Charles Spencer—Spencer's my middle name—and I stayed here because I didn't know any other place where you could dine. The police had sent me word on the train that I wasn't to go in to Grand Central, because of the crowds waiting to see me there, so I had to get off at 125th Street —and all I was coming here for was to look for a job."

Chaplin said that he hoped in the course of his current visit to find a leading lady for a movie he's planning to make, but that he didn't know how to go about finding her. "I see shows and interview a certain number of people, out of a sense of duty, but all the

people I've found I've always found by luck," he said "This new role is a very difficult one. The girl will have to be able to act *and* dance ballet. I said something about the role a while ago, jokingly, and it came out in one of the gossip columns that I was looking for a person who could act like Duse and dance like Pavlova, and some agent called me up and said, 'I've got her!'—really quite humorlessly. I'm going to see the poor dear after lunch." [A years-later footnote: the "poor dear" he finally chose for the part—for his movie *Limelight*—was Claire Bloom, whose ballet sequences were performed by the dancer Melissa Hayden made up to look like Bloom. Bloom/Hayden became, according to one writer, "a wonderful image of everlasting life spinning forever, while her mentor, Chaplin, as the clown, lay dying backstage."]

Chaplin said, over lunch, that it had taken him over two years to prepare the script of his new movie, that he had composed the music for it, and that he will, as usual, direct it, produce it, and act the leading role. He's anxious to get it under way as quickly as possible. "I can't afford to wait too long on it, because I use my own money," he said. "I don't want to say much about it, but I've poured my guts into the script and I mean it to be the best thing I've ever done." His roles will be different from the roles he played in his early films and from his role in *Monsieur Verdoux*, which he considers his best work. "I lost money on that one," he said. "The people who came to see me came to see the funny man. They were shocked. They couldn't adjust. They wanted to know where the big shoes were." Though *Monsieur Verdoux* was a failure in this country, it won several prizes elsewhere, including the Danish equivalent of an Oscar.

Chaplin recalled that when he entered the movies, in 1913, his contract called for three pictures a week. They used to make a pic-ture in half a day then. Chaplin told us that he acts without any conscious intellectual activity. "All you feel while you're acting is ebullience," he said. "You intellectualize when you go into the projection room and say, 'Now why isn't that funny?' When you get older, you know how to approach humor. The best definition of humor I ever heard is that it's getting people in and out of

trouble. That's what I try to do. I'm emotional about most things but objective about my work. I don't get satisfaction out of it, I get relief." Chaplin said he doesn't have time for much of anything besides his work and his family. "I live in my very secure house of cards," he said. "I'm a self-educated man and don't get everything I'd like to get out of reading. Oh, maybe I browse though my Burton's *Anatomy of Melancholy*, but I leave most of the reading to my wife. Besides, I've got an odd quirk in my sight. I see only the first word and the last in a line on a page. Must be something psychological in that, don't you think?"

A man hurried up, whispered something in Chaplin's ear, and hurried away. "That's the girl's agent," he said, as we got up to go. "This will be very embarrassing. I never know what to say to them. Usually, you know, I just look at them from a distance."

Charlie Chaplin died in 1977, twenty-seven years after I did the story above. I first met him and his wife, Oona, at a party in 1948 in Hollywood, when I was doing the reporting for "Come In, Lassie!" In 1943, at the age of fifty-four, Chaplin had married the eighteen-year-old Oona O'Neill, the daughter of Eugene O'Neill, and with her he settled down into a period of astonishing serenity, which lasted as long as he lived. In 1950, when I came to Hollywood again, working on what became *Picture,* I spent a lot of time, during the ensuing year-and-a-half, every time I wasn't working, socializing with the Chaplins. Among other things, they would have Sunday afternoon tennis parties at their tennis court. Like the Hustons and some others I've written about, they became friends, and it was always fun hanging out with them.

After Chaplin's death, I felt that a memoir was in order, and so I was able to write "Moments from Chaplin" for *The New Yorker* (1978). It was published as a book that year.

William Shawn, who wrote the jacket copy for all my books, wrote about this one:

Long before he made *The Gold Rush, City Lights,* and his other remarkable feature-length movies, Charlie Chaplin, on the strength of his one-reel and two-reel silent comedies, became

the most famous person on earth. No statesman, president, king, general, athlete, or other artist was known to as many of the world's people as Chaplin. Not only his fame, but also his popularity was without precedent and beyond comparison. Yet it was not precisely Chaplin who was known, it was the character he created and played, and into whom he poured everything he was, including his comic genius: the vagabond with the big shoes, the baggy pants, the short, pinched coat, the cane, the derby, the little moustache, the funny, flat-footed walk. This person, in fact, became the most widely-known imaginary character in all history. The Chaplin character had such overwhelming reality for us that it was difficult to think of him as having originated in another man's mind, as having been called forth by a man who, except in his art, was a man like other men: the "real" Charlie Chaplin, who had a wife and children, who was to spend his last twenty-five years living peacefully in an elegant old villa in Corsier-sur-Vevey, Switzerland, who took pleasure in family occasions and in quiet times with friends. The private Chaplin was unfamiliar to the public. In a sense, he wasn't believed to exist. The character he created had no name of his own, but he had an identity so vivid and powerful that he was able to take his creator's name and become, to the world, Charlie Chaplin. The vagabond we saw on the screen, whose poverty and hunger and loneliness had their source in Chaplin's own childhood, also seemed to have yearnings toward the very real pleasures—the ease, the beautiful surroundings, the affectionate companionship—that Chaplin himself finally attained.

It's the real Chaplin whom Lillian Ross knew. She was lucky enough to be a friend of Chaplin and his wife, Oona. It was her privilege to see the non-public Chaplin in moments of reflection, relaxation, domestic happiness, and off-screen clowning. She played tennis with him, watched him lend a directorial hand to his son Sydney in a play rehearsal in Los Angeles, took a long, reminiscent walk with him through the streets of New York, and went to a circus with him in Switzerland, and there, too, joined his family circle and listened to him talk about the inspired "bits

of business" he invented by the thousand for his pictures. Out of these moments, with her uncanny ability to bring people to life on the printed page, Lillian Ross has fashioned a delicate, charming, illuminating, unforgettable portrait of Charlie Chaplin. It is unlike anything else that has been written about this great and beloved man.

Here are a few excerpts from *Moments with Chaplin:*

I found Chaplin and Oona in their [Beverly Hills] kitchen fussing over a leg of lamb that they were roasting, while a couple of small children stood by watching. Food was always important to Chaplin, because, as he used to explain, he had been so often deprived of it when he was a child. On this day, he was in charge of the oven, a chef's big white apron tied around his waist, a big spoon in his left hand, and he was giving the lamb his full concentration, with a Charlie Chaplin pursing of the lips, a Charlie Chaplin frown, a Charlie Chaplin raising of the spoon at his wide-eyed, frozen onlookers, to keep them at their distance.

"It's done now," he reported rather nervously. "It's just right. Tender and succulent."

"Charlie did the basting while I fed the baby," his wife said.

"I baste and baste," Chaplin said to me, with authority. "Baste and baste and baste."

In Hollywood, Chaplin was restless whenever he was not working on a movie, and there were often long stretches between movies. On a chilly, damp evening during one of those periods, I watched Chaplin take a hand in directing the James Barrie play *What Every Woman Knows,* at the Circle, Hollywood's leading non-commercial theatre. The play was starring Ruth Conte and Sydney Chaplin, Charlie Chaplin's second son (by an earlier marriage) who was then twenty-four. . . .

Chaplin arrived at about eight o'clock, dressed for the chilly, damp evening in a salt-and-pepper tweed suit over a sweater.

"Hello, Papa," Sydney said.

"Where's the cast?" Chaplin asked crisply. . . . Chaplin got to work at once. He started talking the moment the rehearsal got

under way, with the actors playing the parts of a Scottish quarry owner and his two sons discussing the problems of the quarryman's spinster daughter, played by Ruth Conte.

"Don't let it get doleful!" Chaplin said. "Make it very warm. It's cold outside, but you get a glow, a warm glow. . . . All right, let's go, let's go," he said impatiently. "Keep it going. Keep it going, keep it going." To one of the two sons, he said, "You bring it down. Keep it up. Keep it *up*."

In September, 1952, the year *Picture* was published, Chaplin and his wife came to New York. They came by train, stopping in Chicago briefly en route. Chaplin's newest finished movie, *Limelight*—the one he'd talked about in my story above and the last movie he made in this country—was scheduled to open shortly, and after that they were planning to sail on the *Queen Elizabeth,* with their children (there were four by then: Geraldine, Michael, Josephine, and Victoria), for Chaplin's first visit to London in twenty years, on what he thought was going to be a vacation. He did not yet know that on the ship, in mid-ocean, he would be informed by the United States government that, as a British subject suspected of "left-wing leanings," he would not be welcome to return to the United States.

When the Chaplins arrived in New York, they checked into the Sherry-Netherland, and Oona called me to ask if I wanted to go walking with Charlie around the city. "I can't go," Oona said. "He walked me for four hours in Chicago. I've got blisters on both heels."

The next morning at eleven, I went to pick Chaplin up at their suite.

"Walking around the city is a ritual with me," Chaplin told me as he ushered me in. "I love to walk all over New York. It's a bloody ritual with me."

Oona smiled and rubbed her feet.

Chaplin looked at her with unabashed affection and admiration. "She's a bloody Victorian," he said. "The only woman I know who carries *smelling* salts!"

Chaplin was dressed for the walk in an oxford-gray, double-breasted suit, a white shirt with a black satin necktie and gray socks and well-shined black shoes. His hair, pure white even then, was long, curling up at the back of his neck. His eyebrows, too, were pure white. His cheeks were pink. He was smiling, and eager to get going. "This isn't too bad now, is it?" he asked, waving a hand around the living room of the suite. "At least it's light. At first, they took us to a dark green room with red drapes. The gloomiest bloody place, with holes in the drapes. Can you imagine that? Holes in the drapes! We had to move. I like brightness. My brother and I were brought up in a dark hovel, and I'm not having any more of that, am I?" He smiled at his wife, and she smiled back.

Out on the sidewalk, Chaplin took a deep breath. "I like this kind of day for walking in the city," he said. "A sultry, Indian-summer September day. But do you know the best time for walking in the city? Two A.M. It's the best time. The city is chaste. Virginal. Two A.M. in the winter is the best, with everything looking frosty. The tops of the automobiles. Shiny. All those colors." He took another deep breath. "It's really hot today," he said. "Thank God I left my vest off."

We started out, walking south on Fifth Avenue. "There used to be a florist right here," Chaplin said at Fifty-eighth, looking puzzled. "His name was Schling. He was a philosopher. I could never pass by without his saying 'Come in here,' and he would stick a flower in my lapel. He was full of emotion. Very talkative. He always gave you a reason he loved to sell flowers." Chaplin laughed, and then arranged his face in that inimitable eager-to-please, self-abnegating, teeth-baring, lingering smile.

Not many people among the passers-by seemed to recognize Chaplin as we walked. He was smiling a bit to himself, as though he noticed that he wasn't being recognized, and got a kick out of it.

"The first time I came to New York from Hollywood, I stopped traffic on Broadway," he told me when I remarked on his near-anonymity. "One of the newspapers had a big headline—'HE'S

HERE!' That's all. The police chief, I remember, made me get
off the train at a Hundred and Twenty-fifth Street to avoid the
mobs. That was in 1916.

". . . Sometimes when I have a whole day here I walk a whole
day. I just go along, and I discover places. I discovered Sweet's, the
famous fish place, all by myself. Down near the Battery. To me,
that's the romantic part of New York, especially on Sunday. It's so
quiet down there. So chaste. So clean. Nobody's around. You take
any business center, there's something very romantic about it
when it's inactive. So I went walking down there to the Battery
by myself and saw this place with all the limousines parked out-
side. Dowagers stepping out of the limousines. Very respectable
gentlemen. So I said to myself, 'This must be very good.' And I
went in there and had myself a load of clams. I love clams. I used
to go to Grand Central—to the Oyster Bar. I'd get a dozen clams,
and all you'd want besides is lemon. You'd get a dozen clams for
eighty cents."

We walked along in silence for a few moments. Chaplin
looked with interest at the other pedestrians.

"Every time I walk, I get a terrific exhilaration," he said. "each
new day is a day of promise. There are always parts of the city
to explore. Always parts you haven't seen. The first time I saw
Fifth Avenue was in 1910, when I first arrived in New York,
from England, with Fred Karno's vaudeville troupe. I was very
poor. I was the leading comedian in a sketch called 'The Wow
Wows.' I wasn't getting much money, even though I was getting
twenty-five dollars more than the others in the troupe. In those
days, all the actors in the summertime used to go to Coney
Island to work as waiters. I never did it, because I was getting
more than the rest."

Forty-second Street:

An old woman in a torn dress was standing in front of the New
Amsterdam Theatre selling pretzels from a battered baby stroller.
"I don't think the old girl would know whether this is where
Ziegfeld had his *Follies,* or whether it had a roof garden," Chaplin

said. He stopped walking. He looked puzzled, a bit hurt.

An elderly man with a pale, freckled face, who was bald except for reddish hair at the base of his skull, came along and stopped beside us. He wore a dirty white shirt open at the collar, and he had a bundle of old newspapers under one arm. "Visiting your old haunts, Charlie?" he said to Chaplin.

"Why, yes," Chaplin said. "Yes. Yes, I am."

"I used to come in as a kid, fifteen years old," the man said. "I used to see you. They were good old days."

"Wasn't this where Ziegfeld had his *Follies?*" Chaplin asked. "And didn't it have a roof garden upstairs?"

"You're right," the man said. "And it still does have a roof garden."

"You see, I was right, wasn't I?" Chaplin said to me.

"What are you doing now, Charlie?" the man asked.

"I'm still in the movies," Chaplin said. "At least, I think I am." He gave his laugh.

There's a special kind of satisfaction in waiting months or years to write about someone you admire and love, and the memoir is a straightforward form to accommodate this kind of piece. Writing about Chaplin gave me additional pleasure as a way of bringing him to life again. I also discovered, about myself, that the details and the quotes I selected for him fifty years ago and then twenty-eight years later, are exactly what I would choose today.

I told a bit about Chaplin's life in Switzerland after having been, to all intents and purposes, thrown out of the United States:

He lived, with his family, in a beautiful old manor house—Le Manoir de Ban—on thirty-seven acres of vast lawns, ancient pine trees, and orchards, where he had a swimming pool and a tennis court and also a view of Lake Geneva and the Alps. There he and Oona had four more children—Eugene, Jane, Annette, and Christopher. They made their home an open one to their friends. The Chaplins relished hearing about life back in the United States, but they evidently had no longing for it. . . . "We couldn't have found a more nearly perfect place to live," Chaplin told

me. "The kids can go to the best schools in the world right here. They've already learned to speak French. And if Oona and I get bored, we can pop over to London or to Paris in an hour or two."

They ate outdoors as often as possible, on a large terrace overlooking a long expanse of lawn, and the mountains in the distance.... "Every once in a while," he said, "the old lady and I get out the caviar and champagne. And we don't invite anybody else. We sit here gorging ourselves, just the two of us."

They loved their children; they loved their friends; they loved their work; but more than anything else, they loved each other. There have been two or three times in my experience, including in my own life, when I have known that kind of couple so completely at one with each other, they had absolutely no real need, ever, for the presence of a third person.

My last paragraph:

The Christmas card for 1977 arrived just before Christmas Day, which was the day Charlie Chaplin died. The photograph is of Charlie Chaplin alone, and was taken on April 16, 1977, his last birthday, his eighty-eighth. He is sitting in a chair and is wearing a dark suit over a baby-blue cashmere sweater. The white collar of his shirt comes down over the sweater, and there is a white handkerchief in the breast pocket of his jacket. His white hair is sparser but still full and is combed neatly from a side part. His right hand is holding a walking stick. His left hand is raised—a bit of the blue sweater showing at the wrist—and is held in midair to a position over his heart, in the classic gesture of the actor.

LORRAINE HANSBERRY
AND SIDNEY POITIER

▬ ▬ ▬ ▬ ▬ ▬ ▬ ▬ ▬ ▬ ▬ ▬ ▬ ▬ ▬

E VERY NOW AND THEN, people I wanted to write about had
so much to say that a story about them required nothing
more than their own talk. The drama and the action were
embedded in the talk. Lorraine Hansberry, the twenty-eight-year-
old author of the 1959 hit play *A Raisin in the Sun,* was that kind
of rare subject. She was a *very* rare person—"a relaxed, soft-voiced
young lady with an intelligent and pretty face, a particularly verti-
cal hairdo, and large brown eyes, so dark and so deep that you get
lost in them." My Talk story appeared shortly after the opening of
the play, the first on Broadway by a black person, and in this
instance, a young black woman. (The actor Sidney Poitier was in
the play, coming back to Broadway from having made movies like
The Blackboard Jungle and *Porgy and Bess.*) We met, at Miss
Hansberry's request, in a midtown restaurant, so that, she said, she
could get away from her telephone. There was considerable back
and forth between us, and I asked questions, but I felt that the flow
of her talk, in the writing, should be uninterrupted, a monologue.

"The telephone has become a little strange thing with a life of
its own," she said, calmly enough. "It's just incredible. I had the
number changed, and gave it to, roughly, twelve people. Then
I get a call from a stranger saying 'This is So-and-So, of the
B.B.C.'! It's the flush of success. Thomas Wolfe wrote a detailed
description of it in *You Can't Go Home Again*. I must say he told
the truth. I enjoy it, actually, so much. I'm thrilled, and all of us
associated with the play are thrilled. Meanwhile, it does keep
you awfully busy. What sort of happens is you just hear from
everybody!"

Miss Hansberry gave a soft, pleased laugh.

"I'm going to have some scrambled eggs, medium, because, as
far as I know, I haven't had my breakfast yet," she went on.

"I live in the Village, and the way it's been, people sort of drop
in on me and my husband. My husband is Bob Nemiroff, and he,
too, is a writer. Yesterday, I got back to writing, and I wrote all
day long. For the first time in weeks. It was wonderful. We have
a ramshackle Village walkup apartment, quite ramshackle, with
living room, bedroom, kitchen, bath, and a little back workroom,
and I just stayed in that little old room all day and wrote. I may
even get time now to do some of my housework. I don't want to
have anyone else to do my housework. I've always done it myself.
I believe you *should* do it yourself. I feel very strongly about that."

The medium scrambled eggs arrived, and Miss Hansberry
sampled them vaguely and went on to talk about what life has
been like since her play opened, a few weeks ago. "I now get
twenty to thirty pieces of mail a day," she said. "Invitations to
teas, invitations to lunches, invitations to dinners, invitations to
write books, to adapt mystery stories for the movies, to adapt nov-
els for Broadway musicals. I feel I have to answer them, because
I owe the people who wrote them the courtesy of explaining that
this is not my type of thing. Then, there are so many oranizations
that want you to come to their meetings. You don't feel silly or
bothered, because, my God, they're all doing such important
work, and you're just delighted to go, but you're awfully busy,
because there are an awful lot of organizations. The other morn-

ing, I came downstairs to walk my dog—he's sort of a collie, and he'll be six in September—and there, downstairs, were the two most charming people, a middle-aged couple who wanted me to have dinner with the New Rochelle Urban League before it went to see the play. I just couldn't say no. . . . I sometimes find myself doing things for three or four organizations in one day. The other morning, I started the day by taping a television program. Then I went to the National Association of Negro Business and Professional Women's Clubs Founders' Day Tea, at the Waldorf, where they were giving out Sojourner Truth Awards—awards named for Sojourner Truth, who was a very colorful orator who went up and down New England and the South speaking against slavery. Then I went home and went to the Square with my dog. When I got back home, I fed the dog and put on a cocktail dress, and my husband and I had dinner in a new Village steak house. Then we went to a reception for a young Negro actor named Harold Scott, who had just made a record album of readings from the works of James Weldon Johnson. A very beautiful album. Then we went home and had banana cream pie and milk and watched television—a program with me on it, as a matter of fact. It was terrifying to see. I had no idea I used my face so much when I talked, and I decided that that was the end of my going on television. . . ."

The trick in a story like this is to make the talk flow as though it is nonstop. If the writer's senses, especially the hearing, are completely attuned to the person who is talking, then the writer gets it right—the choice of words, the rhythm, and the exact meaning of what is being said. Whatever alteration the writer makes should sound right to the talker; it should be his and only his own voice. It's the writer's responsibility to make it so. If a writer is tempted to inject his own voice into the talk and does it, as often happens, it will disturb everything, especially the rhythm, and make it false.

Miss Hansberry said she was born May 19, 1930, in Chicago.

"I have two brothers and one sister. I'm the baby of the family . . . my father, who is dead now, was born in Gloster, Mississippi,

which you can't find on the map, it's so small. My mother comes
from Columbia, Tennessee, which *is* on the map, but just about.
My father left the South as a young man, and then he went back
there and got himself an education. He was a wonderful and very
special kind of man. He died in 1945, at the age of fifty-one—of a
cerebral hemorrhage, supposedly, but American racism helped kill
him. He died in Mexico, where he was making preparations to
move all of us out of the United States. My brother Carl had just
come back from Europe, where he fought with Patton's army. My
father wanted to leave this country because, although he tried
to do everything in his power to make it otherwise, he felt he
still didn't have his freedom. He was a very successful and very
wealthy businessman. He had been a U.S. Marshal. He had
founded one of the first Negro banks in Chicago. He had fought
a very famous civil-rights case on restrictive covenants, which he
fought all the way up to the Supreme Court, and which he won
after the expenditure of a great deal of money and emotional
strength. The case is studied today in the law schools. Anyway,
Daddy felt that this country was hopeless in its treatment of
Negroes. So he became a refugee from America. He bought a
house in Polanco, Mexico, a suburb of Mexico City, and we were
planning to move there when he died. I was fourteen at the time.
I'm afraid I have to agree with Daddy's assessment of this coun-
try. But I don't agree with the leaving part. I don't feel defensive.
Daddy really belonged to a different age, a different period. He
didn't feel free. One of the reasons I feel so free is that I feel I
belong to a world majority, and a very assertive one. . . .

 "I mostly went to Jim Crow schools, on the South Side of
Chicago, which meant half-day schools, and to this day, I can't
count. My parents were some peculiar kind of democrats. They
could afford to send us to private schools, but they didn't believe
in it. I went to three grade schools—Felsenthal, Betsy Ross, and
A. O. Sexton—the last of them in a white neighborhood, where
Daddy bought a house when I was eight. My mother is a remark-
able woman, with great courage. She sat in that house for eight
months with us—while Daddy spent most of his time in Wash-

ington fighting his case—in what was, to put it mildly, a very hostile neighborhood. I was on the porch one day with my sister, swinging my legs, when a mob gathered. We went inside, and while we were in our living room, a brick came crashing through the window with such force it embedded itself in the opposite wall. I was the one the brick almost hit. I went to Englewood High School and then to the University of Wisconsin for two years. Then I just got tired of going to school and quit and came to New York, in the summer of 1950. The theatre came into my life like k-pow!" Miss Hansberry knocked a fist into the palm of her other hand. . . . "Mine was the same old story—sort of hanging around little acting groups, and developing the feeling that the theatre embraces everything I like at one time. I've always assumed I had something to tell people. Now I think of myself as a playwright."

By permitting Lorraine Hansberry to give us, in her own words, the salient facts in her background, the story builds to the point where she says she now thinks of herself as a playwright. Journalistically, the story about Lorraine Hansberry has a connection with the following one, about Sidney Poitier. It, too, didn't need interaction with anyone else. What he had to say gave me all the action I needed. I saw him a couple of years after he was in *A Raisin in the Sun*. His piece appeared in my 1962 book, *The Player*, and started off with his statement:

"When I experience a moment of total communication between me and the audience, I feel, Well, maybe they do accept me as an actor."

Both Poitier and Hansberry were young and in love with the theater. Both had something interesting to say, in their work and for a story. Both were black, and their talk, it turned out, played contrapuntally. Listening to both of them was sheer pleasure for me.

Poitier, who was born in Miami, Florida, on February 20, 1924, was the youngest of eight children.

"To my parents, what started happening to me after I left home was all very strange. I was still their baby—so much so, I'm afraid,

that it was sickening. They'd see me in movies, and they'd wonder
what on earth I was doing there. Most of the time, I've felt exactly
the way they did. My eldest brother, Cyril, is forty-six and does
odd jobs in Miami. He has twelve children. The other children
are Ruby, a housewife in Miami; Redis, a waiter in Nassau;
Reginald, a maître d' at the British Colonial Hotel, in Nassau;
and Carl, a waiter in Nassau. When I was three months old, my
family moved to Cat Island, in the Bahamas, where my father
worked as a tomato farmer. We stayed on Cat Island until I was
eleven, and then we moved to Nassau. I could swim when I was
three. I could climb trees as well as Tarzan himself. There were
no automobiles on Cat Island, which is about fifty miles long and
averages ten miles wide, and there was nothing to get in my way.
I had freedom. I was never watched. From the time I could walk,
I had complete freedom to learn by trial and error. When I was
three, I would go out and be alone on the island all day. I had my
own imagination as a companion. I'd imagine I was a big fisher-
man going after big fish, or I was a farmer working in the fields.
When I was five, I once walked across the island, all by myself,
which would be like walking from Brooklyn to the Bronx. I got to
the middle of the island, and there wasn't a human sound—only
birds and little insects. Finally, I came to the other side of the
island, and I played out there for half a day, all alone, hunting
turtle eggs. My mother used to cook the turtle eggs I brought her.
Our kitchen was outside, with an open grill. Our house was stone
and had a thatched palm-leaf roof—very primitive. When I got
home after being out on the island all day, nobody ever noticed.
My mother just said, 'Sit down and eat your dinner.'

"In Nassau, I went to school for a year and a half, then quit
to work at odd jobs, to help support the family. My father was
unable to work, because of arthritis and rheumatism. I was always
hungry as a kid. To this day, between huge meals, I'm hungry, and
I fill in with Mars bars, Snickers, Oh Henrys, and Life Savers. So
far, I've never been to a dentist. When I was fifteen, I was sent to
Miami to live with my brother Cyril. I felt I wasn't wanted there,
so before very long I set off for New York City. It took me three

and a half months to get here. I rode a freight train, then walked, and then worked in the kitchen of a summer-resort hotel in the mountains in Georgia, where I saved up thirty-nine dollars— enough to take a bus the rest of the way. I arrived early one morning, with a dollar and a half and no clothes except what I had on—a shirt and blue jeans—and one extra shirt. I took the subway to Harlem, and then came downtown that same afternoon, walked down Broadway from Fiftieth to Forty-second Street, and spent all the rest of my money on hot dogs and malted milks. That night, I got a job at the Turf restaurant, as a dishwasher, for four dollars and eleven cents a night. For the next few months, until I had saved enough money to buy myself a coat and a suit, I slept either in Penn Station or in the Greyhound Bus Terminal that opens off it or on the roof of a building on Fifty-first Street, across from the Capitol Theatre.

"Soon after Pearl Harbor, I enlisted in the Army. I was trained to be a physio-therapist, and I served with the 1267th Medical Detachment, stationed at the Northport, Long Island, Veterans Hospital, which was a mental institution. I was discharged in December of 1944. In the Army, I was very rebellious. I was always restless, and the restlessness manifested itself in a violent thrashing about—something I still have as a carryover today. . . . It was a strange period for me. I couldn't read as well as I wanted to. . . .

"After getting out of the Army, I continued to read the newspapers, not only to help myself learn words but to follow the want ads. . . . One day I read in the *Amsterdam News* that the American Negro Theatre was looking for actors. . . . the ad said that they were holding auditions. A giant of a man—Frederick O'Neal, co-manager of the A.N.T., who is now a good friend of mine—was in charge. . . . He told me they were looking for actors for a play called *Walk Hard* adapted by Abram Hill from Lew Zinberg's novel *Walk Hard—Talk Low*. He handed me a script, pointed to a place somewhere in the middle, and said 'Read.' So I started to read. I read it terribly I was a lean, lanky kid. I had just about my full growth then—six feet two and a half—but I had a baby

face, and my voice was sort of high; it has deepened considerably
over the years. And in reading I sounded like a West Indian.
O'Neal was bugged with me. He said 'Forget it.' If he had said
'Thank you very much. Sorry, but not right now,' or something
like that, I would have walked out of there and never come back
or tried to do anything like that again. But the way he said 'Forget
it' made me feel as if I had been attacked. I felt chopped down a
peg. Don't chop me down a peg, or, if you do, do it for good rea-
sons that you tell me about. I was extremely sensitive then about
not being able to rise above working with my hands, so I walked
out of there determined to go back and show that man I was not
destined to be a laborer all my life. I had to vindicate myself. . . ."

Poitier went on to tell how he persuaded the A.N.T. and O'Neal
to take him as a student, his early acting, his going to Hollywood to
make movies, and his return to Broadway in *A Raisin in the Sun*.
Later on, he said:

"When I act on the stage, it's a total experience. With me—as
with other actors, I believe—it's quite a job to prevent the work
from becoming mechanical. You have to find ways to keep refuel-
ling the impulse. . . . But it has to be manufactured synthetically
when things aren't going right—when your energy is low, when
you've eaten too much, when you haven't cleansed your mind of
your own thoughts and worries so you can flood it with the part
you're playing. You cannot will a response. When I feel good and
right, I experience complete communication with the audience.
But each performance is different, and if I expected to feel that
good every night, I'd be disappointed. There's no one way of act-
ing, but my way is to try to feel the experience of the moment and
to have each moment flow out of the last and into the next.

". . . For me, acting is a refuge and a respite from the battle of
the opposites: to be successful or not to be successful, to go home
or not to go home, to smoke or not to smoke, to eat lobster or not
to eat lobster—to be or not to be. The only way I can transcend
the battle is to act. When I play someone else, I am no longer
caught in the battle; the person I'm playing is caught. I accept

someone else's circumstances and I cease to function as Sidney
Poitier. I feel peace. I feel it. It's now. It's great. It's encompassing.
It's got you. You're secure. Everything you do is absolutely meant
to be done. It leads you, every now and then, to transcend the
battle so completely that you give a performance that is absolutely
shattering, even to yourself. . . ."

Poitier and Hansberry had in common a kind of overwhelming
heroism that went far beyond the fact that both were black. Both
profiles are self-contained and needed no revealing action or
exchange involving another person. Different as they are, Poitier
and Hansberry both had a similar quality of character and elo-
quence. I admired them, and I was drawn to what they represent.
So I linked them together here. Their stories belong together the-
matically, whatever their color. Or, perhaps, their color in itself
was deeply appealing to me, or, perhaps, their color had something
to do with the exhilarating feeling that both of them communicat-
ed to me: their unusual appreciation of life itself.

THE REDGRAVES
AND HAROLD PINTER

I N 1962, WITH MY SISTER, Helen Ross, as co-author, we pub-
lished *The Player: A Profile of an Art,* a book that contained
pieces about fifty-five actors. They included, among others,
Warren Beatty, Katharine Cornell, Joan Crawford, Henry Fonda,
Jane Fonda, John Gielgud, Angela Lansbury, Walter Matthau,
Zero Mostel, Sidney Poitier, Michael Redgrave, Paul Scofield,
Simone Signoret, Kim Stanley, and Eli Wallach. The pieces were
based on interviews, not tape-recorded, and they were presented as
autobiographical monologues. Taken together, these pieces about
individual actors have the cumulative effect of creating a profile of
the art of acting. *Picture* told the story of various relationships
among the participants in making a film. *The Player* gives us the
story of the actor in relation to his art. Each piece started off with a
quote from the actor that expressed his spirit.

Michael Redgrave, in *The Player,* was the first of three genera-
tions of Redgraves I wrote about. His piece, like the others in the
book, started off with a characterizing quote:

"I prefer the fiction and fantasy of acting to the truth, but I hope I use truth in experiencing fiction and fantasy on the stage."

The pieces about Tony Richardson, married to Vanessa Redgrave, and about Vanessa, Rachel Kempson, and Natasha Richardson together, to follow here, pick up threads that all five of these theatre figures have in common. They fit neatly to give the reader a strong sense of their emotional connections with each other and with the stage—their literally undying love and passion for their work, their understanding of and devotion to each other, their professionalism, their disciplined standards, their habitual ways of harboring their energy, and their attraction to and romanticism about New York. To me, they are admirable and endearing, and I wanted to show them as such to the reader.

When I wrote the piece about Michael Redgrave, I didn't know I'd eventually be writing about his wife, his daughter, his son-in-law, and his granddaughter. I had already written about Edith Evans, the actress who taught him so much as a novice. In his piece, he tells about his profound stage involvement with her, and it helps make a strong and clear picture of the disciplined, classic, British actor. The reader will notice that he said initially in his piece that he tired easily and believed that every actor should lie down for a little while every afternoon, even if it's on the floor. Led by Rachel Kempson many years later, the "lie-down" comes up in the trio's talk (she calls it a "feet-up"). I deliberately use these echoes of each other to build the connections of these stories.

Michael Redgrave tells how he joined the Liverpool Repertory Company, one of the best companies of its kind in the country. After three months, he was playing leading parts.

> "At the end of my first season, I met Rachel Kempson, who came to us from Stratford as our new leading lady. Ten days later, we became engaged. Her father was headmaster of the Royal Naval College, Dartmouth, and we were married in the chapel there.
> . . . I was an ambitious, arrogant, conceited young man. I wanted to play everything. . . . While I was playing in Liverpool, Tyrone Guthrie offered me a contract for the 1936–37 season with the Old Vic, where I played Mr. Horner in *The Country Wife*. I found

myself playing with Edith Evans. . . . There was not a moment's
doubt in my mind that I wanted to play Orlando to Edith Evans'
Rosalind. She had only to look at me. Odd that my eldest daugh-
ter, Vanessa, is at present performing in London as Rosalind. . . .
I was more influenced by Edith Evans than by any other per-
former. I was very much in awe of her. . . . For me Edith Evans
has the authentic magic. Claptrap word though 'magic' may be,
it's the only word for the stage. When she comes onstage, the
stage lights up. She's a very strict person about her profession,
and is without any of the nonsense. She's a real and dedicated
artist. Her art is her life. Everything she does on stage is inter-
preted through her own morality. . . . It's the thing the great
artist has that makes him different from other people. I don't
mean morality in a pettifogging way. I mean moral values, with-
out which nothing is achieved and nothing is created. Part of it
is caring enough about what you do to achieve something beyond
the mundane. One reason for the great influence Edith Evans has
had on me is that she accepted me in the early phase of my career.
Until you act the great parts in theatre literature, you really don't
know what acting is. Orlando for me was a great part.

"I was twenty-eight. Edith Evans was forty-eight. I had been
married about a year, and Rachel and I had just had our first child
[Vanessa]. But none of that seemed to have anything to do with
my special life on the stage as Orlando. We played for something
like five weeks in repertory, and then we took the play to the West
End and played it for three months, which was pretty good for a
Shakespeare run. Acting with Edith Evans was heaven. It was
like being in your mother's arms, like knowing how to swim, like
riding a bicycle. You're safe. The late Michael Chekhov said once
that there are three ways to act: for yourself, for the audience, and
to your partner. . . . I believe that the only way to act is to your
partner. As a partner, Edith Evans was like a great conductor who
allows a soloist as much latitude as is needed but always keeps
everything strict. Strict but free. . . . For the first time in my life,
acting in *As You Like It*, I felt completely free. For the first time,
I felt completely unselfconscious. Acting with her made me feel,

Oh, it's so easy! You don't start acting, she told me, until you stop *trying* to act. It doesn't leave the ground until you don't have to think about it. . . . In the forest scenes between Orlando and Rosalind, she would encourage me to do almost anything that came into my head. Yet if I had done anything excessive, she would have stopped it by the simplest means. Somehow it didn't occur to me to do anything excessive. For the first time anywhere, onstage or off, I felt completely free."

In the 1960's, Vanessa Redgrave's husband, Tony Richardson, was here, directing the New York production of *Luther*, by John Osborne, whose *Look Back in* Anger he had directed in the late 1950's. For The Talk of the Town, I found Richardson in his suite at the Algonquin "wandering around in white socks, All-American chino pants, a black wool pullover on top of a white shirt open at the collar," and wrote that "he looked like a combination of all those gaunt, underfed, student-poet characters in Chekhov plays, though not tortured." He was also here to work on the opening of his film *Tom Jones* (which went on to win Oscars for best picture and best director), and he was planning to go to Hollywood to direct *The Loved One*, the movie based on Evelyn Waugh's novel. He was also preparing to direct *The Sea Gull* in London later in the year. At the moment, he was awaiting the arrival of his wife, Vanessa Redgrave, and their six-month-old daughter, Natasha Jane. It was Natasha Jane's first visit to this country, he said.

"I like being in the States," he said.

"I like New York. I feel at home in New York. From the minute I first saw New York, in the summer of 1953, I knew it was the place I liked best in the world. I was just a kid, down from Oxford. I came over on one of those student trips, travelling on a hundred dollars, and lived in some crummy little hotel in the Village. There was a heat wave, and I couldn't afford air conditioning. I just wandered around the city, walking and looking and loving New York. . . . One's personal responses are always inexplicable. It's like that marvellous thing that Henry James felt about London from the moment he went there. He left after a few days

and lived in Paris and Geneva, but all the time he knew in his heart that the place where he felt at home was London. That's the way I feel about New York. I love the excitement and fun of Broadway, the unexpectedness of the whole city, the feeling that something can happen at any moment. And the sheer physical beauty of it. The way all those buildings look all lit up when you're driving down through Central Park. However much I'd like to be an American, I'm not. Everything about me is English. Mainly, I'm stuck."

Thirty-five years later, I wrote, in The Talk of the Town:

Lady Rachel Kempson Redgrave (widow of Michael Redgrave), her daughter Vanessa, and her granddaughter Natasha Richardson—three generations of theatrical Redgraves—were in town at the same fleeting moment last matinée Wednesday, so they met over coffee at the Mayflower Hotel's Conservatory Café and had a quick "catch-up," as they called it. Natasha, beautiful, cheerful, all-together wife of Liam Neeson, the mother of their two small boys, and a Tony nominee for her knock-out performance as Sally Bowles in *Cabaret*, was in gray sweats and sneakers, Vanessa, her white hair tousled, and Rachel, *her* white hair elegantly coiffed, had just returned from Springfield, Massachusetts, where they had performed *Sarah Bernhardt Comes to Town*, a Vanessa Redgrave—created show compiled from the stories and plays of Anton Chekhov. They were planning to take the show up to Bard College later that day, and to put it on this week, back in New York, at Symphony Space, at Broadway and Ninety-fifth Street.

 "It's so special, when we come together like this," Natasha said. "How was it in Massachusetts, Mum? Granny?"

 "Standing ovations," Lady Redgrave said.

 "The entire audience, standing."

 "Everyone up and shouting, 'Woo, woo! Whee, whee!'" Vanessa said. . . .

 Outside, on Central Park West, a festooned horse and carriage came clomping along. The heads of all three Redgraves turned as one to the café window and longingly watched it pass by.

"Wish we could go," Vanessa said.

"We always go, every visit," Lady Redgrave said.

"Granny, perhaps next week," Natasha said. "I have two shows today. No time even for a feet-up."

"I say first things first," Lady Redgrave remarked. "We should all have a feet-up. At least, that's my view. . . ."

"We'll have the weekend together, at the farm in the country," Natasha said. "We worry about you, Mum. You don't eat. You don't sleep. You drink coffee, coffee, coffee."

"You won't have a million guests at the farm this time?" Vanessa asked.

"Just Ron Rifkin and his wife," Natasha said.

"Good, I can cook," Vanessa said. "You always make something right for everybody, Tash," she added, holding her daughter's head between her hands and kissing the top of it.

"Got to go. Two performances today," Natasha announced.

"Hope it goes brilliantly," Lady Redgrave said.

"Have two wonderful ones," Vanessa said.

Somehow or other, these stories morph into a single entity. All three Redgrave pieces contain elements that echo each other— Michael Redgrave's feelings about Edith Evans and art and the sense of his acting to her being outside of his marriage and new baby (Vanessa); Tony Richardson's devotion to work and his longings to be part of life in New York and his reference to Central Park; then the three generations and feelings for their work and for each other. Natasha Richardson, now an American citizen living on Central Park West, echoes her father's longings. Members of theatrical families—Redgraves, Fondas, Hustons, Chaplins, etc.,— have a special appeal to me. They seem to have such strong, real and impressive connections to each other.

Here is the missing piece to fill out the story: a Talk story, called "Dame Edith," about Edith Evans, that was written a good year or so before I wrote about Michael Redgrave. She, like the Redgraves, revelled in her little American experiences, her charming discovery of the "blintz" and the "bagel." She expressed her admiration for

and appreciation of the classic, disciplined "good actors" from
whom she learned to "speak" and to be "heard"—From Ellen
Terry, for one, who "was a lovely person and a great professional."
 She had come to New York—for the first time in over a decade
—to be in her first American television play, Jean Anouilh's *Time
Remembered,* an N.B.C. *Hallmark Hall of Fame* production
scheduled for broadcast the day before her seventy-third birthday.
I noted that, in the opinion of many actors, she was considered the
greatest of all. I described her as "looking at least twenty years
younger than her age, with her gray hair bobbed short and her
shoes low-heeled and Britishly sensible, and wearing a gray tweed
skirt, a dark-gray sweater with a gold pin at the neckline, heavy
Indian silver bracelets on her wrists, rings on her fingers and bells,
I'd swear, on her toes." I took her to lunch at Ratner's, the cele-
brated Jewish restaurant, which was just downstairs from her
rehearsal hall. She asked our waiter for pancakes.

 "Blintzes," the waiter said. "What kind?"
 "What kind do you have?" Dame Edith asked.
 "If I told you, would you remember?" the waiter asked.
 "Yes," Dame Edith said.
 "All right," the waiter said, and recited, "Potato blintzes, kashe
blintzes, cheese blintzes, lekward or jelly blintzes, and huckle-
berry, pineapple, cherry, and strawberry blintzes. All right?"
 "Sounds wonderful," Dame Edith said. "I shall be very pleased
to try cherry blintzes."
 "In the meantime, eat a pumpernickel bagel," the waiter said,
indicating a basket of rolls on the table.
 Dame Edith peered longingly at the basket. "It would be too
much," she said.
 Between bites, she said that she had made several television
appearances in England, and that she liked acting in any medium.
 "Good acting is good acting all over the world," she said. "And
bad acting is bad acting anywhere. I'm satisfied as long as I have a
sensitive director, and not someone who wants to be tricky. Tricky
is always bad. In rehearsing for television, you have two or three

weeks to make up your mind about how you're going to play a
part, and you don't have much more than that for a play. I like
to find a way to do things that gets the biggest result with the
least amount of effort—that is, effort that can be seen. I'm a great
believer in the process of deletion. I don't do more as I go along
in rehearsal. I do less."

She also said: "In the old days, you made your way up by steps.
It was lovely, because you learned to speak, to be heard. Nowadays,
a good many actors are too busy talking with microphones. I
learned with good people—all good actors. The older actors
would teach me how to make the best of myself. You were told
the way you moved, the way you looked, the way you spoke. The
older ones were professional. On the dot. The word amateur may
come from the word love, but the professional makes the final
sacrifices. Ellen Terry was a lovely person and a great professional,
too. In 1918—a few years before I was married—my husband died
twenty-six years ago; he was an oil mining engineer—I toured
with her, when she was a very old lady, in variety theatres. She
was gracious, kind, charming, thoughtful. She was someone you
loved. And you could hear what she said. There was no television
then and no cinema—just theatre and concerts. She'd say to me,
'Smile, child. *Smile,* child. You have a lovely smile.' I was shy and
nervous and young and just beginning and gauche, and the older
ones knew how to say things to make you feel good and to make
you happy. All the older ones were like that."

Our waiter returned and said to Dame Edith, "You left one
blintz. You should eat it."

"I can't," Dame Edith said.

"You should have ordered one for two," the waiter said.

"I didn't know any better," Dame Edith said. "Would it be
awful if I broke off this—just a piece?" She pointed a finger at a
pumpernickel bagel.

"You should eat the whole thing," the waiter said.

"Just a little piece," Dame Edith said firmly, and broke it off.
"And I'll have a little bit of butter." She put the bit of butter on
the bit of bagel and sighed. "I've been very fortunate," she said.

"I've had the most wonderful opportunities, and they're still coming."

In the 1960's, when I wrote about Michael Redgrave reminiscing about how he worshipped Edith Evans and how much he had learned from her, I did not know that I was going to write about Tony Richardson, who married Vanessa Redgrave, and who was in New York, directing the John Osborne play *Luther,* awaiting the arrival of Vanessa with their new baby Natasha Richardson. Tony Richardson said how much he liked New York and felt at home in New York. I did not know then that thirty-five years later, I would be writing about Rachel Kempson, Vanessa Redgrave, and Natasha Richardson having lunch together on Central Park West and talking about how they loved New York and Central Park West. I remembered my story about Edith Evans coming to New York to be in her first American television play and how she had told me she'd been so fortunate and had had so many wonderful opportunities. Edith Evans, Michael Redgrave, and Tony Richardson—those remarkable people—are dead now, but all are quite alive in the stories. Journalism can do that for a reader.

In February, 1967, I wrote a Talk of the Town story, "Two People in a Room," about Harold Pinter, the spirited English playwright, who was then living in New York, with his wife, an actress, and his nine-year-old son, during the Broadway run of his twelfth play, The Homecoming. Thirty-two years later—almost to the day—I wrote another Talk story about Pinter, who by then had written twenty-eight plays and had flown in to New York to look in on two of them in rehearsal—Ashes to Ashes and The Hothouse.

In my first story, I described him as "a handsome and amiable-looking man of thirty-six with black hair, black sideburns, and eyeglasses that are rimmed with horn on top and colorless plastic on bottom." He talked about growing up in a working-class area in London's East End:

"My mother was a wonderful cook, which she still is. My father worked terribly hard. He worked a twelve-hour day, making

clothes in his shop, but eventually he lost the business and went
to work for someone else. In the war, he was an air-raid warden.
When I was nine, I was evacuated to the country. . . . I was quite
a morose little boy. My parents came down occasionally from
London. It was over four hundred miles there and back, and I
don't know how they made it. It was terribly expensive, and they
had no money. . . . On the day I got back to London, in 1944,
I saw the first flying bomb. . . . There were times when I would
open our back door and find our garden in flames. . . . At the age
of eighteen, you were supposed to join the Army for two years
under conscription. I decided not to join. I was a conscientious
objector. . . . For me, well, you know the idea of rearming was pre-
posterous. I was aware of the suffering and of the horror of war,
and by no means was I going to subscribe to keep it going. I said
no. And I will still say no. . . . I'm not interested in the general
context of the theatre. . . . I can't regard what I've done as singu-
lar. I'm continually surprised at the response of a number of peo-
ple to my plays. . . . Each play is quite a different world. The
problem is to create a unique world in each case, with a totally
different set of characters. With a totally different environment.
It's a great joy to do that."

Thirty-two years later, in The Talk of the Town, I reported that
Pinter "looked very much the same . . . still handsome, still ami-
able-looking, but a bit heavier now, and his black hair and side-
burns are tinged with gray. . . . His voice sounds deeper now,
almost Churchillian. . . ":

"I always felt strongly about political abuses of power, about gov-
ernments killing people. I was a conscientious objector when I
was eighteen. I never stopped feeling strongly about war, about
bombings. I used to be more thin-skinned, but I was always res-
olute. Now, though, I've put all my cards on the table. I protest,
I write letters. . . . I'm on the picket line in front of 10 Downing
Street. . . .

 "Some critics seem to think that an artist should not raise his
head above the parapets. I feel lucky to have the freedom to say

what I feel, to say what I think. That's not a distraction from my work. That's an obligation. It *is* my work. The plays are the plays. The plays are separate. I'm me."

He now had a different wife, the writer Antonia Fraser.

"My parents were pleased with their boy," Pinter said, smiling. "I always remained close to my parents. They loved Antonia and she loved them. I have a forty-one-year-old son from my first marriage . . . and I have six stepchildren with Antonia—three writers, two bankers, one barrister—and twelve grandchildren between the ages of one and eleven. Antonia is 'Grandma' and I'm 'Grandpa.'" He grinned in a carefree and happy mode, clearly illustrative of the fact that the plays are the plays and that he is he.

In addition to the pleasure of a repeat visit, two stories about the same person—interrupted by time—gave me the opportunity to see deeply into the man. By using only his own words, I was able to make an unusual whole out of the halves. It's always a challenge to write about a celebrated person about whom there have been so many articles and so many books. I find, that if you stick closely to what interests you, to what you see and hear for yourself, what you report will be fresh and interesting and vital.

PLAYERS

S THE PRECEDING SAMPLING of my reports shows, I've
been blessed with opportunities to write about a wide variety
of subjects—politicians, fashion, music, children, etc.
—and I've been further blessed by the freedom to write about so
many aspects of the entertainment business. I make no secret of my
admiration and respect for actors, in whatever areas they choose
to work. What Kim Stanley, a remarkably talented actress, said in
my book *The Player* (1962) has always stayed with me: "Unlike
other artists, the actor has only his own body and his own self to
work with. To exhibit oneself on the stage is quite a brave and
wonderful thing to do."

I was so taken with that statement that I used it to set the theme
of the entire book. Kim Stanley was unique. She was powerfully
endowed and painfully honest, about herself and everything else.
In the mid-1950's, there was tremendous excitement about her
among critics and the public, after her early appearances in the
William Inge plays *Picnic* and *Bus Stop*. She tried acting in a few
movies, but found the bits-and-pieces acting system too frustrat-
ing. She then retreated from acting to live quietly in Santa Fe, New

Mexico. She died there in the summer of 2001. It was deeply moving to me to continue to hear from her, for years, about *The Player* and also about *The New Yorker*. Until a few months before her death, she would send me notes saying why she liked this piece or that, including mine, in *The New Yorker*.

I'm always grateful for an assignment to write about actors. As we all know, there's a lot of humor and irony in the business of entertaining, and I thoroughly enjoy finding them. In the early summer of 2000, a friend of mine took me along to the South Bronx on a visit to Gus Van Sant, who was directing the movie *Finding Forrester* up there. Sean Connery was in the cast, and his co-star was a sixteen-year-old newcomer named Rob Brown, who had been relocated from an inner-city public school and placed, on scholarship, in a prestigious private school. Naturally, I was impelled to find a story in this for The Talk of the Town.

It was entitled "Naked and Truthful in the Bronx." Rob plays basketball in the movie, and a neighborhood basketball player was teaching him "some aggressive things, some moves, and elbowing, shoving, things like that. I didn't have to teach him things like the Hood. It's the handshake with three stages—clasp with thumb up, regular shake, then clasp fingers."

> Everybody on the set seemed to be supremely mindful of the danger of disturbing Ron Brown's calm. "If anybody shows panic, everybody feels it," a young production assistant whispered solemnly.
>
> "Rob originally answered an ad for an open-audition call," said a producer, munching on a juicy Cuban sandwich. "When he walked into our office, we liked the way he said his name: 'Rob Brown.' Just like that. That was it." After casting Brown, who usually lives at his school, the producers placed him in the custody of an acting coach, with whom he is sharing an apartment while he shoots the movie.
>
> Connery is larger in life than 007. Waiting in his trailer to be summoned to the set, he entertained a couple of friends by recounting his visit, that day, to his four-year-old granddaughter's

nursery school, in midtown. "It's like no school I ever saw—you should see this school!" he said, in an overpowering Scottish accent.

"All the equipment! All the paints! Buckets of brushes. Every damn thing you could imagine! And they cook and they bake and they wear these little aprons and chef's hats!" He laughed joyously and did an excellent impersonation of four-year-old cooks and bakers. . . .

Both actors—attending the routine shouts of "Stand by!" and "Here we go!" "Roll sound!"—plunged into action. . . . they did what Barry Papick, Brown's acting coach, said was the "cathartic" scene of the movie.

"The scene is all about loss, so I tried to get Rob down to his own loss," he said. "I follow the Lee Strasberg method: Sense memory! Get to the bottom! Find the real emotion! The rediscovery-of-the emotion thing! Like Brando! Rob is fearless. In front of the camera, he's naked and truthful.". . .

At about 4:30 A.M., when the shooting was done, Brown hung around on the set with Russell Smith and Busta Rhymes and Barry Papick and some of the local kids who were playing his friends. They did a lot of gleeful elbowing and carefree shoving and, fearless and naked and truthful, they gave each other the Hood.

Here's a "we" Talk story, "Young and Happy," from 1954, the first piece in the American press about Julie Andrews—"the nineteen-year-old English ingénue who plays the lead in *The Boy Friend*, and she is the only member of either the local company or the company in London, where the original version of the musical comedy is still running, to be so honored."

One of the great moments in the theatre is supposed to be when a shining-eyed young actress first sees her name on a marquee. . . .

We saw her in the two-room apartment she shares with Miss Dilys Lay, also of *The Boy Friend,* and three stuffed poodles.

Miss Andrews is a tallish girl with a gentle voice, large blue-gray eyes, and brown hair, which she parts in the middle. On the

occasion of our visit, she was wearing a red cardigan, a blue skirt, and high-heeled blue sandals. "Do sit down," she said, sweeping a box of Chinese checkers from a couch. "I was just mailing some photographs of myself in the show to Mother. She hasn't seen me in it and wants to know how I look. There's a chance she may come over after the first of the year, and I'll be so happy if she does. I do hope I've put enough stamps on the envelope. I'm terribly homesick. Not that I don't love New York, but one *does* get homesick. . . .

"Dilys and I share a dressing room at the theatre, too. We share almost everything. Each of us has a dog at home, whom we miss dreadfully. Mine is a Welsh Corgi, the sort the Queen has. No tails, you know, and sweet little faces and tiny little bodies. Such lovely dogs! I was thinking of getting one here, but then I realized how stupid it would be to try and keep a dog in a flat in New York. Dilys gave me that stuffed white poodle over there, instead—as a present on my birthday, which was the day after the show opened. It was a marvellous birthday; except for the fact that I wasn't home, I think it was the best I've ever had or am ever likely to have."

Home to Miss Andrews is Walton-on-Thames, a small town eighteen miles south of London. "My pop used to be in show business with Mummy," she said. "His name is Ted Andrews and he has *such* a lovely voice. He used to sing ballads like 'Love, Could I Only Tell Thee How Dear Thou Art to Me.' It's a beautiful number, and I'd rather listen to it than *any*thing. Mummy always wanted to be just Mummy, so Pop gave up show business. . . ."

En route to the theatre, Miss Andrews told us that her father started giving her voice lessons when she was seven. At the same time, she began attending a ballet school. When she was twelve, she embarked on a career in the music halls. "This is my first musical comedy," she said. "I'm more of a singer than an actress. I had to learn a wholly new way of acting for this show. My own style is rather quiet. I'm the only girl in the show who wears a wig, and nobody recognizes me without it when I leave the theatre.

We're having a terribly good time, *The Boy Friend* company. We're all so young and happy. I didn't *need* to be especially thrilled when they told me the other day that they were going to give me featured billing. I think it would be being a bit of a big shot, don't you, to actually *look* at my name up there? Not that anyone would recognize me without my wig, but"—Our taxi pulled up just short of the theatre, and we got out. For a moment, Miss Andrews kept her face turned away from the theatre, then we heard her whisper, "Ah, there it is!" Over her head the marquee proclaimed

THE

BOYFRIEND

SMASH HIT MUSICAL COMEDY

WITH JULIE ANDREWS

And sure enough, her eyes were shining.

In 1962, *The Player* was published, with the subtitle "A Profile of an Art." For the fifty-five little profiles that comprised the book, it seemed appropriate to write them as first-person monologues; after all, that's what an actor does. Every piece, accompanied by a simple photograph taken by me, appeared in this form. The book is still popular with actors.

Here is Zero Mostel, starting off with his characteristic statement:

"The theatre is like a cathedral—I mean a *shul*. At the end of it, there's a cup of hot tea."

"My real name is Samuel Joel Mostel. The kids in school started calling me Zero, because I was always cutting up in class and appeared to be a hopeless student. I weigh two hundred and thirty-five pounds now; as a kid, I was terribly skinny. When I was seven, I played the part of a Red Cross nurse in a school pageant. I loved doing imitations and getting laughs from the other kids. My family always frowned on acting. My father, who died in 1945, was a very good-natured man, but he never came to see me on the stage, or when I worked in night clubs or in movies. Being an entertainer of that kind came under the heading of making fun

of human beings, which is objectionable according to the ortho-
dox Jewish religion. Both my parents had great humor. My moth-
er was a wit, but never a sentimental one. Once, when somebody
in our house stepped on our cat's paw, she turned to the cat and
said sternly, 'I *told* you not to go around barefoot!' For all the
occupations I chose, my mother had one word: 'Bum!' When
I kept asking my father to give in and come see me entertain,
he would say, 'I don't want the publicity.'

"In school, I found that I was very good at drawing and paint-
ing. I've never stopped painting. I've always had a studio to go to;
even while I'm in a play, I try to go every day to my studio. . . .
I taught life drawing and painting at the Ninety-second Street
Y.M.H.A. We gave Artists' Balls, at which I would get up and
joke and deliver chalk talks. Barney Josephson, who was running
Café Society Downtown and Café Society Uptown at the time,
heard me at one of the Artists' Balls and, in 1942, hired me to
do an act at Café Society Downtown, at a salary of forty dollars
a week. Then I moved to the Uptown, at a salary of a hundred
dollars a week. Here I was, a big night club star, and yet when I
had a date, all I knew to offer was 'Let's go for a bite at Rudley's.'
A year later, I was booked into the Martinique at a salary of
thirty-seven hundred and fifty dollars a week.

"By this time, I knew that I wanted to be an actor. I was a
comic. Most comics never bother to equip themselves as actors.
Most of the young comics today have the misconception that if
they do a series of gags in a certain pose, that's enough. But the
best comics are also good actors. Chaplin is a wonderful actor.
W. C. Fields and Willie Howard and Bobby Clark were real
actors, and so are Bert Lahr and Joey Adams and Shelley Berman.
In France, the word 'comédien' actually means both 'comedian'
and 'actor.' I wanted to play in the classic comic literature. I
wanted to act in the plays of Molière, the daddy of all comic
invention. . . . I wanted to know how to do Lear and Toby Belch
and Falstaff. I had read all of Shaw and Molière by the time I was
nineteen. In college, when my English professor was writing 'You
can't beat Thomas Wolfe' on the blackboard, I was reading *Ulysses*

out loud in an alcove with other rebels. Years afterward, when I
was going to play Leopold Bloom in the Off Broadway produc-
tion of *Ulysses in Nighttown*, I found that I knew whole sections
of it by heart. . . .

"I've always been very choosy. I turned down the part of the
peddler in *Oklahoma!*, which the producers wanted to build up for
me. The idea, they told me, was to get into a musical and make
nineteen million dollars. I didn't want that. I wanted to be free
to act and to paint. . . .

"I don't like to do a lot of things you have to do to become a
success as an actor. . . . I'm not willing to make a business out of
myself. If an actor gets that involved with himself, he's doing pho-
tographs in the morning, and then comes the meeting with the
publicity man, then the session with his psychoanalyst, then the
hot lunch at Sardi's. If you do that kind of thing as an actor, you
get farther, but then you don't have time to paint.

"I don't like acting when I have to do *John Loves Mary*. I'm just
as antagonistic to an Andy Wyeth painting or anything else I don't
like. I like to do what I like even if it's a commercial flop. I don't
care what the theatre critics say. Critics don't know anything about
acting. . . . I have an inclination to do wild things in plays. . . . I
like to be with actors, to see what they do. I'm suspicious of ambi-
tious people, though; I'm suspicious of too much conversation. I've
worked with all kinds of directors. Some of the big-name directors
destroy the most wonderful thing an actor has. Just because he has
power and importance, the destructive director tries to bend you
to what he calls his sense of production instead of letting you
use your own configuration, your own way of merging your own
personality with the character you're playing. A good director
knows how to bring out your talent. . . . The best guide to acting
is Bernard Shaw's phrase 'the life force.' When all the elements
of art enter into it—the distortion, the reality, the naiveté—you
have the life force. . . .

"For me the greatest actor in history was Raimu. There's never
been an American playwright who conveyed a corner of Ameri-
can life the way Marcel Pagnol conveyed a corner of French life in

his film trilogy, *Marius, Fanny,* and *César,* starring Raimu. Raimu
captured life for me. He did everything full-scale, without an arid
moment and with no tricks. The greatest actress was Laurette
Taylor. I saw her eleven times in *The Glass Menagerie* on Broad-
way. The great ones just do it, and it's never vulgar."

Zero Mostel was brave, heroic, and unique; he always said what
he thought, and he always took the consequences. He was honest,
and he admired honesty in others. He was able to translate his
beliefs and his truthfulness into original comedy that is still, years
after his death, revered and imitated by dozens of actors, both seri-
ous and comic. He was also a serious painter. His comedy was orig-
inal and hilarious, and it was always telling you some truth. When
I was in my teens, I was taken to see him for the first time, in a
small, downtown night club, where he was doing stand-up. He did
a parody of a reactionary, bigoted U.S. senator. I found myself
doing somersaults with amazement and delight. On the stage, on
the screen, and in the clubs, he was funny, very, very funny. He gave
people the laughter of their lives. I hope the simple, direct story
above gives some indication of what he was.

Very often, when one meets a young actor, it's not easy to see—
specially off the stage or off the screen—signs of talent or special
qualities of any kind. It's interesting to me to reread what I was
able to make of Warren Beatty, when he was twenty-four—five
years before *Bonnie and Clyde* and about twenty years before
Reds. Here is part of what he said for *The Player*:

> "As an actor, I have plenty of time. I'm in no rush. My sister,
> Shirley MacLaine, the movie star, is three years older than I am.
> Until I was in high school, my mother, born Kathlyn MacLean,
> taught acting and directed plays, put on by local amateur groups,
> and *her* mother had done the same. My father, Ira O. Beaty, used
> to be a psychology teacher and public school administrator, and is
> now in the real-estate business. He's a very good violinist, and he
> might have become a concert violinist, if he had taken the gamble
> as a young man. I changed the spelling of my name so that people
> would pronounce it 'Batey' instead of 'Beety.' Shirley, who

changed the spelling of the name MacLean for the same sort of
reason, took dancing lessons from early childhood, and she gravi-
tated naturally toward the stage. All through our childhood she
was bigger and stronger than I was, and it seemed to me that she
always knew what she was doing. What I'm doing now is still a
little bit of a mystery to me. We were brought up as Baptists, and
attended church and Sunday school regularly. To this day, I don't
smoke much or drink. When I had to smoke cigarettes as the dis-
solute and amoral young Italian in *The Roman Spring of Mrs.
Stone*, I could do it, but I didn't like it. When I was five, my moth-
er gave me a walk-on part in a play she was directing. I walked
across the stage, saying nothing, and that was it. She told me I
was very good. . . .

"In my early teens, I decided that I didn't want to miss any of
the advantages of a normal life. I was an above-average student in
high school and took part in a lot of extracurricular activities. I
went out for football and made the first team. I was a letter man
in baseball and basketball, and was elected president of my senior
class. In high school, I didn't do anything in dramatics, because I
considered it sissy. Because of my football record in high school,
I was offered athletic scholarships at ten different colleges and
universities, but I decided to turn them all down. I'd had enough
of football. Football can get into your blood and ego. The cheers
and admiration can go to your head too easily. Besides, I wasn't
really passionate about athletics. In basketball, I'd often been
more interested in kidding around and having fun than in win-
ning games. I'd never taken anything very seriously. I'd always got
good grades without studying. I'd talked vaguely about studying
law, but I'd been sort of a goof-off, always clowning around. After
high school, I said to myself, 'Now I'll do what I want to do.' And
in 1956, I entered Northwestern University, where I attended
class regularly and joined one of the fraternities. I did two plays
in college: *Bus Stop*, in which I played Bo, the leading man, and
Under Milk Wood, by Dylan Thomas, in which I played three
characters—a clothing salesman, a sea captain, and a poet. After
a year, I suddenly realized that I wanted to be an actor, and that

I wasn't going to learn acting at Northwestern. In 1957, I left college and came to New York. . . .

"Right after the play [*A Loss of Roses* by William Inge] closed, I played the leading role in the movie *Splendor in the Grass*, with Natalie Wood and Pat Hingle, which was directed by Elia Kazan. From that I went right into *The Roman Spring of Mrs. Stone*, with Vivien Leigh, directed by José Quintero. . . . All in all, I got a concentrated education in making movies. I felt terribly frustrated when I first saw myself in *Splendor in the Grass* and *The Roman Spring of Mrs. Stone*. From every indication, I was very successful. I was very much in demand; I was getting a lot of publicity; I was on my way to becoming a movie star. But when I saw myself in those first two movies, I realized that if I had done the same parts on the stage I would have had the opportunity to come back and do them again, in a better way, trying to find new meanings in them. In the movies, they were recorded in one way for all time. On the other hand, I knew I was learning how to combat out-of-sequence shooting, how to sustain a performance, and how to come to the set prepared, in my own mind, to play it. In acting, I've always tried to make the most of whatever I was doing, no matter what. My father tells a story about a man who is captured by cannibals in the jungle and is about to be boiled. He says to himself, 'There is nothing I can do about it, so I may as well enjoy it.'"

Warren Beatty was on the verge of becoming a star when we did the piece about him. At this early point in his life, he didn't put on any show for us; he was modest, matter-of-fact, and unformed, but he clearly had what was going to be called "charisma." The story, by design, shows a young man on the verge of breaking away from the pack, and at that point, he really didn't know he was going to do it.

For *The Player*, Henry Fonda said: "Acting is putting on a mask. The worst torture that can happen to me is not having a mask to get in back of."

Fonda was the quintessential movie star in the 1960's, when this piece was written. What possible reason was there to do a piece

about someone as familiar to the public as Corn Flakes? Answer:
to find out if there was a genuine man behind the usual public rela-
tions-created façade. It turned out that Fonda was unusually inter-
ested in, and sensitive to, the family forces that produced him. And
then we did a piece about his daughter, Jane, and we discovered
that, in this respect, she was just like him.

Henry Fonda:

"There is a strong Fonda look. It's in my sisters, in their children,
in my children. The name Fonda is Italian in origin. There were
Fondas in the Apennine Valley, near Genoa, who migrated to
Holland around 1400 during a religious revolution. Around 1628,
Fondas were among the Dutch settlers who settled in Upper New
York State, where, in a town called Fonda, both my father's moth-
er and his father were born. Omaha has never ceased being my
home. I always stop in Omaha when I'm going from one coast
to the other. . . . I had what I regard as a normal youth. My close
friends today are the friends I grew up with. . . . My mother was a
Christian Scientist. My grandmother was a Second Reader in the
church. Dorothy Brando, Marlon's mother, who was an amateur
actress, was a close friend of Mother's in and out of church. . . .

"I took up journalism at the University of Minnesota, and I
worked at two jobs while studying—troubleshooter for the North-
western Bell Telephone Company, and director of various sports
and other activities at a settlement house. I'd take the streetcar
from the campus to the settlement house on the other side of
town, in temperatures that went as low as thirty below zero, and
in the basketball season, I'd play on the team as well as coach it.
For all that I got thirty dollars a month, plus room and board. Dad
sent me ten bucks a week. It was exhausting. I did it for a year, and
then I went home for a rest. While I was home, I got a message
from Do Brando to call George Foley, the director of the Omaha
Community Playhouse. She knew that I was at loose ends, and
that I was the right age and type to play a juvenile lead they were
looking for. . . . First thing I knew, I was cast in the play [*You and
I* by Philip Barry]. I was sure I didn't want to do it. At rehearsals,

I found myself in another world. It was a nightmare. I didn't dare
look up. I was the kind of guy that thinks everybody is looking
at *him*. I was very reluctant. I had no ambition to be an actor.
But it was summer, and I had nothing else to do, so I joined the
company. . . .

"I went to work at Retail Credit at seven in the morning and
rehearsed for the play at night and on Sundays. On opening
night, I got my first feeling of what acting was all about. I liked
the whole idea of being up there and being Merton. I was given
an ovation. When I got home, Dad was sitting in the living room
behind his newspaper, and one of my sisters was starting to criti-
cize my performance when, from behind the newspaper, Dad said
'Shut up. He was perfect.'. . .

"I might easily have become a credit manager in Omaha and
done community theatre for kicks, but then, in the spring of 1927,
I suddenly had an offer to spend a week in New York seeing all the
shows, as a present from the mother of a local Princeton boy. I was
supposed to pick him up and drive him home for Easter. When I
told the manager of the credit office, he was shocked. He had big
plans to send me to the home office in Atlanta for managerial
training. But I made the trip to New York and saw nine plays
in six days, including *The Constant Wife*, with Ethel Barrymore.
I loved every minute.

"When I got back from New York, Foley offered me a job at
the Playhouse as assistant director, at a salary of five hundred dol-
lars, for the next season. It seemed fine to me. I did a lot of things,
including acting and designing scenery. Ever since kindergarten,
I'd been able to draw. My main acting assignment was to play
opposite Do Brando in Eugene O'Neill's *Beyond the Horizon*.
I was living at home, and I was beginning to think there was
such a thing as making a living in the theatre. By the end of the
season, I knew I wanted to go to New York. . . .

"I was damn sure I was a good actor, and sure that eventually
I was going to prove it. My first season in New York, I became
the best known unknown actor in town. All the offices knew me.
All the agents knew me. I lived on 114th Street in a ten-dollar-a-

week room. I joined Equity. I learned that Equity listed all plays
in production on its bulletin board. I didn't present myself well
to producers, but I knew I was good. I had learned I was good
when I played Merton in Omaha. Thirty-five years later, I can
still remember the way I felt as Merton. There was a breathless
feeling I couldn't ever recapture. It was like being ten years old
and playing cops and robbers. . . .

"It was easy to make the transition to movies. I started to act in
the film version of *The Farmer Takes a Wife* the way I always did
for a play, and Victor Fleming, the director, told me I was mug-
ging. And that's all it took. I just pulled it down to reality. You
don't project anything for movies. You do it as you would in your
own home. Because of all the experience back of me in the same
part, it didn't bother me to work out of continuity, the way you
do in making a movie. Of course, there's very little satisfaction in
doing those bits and pieces for a movie. You don't really have any
recollection of having created a role. But in the beginning the
money made it pretty attractive. . . .

"In 1942, I was thirty-seven. I enlisted in the Navy and served
as quartermaster third class on a destroyer in the Pacific. Later,
the executive officer on the destroyer recommended me for a
commission; I was flown to 90 Church Street and discharged, was
then immediately commissioned as a lieutenant (j.g.), and joined
Air Combat Intelligence. At that time, I wasn't eager to go back
to movies, but after the war I did go back. I made a John Ford
picture, *My Darling Clementine,* and other pictures, and then I
went into Thomas Heggen's and Joshua Logan's *Mister Roberts* on
Broadway. I'd never been a long run before, except for a hundred
and four performances in *The Farmer Takes a Wife. Mister Roberts*
was a love story backstage. We were all just crazy about the play. If
anybody let down, he had thirty other guys on him. It really was
like being in love. You had this good feeling in the guts practically
all the time. I love to act, and in this play I always knew every-
thing I was going to do but could make it look like not acting at
all. . . . I'd still be in my dressing room waiting to go onstage and
I could feel the hackles rising in anticipation, the skin tingling.

One of my joys was for Josh Logan, who directed the play, to come to a performance and say, 'Fonda, you son of a bitch!' To have him recognize the way the part got better all the time. . . . The thing I try to do onstage is to create the illusion that it's happening for the first time. In two years, not a performance got by of all the performances we did that the audience didn't get what it came for; for them it was happening for the first time. I never got tired of it. . . .

". . . I was damn lucky I became an actor. Theatre is the only thing I understand. I can't really talk about anything else. In company, I don't have small talk. It's pretty silly to begin with, and I don't know how to do it at all. When you've exhausted the weather, and where you've been, and where they've been, you're stuck. When I get stuck, I feel everybody is looking at me, and I want to hide. I like to be the observer. . . ."

Here is Jane Fonda at twenty-four:

"What I like even more than the acting itself is just being in the theatre, especially during rehearsals, as a member of a group working together, in the same place, for the same goal, under one spotlight surrounded by darkness, like a family in the living room. . . .

"I have a brother, Peter, two years younger than I am, who left the University of Omaha in 1960, his junior year, to act in a comedy on Broadway, then got married and went out to Hollywood on a movie contract. . . . As children Peter and I lived on a twenty-four-acre farm in Brentwood. It was quite isolated around there, and Pete was my main companion. We had three dogs and a cat and a lot of chickens, and some rabbits—who were my best friends for a while—and we had flower and vegetable gardens. I loved my job, which was to collect the newly laid eggs. Our house was unusual around there; it was a sort of New England setup transplanted to California. My father did everything possible to make it look like a genuine old New England house; it had shingles made to look weatherbeaten, and a lot of Early American furnishings—cobblers' benches, braided rugs, lamps made from

butter churns. We had a large dinner bell on our roof that could
be heard for a mile around. We had a swimming pool, but my
father disguised it to look like a pond. My father loved the farm
and often plowed the fields himself. We had two mules, and Pete
and I would go out in the hills on them and explore. . . . In the
hills, Peter and I played big roles in our own kind of westerns,
living the way we thought our father lived in the movies we'd see
him in. I was scared to death when I saw my father in John Ford's
Drums Along the Mohawk. For two days, in the movie, my father
ran from one fort to another as a settler, and then there was a big
life-and-death battle, with the Indians massacring the whites, but
the whites finally winning. It was the longest movie of my life, as
I waited for my father and the whites to win. . . . At home, my
father always wore levis and work clothes that made him look like
a cowboy, and Pete and I would try to copy him in every respect.
My father would bring his Hollywood friends in—John Wayne,
Ward Bond, and John Ford—who dressed the same way, and
they would sit around the house playing cards and talking like
cowboys.

"I don't remember owning a dress until I was about eight. . . .
When I was ten, my father left for New York to appear on Broad-
way in *Mister Roberts*. Six months later, the whole family moved
to Greenwich, Connecticut. . . . When I was fourteen, my father
was staying at Oscar Hammerstein's town house in New York, so
I stayed there, too. If you have glamorous parents, you just have to
live a special way. I loved New York, but I didn't have any friends
here. I felt sort of special living my way, but I rather envied girls
with what looked like normal family lives, and I often pretended
to my classmates that my life was like theirs. Four months after
my father married Susan Blanchard, Oscar Hammerstein's step-
daughter, in December, 1950, I went to live with them. I was very
fond of Susan, and it felt almost like having a whole family again.

". . . People always said I was a fine, healthy girl and called me a
mature child. So helpful, they said, and so understanding. I wasn't
a mature child at all. At home, I never showed anything I felt. I
kept a poker face, and that made people conclude that I was

mature. We were not a demonstrative family. I grew up not knowing how to show hatred, anger, or grudges. I just stored it all up. It was a great disadvantage to me as an actress, I discovered later on. . . .

"My father had nothing to do directly with my wanting to act, Something must have rubbed off, though—a temperament, a need for the theatre. I really admired my father's acting. He's never bad, no matter what he's playing in. My favorite movie of his is *The Grapes of Wrath,* which he made when I was two years old. It was beautifully written and directed and deals with a subject that was important to my father. He believed in it socially and politically. He was Tom Joad, and he loved that character, and it shows, and that's why I like it the best of all his movies. . . .

"Everything is best for me when I'm onstage. That's when I come alive. . . . In the beginning, when I first went out onstage, I always felt like apologizing to the audience. I suppose I felt unworthy to appear before it. If I sensed resentment on the part of anybody in the audience, I'd start to fade out. . . . Sometimes I'd go up to the balcony to look at the faces and guess how they were going to respond to me. If I saw mean faces, I'd feel terrible.

"I'd like some day to be as good an actress as Geraldine Page or Kim Stanley. The better I get as an actress, the freer I feel. Actresses have to exhibit themselves, to hang themselves up on a clothesline. . . . At parties, even today, I work at being charming, though I may not feel in the least like being charming. I show an interest in people I'm not the least bit interested in. Onstage, I found, I didn't have to do anything of that kind. Playing a role, I was free to reveal exactly what I felt."

MORE PLAYERS

WHEN A PERSON being listened to, and written about, speaks at some length, and what he or she has to say is original and riveting, there is only one course for the reporter to take: By all means, quote these precious people, and quote them at length.

Here is another example, the great Paul Scofield, in *The Player:* "People talk of magic in the theatre. 'Magic' is a misleading word. The pure work is all that matters to the actor. Magic is for the audience to discover. Magic is no concern of ours."

"I was married to the actress Joy Parker in 1943, and we have two children, Martin, seventeen, and Sarah, ten. My children aren't the least bit interested in what I do in the theatre. Children like to forget about their parents' careers, I think, and all the claims that their parents' work make on them. When I came to America to appear in *A Man for All Seasons,* my children stayed in England, in school. It was our first long separation. I wasn't the least bit startled to get a letter from Sarah in which she wrote, 'I hope you're enjoying yourself in America. I doubt it.' It pleases me that the

theatre means nothing to the children. I like to leave it behind. I just like to go home.

"Children eventually get recognized as totally independent creations. They seem to lead the way for you to understand them. It's easy for me to see what they want and what they are. That's the kind of thing actors are so good at—putting themselves in other people's shoes. . . . Professionally, I've never done anything I haven't wanted to do since being in a position to refuse work. I could live without acting, I think. I could very easily work on a farm.

"At the age of twelve, I started going to school in Brighton, commuting by train and bicycle to Varndean School for Boys, where I was a leading member of the Dramatic Society. My first part, when I was thirteen, was Juliet. The Romeo was not very good, but my Juliet was a sensation. It's the only part I've ever played of which I can remember every word. It has just stayed. At fourteen, I played Rosalind in *As You Like It*. Then my voice went a little low, and I next played Prince Hal in *Henry IV*, Part I. From then on, it seemed pretty clear to me that I would become an actor. For a boy who was hopeless at everything else, acting was a tremendous release. I wasn't used to the kind of freedom that doing something well gives one. That made it all the clearer. . . .

"When I was fifteen, I made my professional debut, in a touring production of *The Only Way*, at the Theatre Royal in Brighton, which is one of the loveliest theatres in all England, with a horseshoe-shaped circle, and red plush and gilt, and all the old theatre atmosphere, pretty much as it has been for a hundred years. It's very much alive as a theatre today. There's always something to see there. The play *The Only Way* was an adaptation of *A Tale of Two Cities*, starring John Martin Harvey, who was more or less the Henry Irving of his day. He was making one of his ostensible farewell tours. They asked for volunteers for the crowd scenes. I turned up at the stage door, was taken on at ten shillings a week, or about thirty cents a performance, and was given a cudgel to brandish in a crowd scene. The play, and being part of

it, was awe-inspiring. Sir John had a remarkable style of acting, in the tradition of Irving—highly dramatic and rather operatic— and I was deeply affected. . . . I was in the play for two weeks. At the end, I liked that cudgel they'd given me so much that I took it. I walked out with it under my mackintosh. I still have it. . . .

"For most actors in the formative stage, the spotlight is harmful. It makes one set hard too soon, and possibly it makes one become a personality. There's no harm in it if you want to become the kind of actor whose primary concern is expressing yourself to the audience. I hadn't, and haven't, any interest in doing that. The point is that if you're a personality to the audience, it becomes increasingly difficult to put yourself in other people's shoes, which is what I like to do. It's a much more interesting job to try to illuminate as many types of people as possible. I'm very, very cagey about my own personality. I've always been very secretive."

Writing about actors, I discovered that each—no matter how much they have in common—is profoundly different from the other. In trying to write a profile of the art of acting, I used the contrasts.

Walter Matthau was a marvellous actor, original and very funny. In writing about him, I felt that I had to quote him in a way that showed very clearly his view of himself. His introductory line in *The Player* was: "An actor must have senses that are spongelike and soak up everything, and that means he's vulnerable. This very vulnerability can make it tough for him to work in the highly commercial, competitive field of the theatre."

Here is Matthau talking:

"When I was five, I would do an imitation of our landlady coming to collect the rent. That always used to break my mother up. . . . When I was eleven, I started working for the candy concessionaires, selling ice cream and soda pop in most of the Yiddish theatres along Second Avenue for a fifteen-per-cent commission on all sales—places like the Second Avenue Theatre and the Public and the National. I worked in those theatres for five years. I got to see many of the leading Yiddish actors, like

Julius Nathanson, Herman Yablokoff, and Michael Rosenberg. I
watched the way they worked. The idea of becoming an actor was
lurking somewhere in my head. The Yiddish actor who made the
strongest impression one was Michael Rosenberg. The minute he
walked onstage, he had his audience. He brought a whole world
out with him. He was just a little guy who wore wigs and beards
—very unprepossessing offstage—but he was the most interesting
actor I'd ever seen. He had electricity. I learned something of what
I know about comic timing from him. I played bit parts in Yiddish
musical comedies, which were actually tragicomedies with music,
with marvellous actor-comedians, like Leo Fuchs. I earned fifty
cents a night, for seven performances a week. I soaked up every-
thing around me, just being there. I used to feel wonderful in the
theatres—with the actors talking to each other, the girls changing
costumes, the smell of stale smoke, the dampness, the upholstered
chairs, the musty rugs, the buzzing in the audience, and the dead
silence just before the curtain went up. During intermissions,
I'd run out to the audience and sell my ice cream and soda pop,
which netted me about two dollars and fifty cents for a good
week, in addition to what I earned as an actor. . . .

"In high school, I didn't go out with girls very much, and I
refused to go to dances. Instead, I read plenty of Shakespeare. I'd
lock myself in the bathroom and read the plays and poems out
loud to myself for two or three hours at a stretch. I liked the sound
of them. I managed the campaigns of kids running for office in the
student government, and every time I got up in the school audito-
rium to make a campaign speech, the audience would start to
laugh even before I opened my mouth. There was always something
about the way I stood or looked or sounded. . . .

"In April, 1942, I enlisted in the Army. I was trained in the
Army Air Forces radio school in Savannah, Georgia, then joined
a heavy-bomber outfit in Salina, Kansas. I was a radio operator at
Atteborough, England, and then a Link-trainer instructor, and
I served in France, Holland, Belgium, and Germany as a radio
operator-cryptographer. Then I was shipped back to the States.
. . . I met a Red Cross worker who told me I ought to go to school

in New York under the G.I. Bill of Rights. I came back, and when
I heard that the Dramatic Workshop of the New School for
Social Research, run by Erwin Piscator, was at the old President
Theatre, a block and a half away from Madison Square Garden,
where I liked to hang out and watch the hockey and basketball
games and the fights, I decided to go there.

"There were nice people at the school, and every month there
was a check from the government. It was simple. And I began to
soak up more of the climate of acting. Gradually, it started to sift
down into something I could use. Piscator was a weird, eccentric
man, but he knew more about the theatre than almost anybody
else around at the time. . . . He would come around two days
before the opening of the plays we put on every couple of months.
He would redo everything the director had done. I began to get
more of the real feel of acting from him. Once, I was playing
Sadovsky in Nikolai Pogodin's *Aristocrats*. And he came around
and said, 'Matthau, you say here every line wrong.' Another actor
might have been destroyed. I was destroyed for about twenty
seconds. Then I said, 'Teach me how to say every line right.' One
way and another, I began to learn how to talk, how to look, how
to walk—how to act. . . .

"It's on the stage that I feel comfortable, relaxed, fulfilled,
delighted. I'm happy doing stage plays. Working for the screen
is almost like being in the Army; you set your mind to it and you
do it. On the stage, you're wide open. There are no tricks with the
camera to make you look a certain way. Nobody is going to cut
you out, either. The people are sitting out there, and they're going
to see you full on. Nobody can fool around with our face. Nobody
can fool around with your voice. You can taste and smell what the
audience feels. You know if you're coming across. You know if
you're being heard. You know if you're being understood. An
audience deviates about a yard compared to an actor's perform-
ance, which deviates about an inch. An audience of ladies is good
if you're in a hit. The critics have told them they have permission
to laugh, so they start to laugh before the curtain. They come in
laughing at the ushers. . . ."

It was a special challenge to write about Tommy Lee Jones, an intriguing, one-of-a-kind actor. In my 1994 Profile of him in *The New Yorker*, he didn't talk about acting theories or what he as an actor did; he simply revealed his take on his art simply by talking about what he was actually doing and feeling as Mr. Ty Cobb while making the movie *Cobb*. Because he is impressively literate and articulate, I set the stage and put him into action as quickly and as impatiently as Jones does with himself. I tried to absorb his rhythm. He talked fast, always to the point. Before retiring at night, he then was in the habit of making a little summary out loud, of what he as Jones had done all day.

Here's the start of the story:

Last January, seventy-six days before winning an Academy Award as best supporting actor for the role of a relentless lawman in *The Fugitive*, and the day before the scheduled beginning of rehearsals for the filming of *Cobb*, on location at Lake Tahoe, where Ty Cobb, the baseball legend, had lived, Tommy Lee Jones was in San Antonio, where *he* lives, practicing hitting and sliding á la Cobb. While sliding, under the supervision of a production-assigned coach, one of Jones' cleats got stuck in the dirt; his ankle turned over, and he suffered a fracture of the fibula.

The next day, Jones made it to Tahoe, wearing a Bledsoe leg brace with Velcro straps and walking with the support of a carved wooden stick with serpentine decorations. With Jim Burns, a soft-spoken North Carolinian who was his assistant, he occupied a pleasant rented house, with a fine view of the lake, the mountains, and the glorious sunsets. The *Cobb* production offices—including one for Ron Shelton, the writer and director of *Cobb*, who is a former second baseman for a Baltimore Orioles farm club and also wrote and directed *Bull Durham*—had been set up in the Cal Neva hotel nearby, and rehearsals were being held in the hotel's Frank Sinatra Celebrity Showroom. . . . Jones was taking anti-inflammatory medicine, rehearsing scenes for *Cobb*, and putting in some time working on a screenplay he was writing for a TNT movie called *The Good Old Boys*, based on the Western

novel of that title, by Elmer Kelton, who, like Jones, is from West Texas. [Eventually, that movie, which he directed himself and which was shown on television, turned out to be, in my opinion, the best film about a cowboy ever made.] In Tahoe, I found Jones in his house, standing in front of a huge stone fireplace, his back to a picturesque wood-burning fire. He had the brace on his right foot and a low black lace-up boot on his left, and he was wearing blue jeans, a maroon sweater, and a black felt railroad cap. He greeted me with a creased smile and a lot of unforced enthusiasm about his new character, whom he referred to consistently as Mr. Cobb.

"I'm learning the quality of Mr. Cobb's life," Jones said, speaking quickly, in his light, lilting voice that repeatedly strikes the listener, when he first starts talking, as a surprise. "He's seventy-two years old, and there are wrinkles, with the help of a latex application. This old arthritic, with his liver spots and freckles and every disease known to man, is also still an athlete. He's a scrapper. He has a black eye. Mr. Cobb is drinking lots of whiskey, holding his millionaire's investment empire together, and he's planning his visit to Cooperstown, for the testimonial dinner at the Baseball Hall of fame. This mean, violent, powerful old man who has been powerful all his life is now dying. But he's Mr. Cobb."

Jones, who is forty-seven years old, moved gracefully away from the fireplace with a single-footed jump, then took off his cap. "They shaved my head for me to wear a thin, white hairpiece for the movie," he said, running his hand over his pate. He held his walking stick in his left hand, as though it were a baseball bat.

"Now let me explain to you how to hit a baseball," he said, talking fast, confidently, belligerently. "It's a lost art. Ever since Babe Ruth started hitting home runs. The skill, the art, and the science have been lost. You see, the bat is like a wand, a magic wand." He swung the walking stick. He was Ty Cobb, giving his lines. "Hitting a baseball is really very easy. You can't force it. You can't overpower it. You go with the pitch. You let the bat do the work. It's all rhythm and flow." He swung the stick again. "I've been trying to do Mr. Cobb's bunt right down the first-base line,"

he said. "The pitcher would come in to make the play, get caught in the right-of-way, and Mr. Cobb would cut him in two."

"Tommy does not try to make you *like* Cobb, this violent, hard-drinking, hated man who was a genius," Ron Shelton said to me later that day. "But Tommy makes you *care* about Cobb."

. . . Jones moved to another office nearby, to select more wardrobe for Mr. Cobb. He sang and whistled to himself while considering pajamas offered him by Ruth Carter, a quiet, poker-faced woman, who was the costume designer. She showed him pajamas decorated with ycllow pintail ducks on a red background and pajamas with brown cowboys and broncos on a blue back-ground. "I prefer the ducks," Jones said, holding the pajamas up against him. "Mr. Cobb—this elegant man, this powerful man— is deciding to go on a road trip. His valet has quit. So Mr. Cobb starts throwing stuff in suitcases."

Now Ruth Carter offered Jones a jacket, and he tried it on. "Mr. Cobb's going to wear these duck pajamas with this bur-gundy-and-black hounds-tooth jacket," Jones said. "He wants this jacket. The jacket's a good look. Combining it with the duck pajamas makes perfect sense to him. It doesn't make any differ-ence, because he's Mr. Cobb anyway."

Ruth Carter offered Jones a black hat, and he said, "This hom-burg has a good shape. Reblock it so that the crown has more body." He tried on a black suit with white pinstripes. "Great look, great look," he said. Over the suit he put on a large black double-breasted chesterfield with black velvet pocket flaps and a black velvet collar. He put on the homburg, and said, "I like the hat; I like all of it. Mr. Cobb wants to be timelessly elegant. Mr. Cobb has got a pistol in this pocket"—he lightly slapped the right pocket—"and he's got thirty-five thousand dollars in cash in the other." He slapped the left one, and said, "This old man, with his white hair and his latex face. Mr. Cobb is ready to go to the casino and gamble." Jones picked up the walking stick with the bulldog head. "Plus, if Mr. Cobb gets in trouble he can whack his way out of it," he added.

He took off his forties outfit, put on his jeans, laced up the low black boot for his left leg, and replaced the brace on his right. He

put on a black vinyl windbreaker with white letters spelling out
"Harvard Polo," but he was still breathing Cobb. "You come to
the rehearsal, Ruth!" he said bossily to the costume designer. "To
the testimonial dinner! All the great ones will be there." He was
giving her his lines. "The great Mickey Cochrane will be there.
You're gonna meet great athletes, great warriors, great men at
the Hall of Fame dinner."

That night, Jones gave me his habitual summary of that day:
"We had a meeting with the costume department and found
some good gambling clothes and walking sticks. We rehearsed
in the Frank Sinatra room at the Cal Neva. I finished the first
draft of *The Good Old Boys* at a mere hundred and forty-five
pages and sent it to be printed, and Jim found some good take-
out barbecue ribs."

Michael Black, Jones' agent, is a friendly, voluble, likable man,
who probably has the most polished, mahogany-toned suntan
in the state of California. I saw him not long ago in his office, a
glassed-in cage in the ultra-modern International Creative Man-
agement building on Wilshire Boulevard.

"Tommy was always different," Black told me. "Different in
look, different in presence. He was very original and very smart.
Money walks, money talks. Basically, this town wants to tintype
him. That's the way they are. Tintype. Tintype. Tintype. I never
perceived that Tommy ever doubted his own talent. He's unlike
most actors—no matter how many jobs he failed to get, I never
heard anything in Tommy's voice indicating that he himself ques-
tioned his talent. Then came the one-two punch." Black punched
one fist against the other. "*Lonesome Dove* and *JFK* turned the
people around." . . .

In Cambridge, Jones, wearing jeans, black moccasins, a plaid
cotton shirt, and a tan windbreaker went to a Harvard-Lafayette
football game. In the late sixties, Jones attended Harvard on a
scholarship. (One of his roommates at Harvard was Albert Gore,
Jr.) He played in the famous 1968 Harvard-Yale game, in which
Harvard, in the last forty-two seconds, scored sixteen points to
earn a tie. He also appeared in productions at the Loeb Drama

center, beginning in his freshman year with Harold Pinter's *The Caretaker*.

After the Harvard-Lafayette game, Jones walked to Athens Street, where William Alfred, the playwright and Harvard English teacher—with whom Jones had worked in 1969 on his senior-year tutorial, about Flannery O'Connor—lived in a gray clapboard house. Professor Alfred, when he opened the door, was wearing a navy-blue pin-striped suit and a dark-blue necktie. A brass-plated chain across his midriff was attached to an American Waltham silver turnip watch, which, he later said, his mother had given him on his sixteenth birthday. Alfred had a splendid Brooklyn-Irish accent and was shy and subdued. Jones sat down on a sofa with a white linen slipcover. Alfred sat opposite him on a white-linen-covered armchair. Jones edged forward on the sofa as Professor Alfred poured tea and offered cookies. Then he edged farther toward Professor Alfred. Without diffidence, and as though he was picking up discourse where it had been left not twenty-five years but twenty-five minutes earlier, Jones said, "Well, I've decided to become a writer." He explained that he was writing a screenplay, based on Elmer Kelton's *The Good Old Boys*. The book had been optioned by producers, Jones said, who had sent it to him with the idea that he would play the lead role, Hewey Calloway. "They didn't know about Elmer Kelton," Jones went on. "He's written a lot of books about western Texas, and he also wrote for the local paper, the *Livestock Weekly*. They couldn't afford me as an actor. But I said I would act in it if I could direct it, and that led to my writing it. I got myself a director's job." He edged still farther forward on the sofa. "I want to be this character, Hewey Calloway." He spoke rapidly. "Hewey believes the plow is a mistake. He says it's wrong to plow back what God gave as a gift, that God's too big to stick in a church house. He's telling it to his nephew, a teen-aged kid who just wants to see an automobile. And Hewey's brother wants him to marry the local schoolmarm and settle down." He looked intently at Professor Alfred. "My outlines were coarse at first, sir, but I did the first page, and then the second page, and it finally began to write itself."

"Hewey Calloway," Alfred said slowly, refilling Jones's teacup. "Well, I saw you as Coriolanus here at the Loeb. You were able

then to get over to us a sense of what a man would be like if he believed in his own nobility."

"I'm glad I found something to do," Jones said in a matter-of-fact way.

Later, walking back to his hotel, amid the students near Harvard Square, Jones looked sharply at the young women and said they were so different today from the way they had been when he was at college. "I stopped in at the Coop today to buy something and I said, 'Yes, Ma'am,' to a kind of reconstructed Radcliffe girl, and I got a real dirty look from her," he said. "That reminded me that things are different now."

Tommy Lee Jones was born on September 15, 1946, in West Texas, in the town of San Saba, which then had a population of just over three thousand. He is an eighth-generation Texan. His father, Clyde Jones, was a specialist in drilling tools who worked in oil fields—not only in Texas but all over the world. Tommy Lee himself worked in the Texas fields, with his father and without him, during school vacations. Clyde Jones died of a heart attack when he was in his mid-fifties. Tommy Lee's mother, Lucille Marie Scott, known as Marie all her life, worked at various jobs, including those of policewoman and schoolteacher. . . . With her second husband, Marie now lives in Cameron, about a hundred miles east of San Saba and a hundred and fifty miles north of San Antonio. Her father, Archie Lee Scott, who is ninety-two, and who is recovering from a recent stroke, also lives in Cameron.

"My Granddad is a very kind man and a good cowboy," Jones said to me. He was quiet for a few beats. Then he said, "I'll tell you about my Granddad. My uncle Harold and my aunt Sarah lived with my Granddad in Bracketville on the Rio Grande, near Fort Clark, where John Ford shot the movie *The Alamo* and where people still around there were extras in the movie. Uncle Harold and Aunt Sarah had six boys, separated in age from each other by ten months. The youngest of the boys, Vernon Clyde, was just my age. When we were twelve, Granddad said to me: 'Get a couple of horses and take our stud to our neighbors.' The neighbors lived twenty-five miles away. Vernon Clyde and I got up at sunrise and rode for hours, and we delivered the stud. The *vaqueros* at the

neighbors gave us lunch—chili, beans, tortilla, and iced tea. One
of the nicest meals I've ever had in my entire life. We started
home. It was hot, and we took off our shirts and got all sun-
burned. Then we decided we'd lope our horses back. We nearly
rode their feet off. When we got back to Granddad, our horses'
feet were bleeding. Granddad bent over and picked up my horse's
foot. He put it down. He didn't say a word. He went into the
barn. He didn't raise his voice. He didn't whip us, and we should
have been whipped. He never said a word about my horse's feet.
In the next five days, we butchered a lot of deer and made a lot of
sausages while waiting for my horse's feet to get well." He looked
serious. He did not comment on the story.

"I've talked myself into believing I remember the day I was
born," Jones said to me as we walked along. "I hang on to my
memories with cat's claws. I can remember tornadoes in Knox
County when I was three. . . . Some of my memories are clear—
very, very clear. Both my mother and father used to go to honky-
tonk bars, to do what everybody in that part of Texas did—drink.
I'd wait for them outside in the car, alone. I remember hearing
music and singing coming through the walls of the saloon to
me in the car. I remember lying there, just waiting, just waiting,
alone."

When we reached the hotel, Jones said, "It's been a wonderful
day." He added quickly, almost throwing the words away, "I took
a long walk around Cambridge. I went to the football game. We
had tea and cookies with Professor Alfred and some good talk."

. . . The day before what is fondly referred to in the movie com-
munity as "the most important night of the year," a 5.3 earthquake
rattled everybody in the place. To me, it seemed imitative of the
Universal Studios version of a quake, and I found it fell rather
short of the unreal one. On Oscar night, Tommy Lee Jones,
sitting with his wife, Kimberlea, in the front row at the Dorothy
Chandler Pavilion auditorium and wearing a new-looking tuxedo,
his head still bald for the *Cobb* part, also seemed somehow short
of his unreal roles; he looked deprived. Kimberlea, however, was
lit up with undisguised excitement.

Accepting the Oscar for Best Performance by an Actor in a Supporting Role, Jones played the role to perfection, standing tall, giving his many-creased smile, and saying, "My thanks to the Academy for the very finest, greatest award that any actor can ever receive. The only thing a man can say at a time like this is"— he paused for a couple of beats and bent forward, and ran his hand over his pate—"I am not really bald."

Later on, after posing along with the other winners for the press, Jones made his way, followed by Kimberlea, through the crowd inching its way to the Los Angeles County Music Center Plaza, next door, for the Board of Governors Ball, which began with a seated dinner. Heading for his table, assigned to Warner Bros. figures key to the making of *The Fugitive*, Jones could be seen projected on a huge, movie-theatre-size screen. He was clutching his Oscar in one hand, and, looking grim, clearly not happy in the midst of the jam of formally clad guests, was pointing with his other hand in the direction of the Warners table. Yet, up on the screen, he looked restored. He didn't eat any dinner and left as soon as possible, skipping all the celebratory parties in the aftermath.

At six o'clock the next morning, Jones was in makeup again, ready to go before the camera as Mr. Cobb and work.

I wanted the cut-to-the-chase phenomenon of Tommy Lee Jones to follow, appropriately, the slow, measured phenomenon of Paul Scofield—as a clincher to the phenomenon of what makes an actor. The way Jones talks about his "Granddad" told me everything I wanted to know about the nature of his spirit and his character. With that, he had me, and, as far as I'm concerned, Tommy Lee Jones can do no wrong.

In writing a Profile, a reporter usually does a lot of legwork, following the subject here and there, interviewing him and others, making telephone calls, researching facts. But it's incumbent upon the reporter not to give the reader a litany of the work involved, the hardships in the reporter's struggles, the inconveniences, the frustrations, etc. A Profile should be written as though everything

just happened, effortlessly. For the record: for the Tommy Lee Jones Profile, I travelled to Lake Tahoe, to San Antonio, to Los Angeles, to Hollywood, to Cambridge. Mr. Jones graciously invited me to come to his home, to meet his family, to accompany him on the visit to Professor Alfred, to drive with him to his film locations, to walk around with him at Harvard. Undertaking to do this story, like every other one, starts with an understanding between me and my subject about what I need to do and how much access I'd like. Then it requires work, thought, planning, and elbow grease, but a writer does not lay all that on the reader. In the written story, it just happens.

Funny Guys:
The Friars and
Robin Williams

O NE OF THE greatest feats a reporter can pull off is finding
humor in a story while delivering the facts. My greatest
satisfaction in my work is being told by my peers that I
have made them laugh. That always sends me flying. Writing about
standup comics puts an extra demand on the reporter: the story
must be funny. It should never be "funny" just because the subject
is supposed to be "funny."

The Friars Club annual "Roast" of a prominent fellow Friar
features a bunch of joke-obsessed comics, competing with each
other to be outrageous and funny. As a reporter covering this event,
it wasn't enough for me to sit there, to listen, and to repeat the
jokes. I felt I had to seek out the participants, including the roastee,
in advance of the event so that I could set the scene for what would
happen. The various comedians' philosophies about how to get

laughs was my way of moving my story beyond the jokes and making it funny.

Here's the story, from The Talk of the Town, in 1999.

When the New York Friars Club, the ninety-five-year-old stronghold for show-biz folks, began planning its annual roast, which took place on October 1st at The New York Hilton, the organizers asked Friar Jeffrey Ross, a thirty-three-year-old standup comic, to help out. This year's honoree was to be the actor Jerry Stiller, and the roastmaster the actor Jason Alexander. Ross, a friendly man with bulging, clownlike cheeks, is the Friar responsible for recruiting dozens of other young comics, such as Janeane Garofalo and Drew Carey, into the Friars. He immediately started making up jokes to offer to the roasters, and he sought out veteran roasters for suggestions.

Shortly before the roast, when the comedian Buddy Hackett was in town, Ross met him at the Friars Club for lunch. Hackett, wearing a bright red blazer and tan slacks, was in a good mood. His new television show, *Action*, had just been picked up for thirteen weeks.

"I call it a dramedy," the senior comic proclaimed, in the familiar, heavily enunciated Buddy Hackett syllables. "I'm da uncle-chauffeur-bodyguard of da film producer, played by Jay Mohr. To make my character, I gotta be honest, true to myself. It all comes from in *me*. Dat's da key. Don't let anybody stop you, in whatever you're gonna do in comedy or in roasting, from making it out of your own self."

"Buddy is very serious about the art of standup," Ross said solemnly.

"Yeah, it's our creative art," Hackett said. "A real art."

He went on: "F'rinstance, in 1945, when I started, as Butch Hacker, at the Pink Elephant in Coney island for ten dollars a night, I would talk about my mother. I'd say, 'My mother caught me in bed with a girl, and she said, 'Soon you'll be smoking.'"

Jeffrey Ross said, "In my act last night, I said, 'The first time my girl saw me naked, she said, "Is everything a joke with you?" It killed.'"

"Be unafraid and make it honest, from inside yourself," Buddy Hackett said. "It's our art."

Ross said, "At the L.A. Friars Club the other day, Milton Berle told me about the old roasts. He was the roastmaster when the Friars roasted Lucille Ball in 1961, twenty-six years before they even allowed women to join. Uncle Miltie came out and said, 'Because we are honoring a lady, tonight you will not hear any dirty words, no four-letter words, but it is still quite an honor to be asked to serve as roastmaster for the great comedian and actress Lucille Testicle.' When Uncle Miltie was a roastmaster, he told me, he would try to say 'cunt' in the first three minutes. That way, he knew the gates were open and tradition would be upheld."

"Yeah," Buddy Hackett said. "But the roast ended many years ago. The day the critics from *Variety* were invited to see the roast, it killed it. What we were doing in those days, we were doing for ourselves. It was private. It was so private they made the waiters leave the room. It was only for us alone. Now it's FUBAR— Fucked Up Beyond All Recognition."

"Well, it'll be edited for television, two and a half hours into one," Ross said. "For Comedy Central."

"Yeah, all two million outsiders," Hackett said.

A couple of days before the roast, a sad-looking Jerry Stiller— on a two-week hiatus from working in L.A. on the sitcom *King of Queens*—and his playwright wife and longtime acting partner, Anne Meara, met Jeffrey Ross for lunch on the Upper West Side. (The Stillers' children, Ben, an actor-director-writer, and Amy, a comedian, were both due to turn up on R Day.) Meara is not a Friar.

"They're a bunch of pottymouths getting together," Meara said. "Every other word is 'fuck' or 'cock.'"

"It's not my style," Stiller said, worried. "I have trouble with those words. In a restaurant I always order *chest* of chicken."

Jeffrey Ross looked stricken. "It's the World Series of comedy," he said. "It will be fun."

"Yeah. Let's cling to that," Meara said. "Jerry's up all night worrying about something to say."

"Now I know why Jacob sacrificed Isaac," Stiller said.
Jeffrey Ross gave a yelp of joy, and laughed. "That's a good one."
"It was *Abraham* sacrificed Isaac," Meara said dryly.

Stiller took from his coat pocket a limp piece of paper with blurred scrawls all over it. "I wrote this down in the bathtub. It fell in the water," he said. "Maybe I'll say this, if they say stuff about my having sex: 'This pithecanthropus is still erectus.'" He gave Ross a hopeful look. Ross laughed. Stiller read on: "The only time I take Viagra is for an encore." Ross laughed again.

Meara gave a soft sigh.

"What I'd really like to do is tell my story about Groucho Marx," Stiller said, with a questioning look at Ross, who gave him an encouraging laugh in advance. "When I was about eight, during the Depression, my father was an unemployed cab driver. He came home discouraged one afternoon and took me out to the movies. We saw *A Night at the Opera*. I laughed so much, I cried. We came home. My mother said, 'No food on the table and you take him to the movies?' Years later, in Hollywood, Groucho invited Anne and me to dinner at his house. He asked us how long we'd been married."

Meara, delighted, took up the anecdote. "We told him twenty years! And Groucho said, 'Why?'"

"Then Groucho showed us, on sixteen millimeter, *A Night at the Opera*," Stiller continued. "So I told him the story of how, in Brooklyn, as a kid, I first saw *A Night at the Opera*."

"'Which theatre?' Groucho asked me."

"'The Follies,' I told him."

"'No,' Groucho said. 'It was the R.K.O. Bushwick.'"

Jeffrey Ross grinned. "Good story. But isn't it kind of long? You shouldn't feel pressured to perform," he counselled. "When they give you the award, just thank the Friars and Jason Alexander, and stay true to yourself."

Stiller consulted his damp page again. "How about this, at the end?" he said, and read, "I'm delighted to be honored by the Friars tonight. I'm not a standup comedian. I'm just a simple Mexican-American, trying to make it in America."

"That's a good one! We got something," Ross said. . . .

When the roast got under way, Jerry Stiller, looking lost and puzzled, was ensconced in an armchair on the dais. The three other Stillers sat to his left. The show went on. Freddie Roman, the Dean of the Friars, told the crowd, "Today we honor Jerry Stiller. Why Jerry Stiller? Simple, we're running out of young Jews." He also said, "Jerry and I have a lot in common—he's been on Broadway, I've been on Broadway, he's been on Anne Meara, I've been on . . ." To Ben Stiller, he said, "Ben, your father *is* very proud of you. In fact, he's downright jealous. *He* wants to star in movies. *He* wants to win Emmy Awards. *He* wants to come on Cameron Diaz's head."

It turned out that none of the roasters used the words "cunt," "motherfucker," or "cocksucker" in talking about Stiller. After Jeffrey Ross and the Stiller family and a few others got up and did their bits, it was time for Stiller to accept the Roast Award, a crystal statuette of a friar. Somewhat faintly, he told his pithecanthropus-is-still-erectus joke. He wound up with the line about being a "simple Mexican-American trying to make it in America." He did not tell his Groucho story.

Buddy Hackett didn't get to the roast. He had to stay in California to work on his television show.

Humor is often what makes my stories into stories. It's the essential ingredient, for me. It's easy to find the humor in just about any subject, including humor itself, as the story above demonstrates. There is always truth in humor. If there's a point to be made by the writer in a story, it can be made with facts and with quotes that have humor. What's more, it's humor that drives a story, making it believable. It's the key to originality and power in reporting. I couldn't live, let alone work, without laughing.

Sixteen years ago, I wrote a Talk story about Robin Williams, who liked—and today, even with all his acting in movies, still likes—working out, in unannounced appearances, in small late-night comedy clubs. He has been unique in comedy, unlike a Jerry Seinfeld or a Chevy Chase, for example, who used their own personalities for

their comic roots; Williams seemed to use the universe. ("Poet in the realm of mirth; greatest comic on the earth"—is part of a little verse Bill Shawn once made up for him on the occasion of his fortieth birthday.) My story was about accompanying him and a few friends, including an alert assistant, Marsha Garces, in visits to clubs like Catch a Rising Star, where he would try out his comic ideas. People in his audiences would often call out subjects they had heard him do before, and these would set him off hilariously on a manic scale. He would go from being a gangster or a drunk to Gorbachev or then President Reagan. He went from being Imelda Marcos to Louis Farrakhan and on to a small child watching his father leave and crying at a window and then turning away from the window, tearless, and saying "Let's put on that Fisher-Price music and get crazy." (His son Zachary was three at the time.) His friend Marsha stayed on the sidelines unobtrusively, laughing at his comedy. He would come off stage looking refreshed and happy.

"I like going to the clubs, because it peels away all pretensions," he told me. "About a week ago, I went to the Comedy Store, in Los Angeles. I was talking about bizarre things. I got going doing this whole thing about travelling at the speed of light, losing your luggage beforehand, doing Albert Einstein as Mr. Rogers, improvising. It was fun. It was like running in an open field."

One night, at a club called the Improvisation, he started out as an Oscar Winner, sanctimoniously:

"Thank you for your kindness. Your words are so meaningful." Then he was South Africa's Botha, and after that he became the state of Michigan and the Statue of Liberty and Frank Sinatra and Jewish hunters ("Let's go out to the country and see if anything died") and Lee Iacocca and Henry Kissinger and El Al Airlines.

After a while, someone in the audience called out "Dr. Ruth!"

"Dr. Rufe?" Williams asked, having obviously misheard the name. Then he got it, and immediately used the error to take off as a black woman preacher giving sex advice in a scolding vein. "Get yoh act together, now," he said. "Yoh look lahk a Ken doll. Don' yoh look at me wid dose mascara eyes goin' flip-flap. Get on dat highway and make sure de bridge is open." He kept it going for a good fifteen minutes. The audience was beside itself. At the end,

Williams came off looking exhilarated and told me that one had been brand new—a breakthrough. He looked as though he had been running in an open field.

In 1993, a few weeks after Bill Shawn died, I was in San Francisco with my son, Erik. By then, Marsha Garces was married to Robin; they lived in San Francisco with their two small children, Zelda and Cody, in addition to Zachary, who was now ten; they were setting out to make a new movie, *Mrs. Doubtfire*, starring Robin and for which Marsha worked with Robin as a co-producer. They invited Erik and me to watch them make their movie.

Wherever I go, and whatever I do, I automatically find myself looking at possibilities for a story. This time was no different. I immediately thought it would make an interesting story to see the change, if any, in the Williamses' relationship with each other and in their personalities, as they evolved into their new roles. I didn't know what I would find. I had no conflict-of-interest problem, because I was clearly writing about them as friends, and they were opening their production to me. I couldn't help but wonder if Robin still found the same kind of freedom and joy in his acting that he had found in the comedy clubs. And it was in that respect that the two stories resonate together. The title of my Profile was "Mr. and Mrs. Williams." Robin had found a real life in this new partnership, and it was interesting to me to see that the real life had actually brought new aspects to his comedy.

From the Profile:

> Mrs. Williams's mettle as a producer was tested early on when she and Mr. Williams and [the director] Chris Columbus were urged to change the film's ending. "Everybody—our managers, our agents, people at the studio—said that the audience would want Daniel and Miranda to get back together, or, at least, to leave their situation up in the air," she said. She paused for a beat, then added quickly and with startling passion, "When two people are harmful and wrong for each other, they do not belong together."
>
> "The Norman Rockwell family doesn't exist," Mr. Williams said, even more strongly. "It's a myth." And Chris Columbus elaborated: "Ninety percent of parents who separate don't get

back together again. We don't want our audience to see a dishon-
est film. We didn't set out to make *The Parent Trap*. We're going
to protect *Mrs. Doubtfire*. We're keeping it honest."

. . . Taking a look at some of what Marsha Williams has done
as a producer involved a kind of mind-boggling course in micro-
management. "Actually, what I'm doing is, to a great extent, what
I've been doing with Robin for several years," she said. "I've been
reading scripts for him, looking into possible projects, and giving
him my opinions about all of it when he asks me. He doesn't
always agree with me, and there have been movies that he
embarked on without paying any attention to what I thought, but
I've supported him in whatever decisions he's made."

"She waded right into it," Robin Williams said to me with a
kind of calm amazement. "She likes the challenge of producing.
My name is on *Mrs. Doubtfire* as producer, and we talk to each
other about everything, but she does most of the work, and all
that talking to other people. She has the patience to discuss a
problem for hours and hours. I have to be busy preparing for my
part. Anyway, I tend to be direct. I'll just say 'That sucks!'"

The transformation of Robin Williams from the thirtyish
Daniel into the sixtyish Mrs. Doubtfire was a work of magic. Of
the seventy days scheduled for filming, forty-one called for that
transformation. It took four and a half hours to achieve, begin-
ning at five A.M., so that Williams would be ready at nine-thirty
for the first shot of the day. At my first glimpse of "her," on that
preproduction Saturday, I didn't know, let alone believe, that it
had actually happened until the actor greeted me, albeit in his
housekeeper's voice, by name. Ten weeks later, I found myself still
staring at "her" and trying to remember Robin Williams's face.

. . . One day during the filming of a scene that had Mrs. Doubtfire
shopping in a grocery store—a location at the corner of Colum-
bus and Vallejo Streets, just between North Beach and China-
town, and near the Hungry I, one of the night clubs in which
Williams used to appear—he emerged in full costume between
takes and headed on foot toward North Beach. People on the
street paid no attention to "her." "I kind of like to wander around
this way," he told me. "To see what it's like."

After a serious, emotionally draining scene, Williams would take a breath, and quickly erupt into standup comedy. "You can have the upstairs!" he suddenly yelled, in a heavy Jewish accent— after a scene that called for a heavily emotional argument with his movie wife, Miranda. "I'll take the downstairs! You can't have the whole house! I'll bring witnesses!"

Ever since the preproduction of *Mrs. Doubtfire*, Mrs. Williams had been warning her husband about how physically taxing the role would be. To keep him in shape, she enlisted the help of a trainer. She enlisted everybody in the family in running or roller-blading or biking in the city's parks or along the marina, often with a child on the back of each parent, and with the family dog galumphing behind.

The ending to the Profile brings together the elements of the comic artist doing what he needs to do for his freedom, and his watchful assistant, now half of a couple, still carefully preserving what he feels to be the "running in an open field."

Late one night, during a break between shots, I sat with Mr. and Mrs. Williams in his trailer, which was parked near the stage. His *Mrs. Doubtfire* bodysuit and dress and shoes were off for a few minutes. His wig and his latex face were on. Wearing a sleeveless plaid flannel vest and plaid flannel shorts, for a brief, cooling respite, he held a Powerbook computer on his lap and was engrossed in playing a game. A few minutes later, he went to the back of the trailer to get dressed again as Mrs. Doubtfire. He was halfway through the filming of the movie. Eighty miles of film was now waiting for editing. There had been a grueling stretch of fifteen- or eighteen-hour days, during which Mrs. Williams worked the same hours as her husband.

I asked her why they had wanted to form their own production company.

"To have the control over when and where we were going to shoot," she replied promptly. "More than anything else, in order to protect Robin."

SATURDAY NIGHT LORNE

N 1988, ON ASSIGNMENT from *Interview* magazine, I wrote a
piece about Lorne Michaels, the originator and producer of
television's now twenty-seven-year-old *Saturday Night Live.*
I first met Michaels in 1975, the year he started SNL. Bill Shawn
and I happened to see the initial shows together, and he was so
enthusiastic about what he saw—in particular, Show Number 2,
with Paul Simon as the host—that he couldn't stop talking and
laughing about this television phenomenon. He even compared
it—in what was, for him, an historic stance—to *The New Yorker*—
"At least, in what they're striving for," he said, amending this com-
parison. At his urging, I quickly visited SNL at Rockefeller Plaza's
NBC offices. It took me an unprecedented dozen years before I was
able to formulate an actual sense of how to do the story.

By the time I got around to writing the piece, Lorne Michaels
had become a friend. By then, too, as in all good friendships, we
knew a lot about each other. He and his second wife, Susan
Forristal, were in my life with Bill Shawn; we shared cheerful non-
working meals. When Bill Shawn was fired from his job at *The
New Yorker,* Michaels immediately offered him the use of his own

large office at his nineteenth-floor Broadway Video headquarters in the Brill Building, on Broadway; we shared good times in Amagansett, Long Island; Michaels and Susan came to see the St. Bernard's School production of *The Boy Friend,* with my son Erik in the cast.

In 1987, Erik and I joined Lorne's close associate, Cristina McGinnis, in attending Lorne's American citizenship ceremony. (He was born in Canada.) I was around during some of Michaels's happy experiences including his re-marriage to his colleague, Alice Barry, and his becoming a father.

If it took me more than a dozen years to write the story about Lorne Michaels, I would have to attribute the reason to the fact that I was just too busy having a good time with my subject to settle down and write. Also, that period of time happened to coincide with my son's elementary school years, and, although I managed to do some writing, I wasn't putting it at the top of my agenda. My son, however—along with all of his friends and classmates—had SNL at the top of *his* agenda, and I was kept busy, during those years, taking all of them to watch the making of the shows.

From the *Interview* story:

Lorne David Michaels, the 43-year-old creator and producer of television's thirteen-year-old *Saturday Night Live,* has brought his show to tens of millions of followers on a single 11:30 P.M. to 1 A.M. time slot, with comedy of a purpose, spirit, tone, and taste that are directly traceable to Michaels alone. This feat is especially impressive when one remembers that television is a business that by its very nature tries to cast a net that will snag a hundred million or so eligible viewers. In 1972, Michaels knew that he wanted to produce a comedy-variety show, theatrical, and with a live audience, for television. He invented *Saturday Night Live* in the spring of 1975. By early that summer, he had full permission from corporate executives at NBC, the official owners of the show, to put what he wanted on television without giving them so much as a peek, not to mention a pilot, at what they would hear and see on the air. By mid-October, he had taken possession of NBC's late-

weekend minutes with Show One to express—through his singu-
lar selection and development of comic acting and comic writing
talents (regular and guest)—what interested *him* and what *he* felt
was funny. "I wanted to do a comedy show reflecting life as I
seemed to be living it, and there didn't seem to be anything like
that on television," he once said to me. "I felt it was my job to cre-
ate the context in which comedy would bloom." A single show in
1988, still presented in its initial structure, and with Michaels at
the helm as executive producer, was employing a staff of 360 peo-
ple—writers, actors, musicians, announcers, directors, stagehands,
scenic artists, costume designers, makeup artists, electricians, prop
hands, teamsters, engineers, cue-card makers, photographers,
security forces, and a production staff—and its comedy (having
once and for all set to rest the old theatrical saying that "Satire is
what closes on Saturday night") was still blooming in the context
Michaels created. Michaels seems to enjoy making that context
sound easy. "The person who picks the people is the person who
controls the show," he says. "I enjoy putting a team together."

Michaels manages to operate in his context against a back-
ground peopled, of course, with constantly changing guards he
has nothing to do with picking: echelons of television executives,
bankers, lawyers, agents, managers, censors, salespeople, and the
all-important advertisers. To enter *their* context, even for a few
moments, is to nearly drown in their peculiar jargon: with them,
you speak of "feed-back," and "prime demographics"; you are
"proud of our industry," and "you give a show another shot"; and
"you can be successful with the right property"; and "you can't bat
a hundred"; and "you stick with old forms." You are "not afraid to
try something different," but "you tend to clone." You have reruns
"as a generic category." You also "send a message to the Hollywood
community to lower costs." With a nice indifference to the correct
meaning of the word "hopefully," you "hopefully shake doldrums,"
and you "hopefully stop viewership erosions," and you "hopefully
lead in with a show like *Cheers*." You are preoccupied with national
ratings—the Top Fifteen Television Shows of the Week, as rated
by A.C. Nielsen—or the percentage of the nation's 88.6 million
TV homes tuned to a given show. All of life is compared to the

31.4 ratings and the 48 share of the number-one-rated *The Cosby Show* (NBC) or the 25.9 ratings and the 39 share of *Cheers* (also NBC). . . . Television Executive Talk wraps up the significance of the numbers with the punch lines: "If you lose the ratings for one hour, you lose that night. If you lose one night, you lose the week. If you lose three weeks, you lose your job."

In the beginning, before *Saturday Night Live* was accepted among network executives as a success, Michaels found it virtually impossible to make what he was trying to do understood. He can explain things to today's executives easily. "The old network business-affairs people tended to think in terms of productivity: six writers at eleven minutes each comes to sixty-six minutes. One old-time executive put it to me succinctly. He said, 'Our job is to lie, cheat, and steal. Your job is to put on shows.' It took me years to learn how they thought. I used to think it was about making money. It wasn't. It was about preserving their jobs."

. . . The reason for the network's support of Michaels—support that for the most part has continued unabated to the present day—was an ordinary one: in the first year, the price of a 30-second commercial started beggingly at $7,500. By the end of the season, in May, 1976, the price had gone up to $60,000. . . . With his own profits from the show, Michaels, in 1979, set up Broadway Video, a company with post-production facilities. . . . From the start, *Saturday Night Live* has been pitched—demographics or no demographics—to a higher level of sophistication than any other comedy on American network television. It was obvious that Michaels did not worry about whether his show was too sophisticated or not. He just went ahead and did—and encouraged his writers and actors to do—what was funny to them. . . , thus giving themselves the maximum freedom. If their humor went over the heads of a few million people here or there, that was all right, because there were dozens and dozens of comedy bits that might be understood by these same people.

Because there is no definition of what is "funny," the key to *Saturday Night Live* was—and still is—what appeals to Michaels, to his own taste. "The show is by and for the television generation. It's the television equivalent of rock music," Michaels says,

explaining his taste. He has made no secret of his affection for that generation or of the fact that he feels, passionately, that it is his. And what is rock music? "It's all about the sound and the way it makes you feel," Michaels says. By extension, *Saturday Night Live* is all about comedy and the way *it* makes you feel.

"At the start, when I was asked by NBC what kind of show I wanted, I had definite answers," Michaels told me one recent Saturday afternoon in his ninth-floor office overlooking Studio 8H, on the floor below, where the show's participants were making things ready. His executive producing effects were close at hand—a television set with a closed-circuit screen revealing the activities on the floor below; a large plate of carrots and celery sticks, cauliflower, and cherry tomatoes, and a large bucket of popcorn, freshly popped; a bulletin board, this one of Michaels' recent fan mail (. . . From Philadelphia, Pennsylvania: "I love your sketch promoting pork to those 'who are healthy enough to eat it,' but I am concerned about the chickens in cages used in the chicken sketch. I hope these are not permanent cages, because they are extremely small. The chickens cannot stand up fully erect, nor can they spread their wings.")

In thirteen years, Michaels' hair has gone from dark brown to dark gray. Otherwise, he looks pretty much the same: boyishly handsome, with clean-cut features and large brown, trusting eyes, and outwardly affable and controlled, his seeming vagueness barely disguising the fact that he is sharply observant and alert, and openly signalling to one and all his hunger for laughter and laughs. . . . "The same things that interested me had interested me for a long time—comedy, politics, music, and films. I wanted the commitment for at least 17 shows without a pilot, and I wanted to find the show on the air," Michaels said that Saturday afternoon, recalling the start of his adventures in Studio 8H. "I wanted what we got and still have: a format and a shape for the show allowing for tremendous variety, with a new host every week to center the show and a new musical guest. It was so natural for me. Rock and roll was the dominant mood. The show was what everything in my life—as a comedy writer and producer—had been leading up to. What we did, and what I was incredibly serious about doing,

was to establish that in comedy it was and still is considered per-
fectly proper to question the official version of everything.

"We have always played to a *movie* and a *book* audience and
not to the audience of television. The reason we went on and
stayed on is that we were not tested. If the show had been tested,
it wouldn't have gone on. ABC stayed away from *Monty Python*
because it tested negatively. People don't like new things right
away. *Saturday Night Live* was way ahead of its time in television,
but we didn't know it for a year and a half. We just did it. The
business lesson in it is to relax with it. There's a natural time to
things. The secret is to act spontaneously, to be as loose as you can
be. We were free to be innovative, topical, satirical, irreverent,
risky, funny, and no competition for Johnny Carson. For Show
One, the NBC network executives suggested Bob Hope as guest
host and the United States Marine Marching band as musical
guest, but they quickly learned that I was thinking more along the
lines of Richard Pryor and Steve Martin, and of Mick Jagger and
Paul Simon. Our humor was not Bob Hope, and it was not Carol
Burnett, either. It was our own."

Creating the humor was a repertory group doing comedy
sketches—The Not Ready for Prime Time Players—along with a
band, the guest host, and the musical guest, all with the unprece-
dented freedom to experiment on the air. Studio 8H, where
Toscanini had given his legendary concerts, was redesigned, fol-
lowing Michaels' specifications, by a theatre designer, Eugene
Lee, who still designs, now together with Leo Yoshimura, for the
show. Michaels wanted, and got, balcony-seating space for most
of the audience, as well as swivel seats on the floor, amid the
mobile cranes bearing several cameras and operators and all the
other technological accouterments. There were eight separate
staging areas and raised stages.

"I love the technology of live television," Michaels told me,
glancing out the glass sliding door to the technological frenzy
below. "I even like just watching a crane move. The technology
meshing with the live comedy is a miracle. Five cameras, all mov-
ing around on the same floor. I wanted to be able to combine tele-
vision technique and theatre technique. I wanted the technology

to serve the show rather than the other way around. With the live show, there's electricity. . . .

"This was all about doing the show continuously, in real time, in front of that live audience. I didn't want laugh tracks. The intensity of the show is so great, I can never remember the previous show. But I enjoy working under the pressure to put on a show live. . . ."

As we looked down at the working cast and crew, Michaels continued, "Comedy is a humanizing force, and it's too important to be left to the professionals. I wanted people who didn't know what couldn't be done, and that's the kind of talent I still look for. I believe in getting the best people I can find and giving them the free environment to work in. *Saturday Night Live* for me is an energy center, a focal point for a comedy style to emerge and reemerge. Someone once said, in talking about Lenny Bruce, that comedians are radical conservatives. People who do satire can't have allegiance to any form of orthodoxy. Anybody who is out of control or is showing off a bit is fair game for satire. It's a safety valve for the culture.

"The major criteria lie in what makes you laugh. In your personal life, deliberate unkindness, however, is the greatest sin. You don't blow somebody else's life pretenses unless they encroach on your own life. . . . In working with talented, volatile, sensitive people, it's one thing to criticize their work but another to criticize *them*. When you say personal things, you can't take back the words; that's a luxury you have only as a child. In a personal relationship, when you tear the fabric, it can't be restored. I have three rules I go by: one, never work with anyone you wouldn't have dinner with, because it's in the nature of show business to have a lot of meals; two, never go to work on a show if you wouldn't watch it; three, the act of a pro is to make it look easy. Fred Astaire doesn't grunt when he dances to let you know how hard it is. If you're good at it, you leave no fingerprints."

TRUFFAUT AND FELLINI

I CONSTANTLY LEARN more and more about reporting from the work of filmmakers. I admire so many of them, and I gratefully absorb countless visual ideas from every new movie I see. While reporting a story, I find myself automatically translating what I see and hear into film-like scenes. So I naturally have been drawn to writing pieces about the directors who were of interest to me. Besides seeing their movies, I've had the privilege of watching them in action, of being around in their relationships with their colleagues and friends, of talking to them about their lives, of listening to them talk about their work. They have never failed to interest me. They invariably inspire me to come up with fresh ideas about my own work.

In 1960, I wrote my first story about the twenty-eight-year-old François Truffaut, in connection with the New York opening of his first film *The 400 Blows*. After that, I wrote a story about him when he returned to New York—in 1964, 1970, 1973, and 1976. He, too, became a good friend. In 1978, in Paris, where he was making his film *L'Amour en Fuite (Love on the Run),* he cast me and my twelve-year-old son Erik in a film—as passengers on a train. My writing about Truffaut over a period of sixteen years—in

The Talk of the Town—was helped by our friendship; it made him accessible, and, from the start, it helped make him trusting.

1960:

. . . Earnest, good-humored, slightly built, and boyish-looking, M. Truffaut told us that he is known in Paris as *"le petit Truffaut."* This is his first visit to America. His wife, who stayed home to take care of their year-old baby, has often visited this country and could have given him plenty of advice on what to see and do but took pains not to, knowing, said *le petit,* that with him everything sooner or later boils down to films.

We noticed that M. Truffaut, otherwise smartly turned out, was wearing brown felt bedroom slippers, and he explained that his feet hurt. "Not from sightseeing, but because my shoes don't fit," he said. "They never fit. I hate to go shopping, and so become impatient and buy the first pair of shoes I try on. When I was a boy, my feet always hurt; I was a weakling in the eyes of my parents, who liked hiking and sent me to live with my grandmother until I was eight. I was always in revolt against adults, and I was always hungry. Today, as it happens, I'm not hungry; I had an excellent lunch at Le Pavillon. It was quite a change for me, because in Paris I usually eat at Manny's Bar, an American snack bar on the Rue Washington, where there are hamburgers and a pianist who plays jazz and songs by Jean Constantin, who composed the music for *The 400 Blows.* A song from the film— 'Comment Voulez-Vous?'—is going to be recorded in this country by Frank Sinatra, which gives Constantin much pleasure."

. . . It's no wonder that *The 400 Blows* is about children, for its maker has long been preoccupied with them. "Even as a child, I loved children," he said. "I have very strong ideas about the world they inhabit. Morally, the child is like a wolf—outside society. In the early life of a child, there is no notion of accident—merely of *délits*—while in the world of the adult everything is allowed. From the age of eleven until now, I've seen three thousand films. Of the lot, there have been only four I have liked that were about children: *Zéro de Conduite,* which was directed by Jean Vigo, a

Frenchman who dies at the ridiculous age of twenty-nine, and
who has had the greatest influence on my work; the 1931 Russian
film *The Road to Life;* Rossellini's *Germany Year Zero;* and Engel's
Little Fugitive. In all the others, the children are betrayed. What
is important about a film that deals with a child is the child him-
self. Why should children be shown on the same level as anybody
else or anything else, whether it is a white mane or as red balloon?

"It is not necessary to add ideas or sugary sentiment to what
the child is. Moreover, in a film about children it is not necessary
to condemn the adults. On the contrary, since the public is always
on the children's side, it becomes necessary to find the maximum
excuse for the adults' conduct. Another thought. Most films about
children make the child frivolous and the adult serious. Quite
the other way around! In a film, when parents give a present to
a child, the parents are shown acting solemn and the child over-
joyed, but in real life the child is nearly always disappointed with
the present and looks angry, and the parents take it away and
cheerfully start playing with it. You have to be extremely tough
in making a film about children, yet I admit that for me it's easier
to make a film about a child than about an adult, as it would be
easier to make a film about a wild animal than about a tame one.
It's my belief, by the way, that an actor is never so great as when
he reminds you of an animal—falling like a cat, lying like a dog,
moving like a fox."

1964:

. . . Truffaut, now thirty-two years old, was here for a few days for
the opening of his new film, *The Soft Skin.* . . . He still speaks no
English, and, as before, his American friend and colleague Mrs.
Helen Scott, who did the English subtitles for *The Soft Skin,*
served smoothly and unobtrusively as his English voice. He
quickly brought us up to date on the major developments in his
life: he now has two daughters, aged four and six, whom he has
trained to cry out "Vive Papa!" as soon as he comes home; he still
has his own film company, Carosse, in Paris; he has made three
films besides *The Soft Skin* since we first saw him—*Shoot the Piano*

Player, Jules and Jim, and a half-hour untitled movie that was part
of an international five-parter called *Love at Twenty,* . . . and, in
collaboration with Mrs. Scott, he has been writing a book about
Alfred Hitchcock.

 ". . . I have long been sure that he is the greatest director of
films in the world . . . and with every passing day I am surer than
ever. Each week for the past few years, I have been going to see
at least two of his pictures. *Vertigo* I see at least every two months.
When I undertook to write the book, I went to the Cinéma-
thèque in Brussels—the best archives for Hitchcock—to see all
his pictures over again. The more I see of Hitchcock's pictures,
the less desire I have to see pictures other than his. . . . In the
summer of 1962, I wrote a letter to Hitchcock, which Helen
translated into English, and I told him I wanted to write the
book. I suggested a series of interviews over a period of eight
days. He agreed. On August 13th, Hitchcock's birthday, Helen
and I arrived in Hollywood. We stayed at the Beverly Hills Hotel.
Every day, Hitchcock would come and pick us up at eight in the
morning and take us to his office at Universal City Studios, and
we would sit in his office and talk until six at night. We spoke to
him with microphones around our necks, and a sound engineer
stationed in the next room recorded what was said. We kept
the microphones on even during meals. Every day we ate with
Hitchcock, and every day we ate what he ate—steak, fried pota-
toes, and ice cream. . . . In the evening, at the hotel, Helen and I
sat up until midnight and talked about Hitchcock. Many people
called up and invited me to come to parties and to meet producers
and to see actresses and to see studios. Many columnists wanted
to interview me. But I didn't want to do any of this. Out of respect
to Hitchcock, I didn't want to see anybody else. . . . I gave instruc-
tions to Helen never to mention my pictures to him, and he did
not bring them up. . . .

 "I think Hitchcock was happy that I knew his pictures so well.
He had never before had an opportunity to speak of himself and
his work in forty years—since he began making pictures. . . .
From the third day on, his sensitivity emerged. He became self-

critical. He described scenes in which he thought he had done
something that was foolish or pretentious or careless. I was struck
by the contrast between the public man, so sure of himself, so
cynical, and what seemed to me to be a very vulnerable man, very
emotional. And I learned what I needed to know—all the things
I had sensed but had never clearly formulated. For instance, the
principle, extremely important, that an emotion must be created
on the screen and then must be sustained—on the technical level
as well as on the scenario level. Many can create an emotion on
the screen, but very few know how to sustain it. It is so important
to sustain it, even after the character eliciting the emotion leaves
the room, goes off the screen. There is so much to learn from
Hitchcock—how to keep the camera on the character you want
the audience to be interested in, and not cut, even when the
character walks all the way across a room. That is just one small
example of what one learns from Hitchcock."

1970:

. . . At thirty-eight, he still looked just about the same, except
for a bit more fullness in his face. He had seen eight hundred
and fifty movies since our second talk, and he had made six—
*Fahrenheit 451, The Bride Wore Black, Stolen Kisses, Mississippi
Mermaid, Bed and Board,* and *The Wild Child.*

"How about the past ten years?" we asked him. "Have they
gone the way you wanted them to?"

He took a good half minute to reflect before he answered, "I
think they have," he said finally. "Except, sadly, for the death of
several people. Actors. Françoise Dorleac, the star of *The Soft
Skin,* and Nicole Berger, who played the pianist's wife in *Shoot
the Piano Player,* and Albert Rémy, who played the father in *The
400 Blows.* Also, Guy Decomble, who played the teacher in *The
400 Blows,* and Catherine Lutz, who played the lady detective in
Stolen Kisses. And there were writers. William Irish, who wrote
The Bride Wore Black, and David Goodis, the author *of Shoot the
Piano Player.* Several of them died in car accidents. And there
were filmmakers whom I didn't know but loved a great deal.

Jacques Becker. Jean Cocteau. . . . It's just that people of my age
seem to have less connection with death, less connection with
older people. So we seem to react strongly. For example, I started
to correspond with Henri-Pierre Roché, the author of the book
Jules and Jim on which I based my film, when he was seventy-
three. Then I became a filmmaker, but I kept delaying making
the film. Roché kept sending me letters telling me it was a very
urgent matter to make this film. I sent him a picture of Jeanne
Moreau and wrote to him that I thought she should be the girl
in the film. He answered, 'Bring her to me quickly.' But he died
before he could meet her. And I am angry with myself that I
didn't make the film during his lifetime. One often feels guilty
toward the dead, if only because they perhaps sent a letter to
which you didn't reply."

Truffaut looked a little sad. Then he smiled. "There's a scene
I would like to have in a film. About an elderly and prominent
man. A young man comes to see him, to get something from him,
to learn how to achieve prominence and success. The old man has
facing him this young man—virile, healthy, ambitious. All the
old man tells him is 'Play golf. Sleep eight hours a night. Do
not smoke. Do not eat too much. Be sure not to put on weight.'
Truffaut laughed out loud. "I have always wanted to do this scene
in a picture," he said. "I will have to do a picture that will let me
do this scene.". . .

"Any plans for movies you're going to make?" we asked.

"Vaguely, I'd like to make a film about life in France during the
Occupation," he replied. "It would not be concerned with the
Germans, or with the Resistance—it would be about the many
Frenchmen who simply waited until it was over. During the war,
France was compelled to be completely French."

"What about the romantic notion of all those French under-
ground fighters?" we asked. "All those wonderful people in the
Resistance?"

Truffaut gave a big laugh. "One out of thousands was like
that," he said. "Many of the others were sitting on their bicycles
going after the potatoes. In my neighborhood, for instance—
Pigalle—if German soldiers asked how to get to the Folies-

Bergère, people *might* direct them the wrong way. It was that
kind of Resistance." He gave another laugh.
 "Any other ideas for new movies?" we asked.
 "Yes," Truffaut said. "I would like to make a film about the
making of a film. One film that is important for all filmmakers is
Fellini's *8½*. There is great truth in it. But it deals with what hap-
pened *before* the shooting. It would show a scene badly played,
the rushes, the cutting—things like that."

1973:

 . . . Well, Truffaut did exactly what he said he wanted to do. *Day
for Night* was shown at the opening of the current New York Film
Festival, and it got a great reception from critics, audience, and
fellow-filmmakers. . . . He is getting more and more lovable with
age (by the time he's eighty, he'll probably be a cross between Mr.
Chips and Jean Gabin) and he is more and more in love with
movies and moviemakers. He's gradually getting heavier around
the midriff, but he still manages to look boyish. He says his hair
gets grayer after each film he makes. He still smokes Celtique
Caporals, though some of his friends have tried to convince him
that smoking shortens one's life. . . . He keeps getting invitations
from colleges and universities to visit them—to talk or not to
talk—but so far he has managed to stay away, except from Har-
vard. Their interest in movies is fine, he thinks, but intellectuality
about movies without enthusiasm may not be such a good thing.
(This opinion was given very deferentially and kindly.)
 The big step forward in his life recently, Truffaut told us, was a
concentrated attempt to learn to speak and to read English. . . . We
will give you some of Truffaut's English phonetically as we got it—
along with some French—because it sounded very pleasant.
 "Ze first English book I have read eez *Memo from David O.
Selzneek,*" Truffaut told us. "Eet eez ay great book. *Extraordinaire!* I
liked heez memo about Ingrid Bergman wiz ze explana*tion* for why
she had to change her name. He wrote in anozer memo ze ver*ee*
best name eez Ver-on-i-ca Lake, ze way eet sounds. Ze syll*a*bles.
Ver-on-i-ca Lake. *Extraordinaire!*" That's the general idea.
 Truffaut told us that he had spent six weeks in West Los

Angeles last summer for the sole purpose of taking an intensive course in English at the Michel Thomas School of Languages. He lived in a small bungalow at the Hotel Bel Air, he kept a red convertible parked out front, and most of the time he led a monk-like life: getting up early, driving to his lessons, spending five or six hours a day just with his teacher, Michel Thomas, having dinner alone in his bungalow while watching television or trying to read the *Los Angeles Times*. He had a little kitchen, with a refrigerator, in which he kept only mineral water. He would order his meals over the telephone. "Always ze same," Truffaut said. "'Weel-you-have-my-breakfast-brought-up-in-my-bungalow? I-would-like-black-coffee-and-some-toast-and-some-orange-juice-zat's-all.' And for ze deenair 'I-would-like-sirloin-steak-medium-rare-wiz-salad-Romaine-wiz-vinagrette-dressing-wiz-creamed-spinach-wiz-black-coffee-and-one-yogurt-zat's-all.'"

We'll try to give you the rest of what he told us in straight translation. "I arrived in Los Angeles two days before the Watergate hearings started. And so I started learning English with the help of the hearings on television and with the reports in the newspapers. . . . While shaving, I would fix the mirror to reflect the television screen. Before I left the bungalow for my lesson, I would hear most of the morning session of the hearings. Then, with my teacher, I would read the newspaper reports about them. Just Michel Thomas and I alone, in his small office, with three goldfish in a bowl on his desk, and, on the walls, signed photographs of the movie stars he had taught French to—Grace Kelly, Gene Kelly, Barbra Streisand.". . . Then he said in a kind of sing-song, "I was*ent* going to tell you zat I was going to buy it for you, because I did*ent* want you to know." He paused and smiled, and then added, "I learned that sentence very well, but so far I have not been able to find an occasion to use it."

Truffaut told us that the Watergate hearings were much more fascinating to him than any film. . . . As soon as he got back to his Bel-Air bungalow, he would turn on his set again and watch the hearings over his dinner. "It seemed that John Dean was a much stronger character even than Humphrey Bogart," Truffaut said.

"John Dean was Jean-Louis Trintignant. And John Dean's wife is Kim Novak—with a face that is rather animal and passive at the same time. The detective—the one who carried a coin changer on his belt, Ulasewicz—is Victor McLaglen. And Senator Ervin is Charles Laughton. What a big lesson for civilization, this democracy in action! . . . I can say very well now, 'To-ze-best-of-my-recollec*tion*-at-zis-point-in-time.' But I have no occasion to use that sentence, either."

1976:

François Truffaut's visit to the Fourteenth New York Film Festival, which opened with the showing of his nineteenth movie, *Small Change,* was also the occasion of our fifth talk with him since 1960. . . . By this time, Truffaut, at forty-four, feels like a kind of relative, so we started by picking him up at Kennedy Airport on his arrival, via T.W.A., from Paris, and bringing up to date our chart of Truffaut statistics.

General appearance: Practically the same as it was sixteen years ago. Hair a mite more iron gray. Horn-rimmed glasses worn almost constantly. Complexion showing hardly any exposure to fresh air or sunshine. Midriff with perhaps a *hint* of a paunch.

Use of the English language: Terrific . . .

Interest in clothes: His main concern is still wearing shoes that don't hurt his feet. He has them made to order. He was wearing a Francesco Smalto suit of oatmeal-colored linen, made in Italy. (Explanation, given to us with an almost wicked grin: "My Cardin period ees over. When Cardin bought a theatre and renamed eet Espace Pierre Cardin, I objected. Ver-ree pre-ten-tious. Ver-ree stupid. I would not wear Cardin to ze best of my recollec*tion* from zat point in time." And from zis point in time we will drop the accent.)

Interest in, and judgement about, food: Nil. ("T.W.A. food very good. Very good chicken.")

Watching television in France: "Our television is cultural, our films are frivolous. The opposite of television here. I do not like the color television. I have on my television set a gadget for turning off the color."

Self-appraisal compared to the way he felt ten years ago: "I feel the pressure of not having much time ahead of me when I am not pleased with my work. I have so many films in my mind to make. It becomes urgent to make progress."

Compared to self in 1960: "I was more timid. I was more worried."

Practical differences in his working life between then and now: "Lately, it has been much easier to obtain the money for the films. All they ask is 'How much does the kid want this time?'"

Freedom to make whatever he wants to make the way he wants to make it: The same as it has been all along—complete. "But I have the advantage of giving them the scripts in French, and they do not read French."

How he thinks about each new film he makes: "It is one more stone in the wall."

How much his films cost to make: *Small Change* cost about seven hundred thousand dollars, which is seven times as much as *The 400 Blows* cost, about one-twelfth of the cost of *Jaws*. About one-twentieth of the cost of *The Godfather, Part II.*

How many movies he has seen since 1973, when he told us he had seen, since he was eleven, four thousand nine hundred and fifty. Five hundred more. . . .

How he happened to get into Steven Spielberg's movie so far entitled *Close Encounters of the Third Kind* as an actor, playing the part of a French scientist, a specialist in U.F.O.'s, for which he will have to go to Benares, India, in January, and for which he has already had to go to Mobile, Alabama, and Gillette, Wyoming, where some of the movie has been shot: Spielberg telephoned him in Paris and told him he liked the way Truffaut wore an old-fashioned wristwatch and always wore a necktie. "I told Spielberg, 'I am not an actor, I can only play myself.' He said, 'Good.'

"I never asked any questions. I made it a point not to bother Spielberg. Jeanne Moreau once told me, 'On every picture, you must love everybody except the one who becomes the scapegoat.' I followed Jeanne Moreau's advice. I made Julia Phillips,

the producer, my scapegoat. Every time I find something not to my liking, I say I am sure it is the fault of Julia Phillips."

Where he goes for a vacation: Only to the Beverly Hills Hotel. He sits by the Beverly Hills Hotel pool and reads. He finds the place calm and appealingly quiet. He never goes *into* the pool. He does not swim. He does not play tennis. He does not go to the beach. He does not go to parties. He does go to visit Jean Renoir, who lives in Beverly Hills, and who recently finished writing an autobiographical novel entitled "Friends, I Have Just Become 100 Years Old," and they talk endlessly about movies and people involved with movies. And he does visit the Larry Edmunds Cinema & Theatre Bookshop, on Hollywood Boulevard. "It is the best shop for film. *Fantastique!*"

Here's another example of how a follow-up story can combine with a previous story to give fuller body, each to the other. I wrote a Profile of the Italian film director Federico Fellini, entitled "10½" published in 1965. A couple of years after his famous film 8½, with Marcello Mastroianni and Anouk Aimée, had been successfully released in the United States, I went to Italy and saw him on his home ground. He was making his film *Juliet of the Spirits*.

I had already discovered that, for me, the form of a piece grows out of the nature of reporting of facts, scenes, and quotes. I built the Fellini piece in the form of a screenplay. I was driven around Rome by Fellini in his black Mercedes; I accompanied him as he visited an electronic music composer; I spent a weekend with him and his wife, the actress Giulietta Masina, at their country place in Fregena, at the seaside; and watched him work at the Cinefonico Palatino, a movie studio. He gave me perfect material for scenes with which to build my story. He always had something to say that expressed his independence, his insight, his rebellious views, his sharp and funny observations.

"I hate film festivals. They all have the kind of atmosphere I do not like—the atmosphere of a competition, which is foreign to my temperament. Festivals and New York cocktail parties, they both have the same atmosphere, with all those people who come

and talk, talk, talk. And they look at me with cross eyes. When
I finish a picture, if it is not released I would not care. I am glad
when my pictures have success, but I would not care if they do not
have success. The things I am asked to do *after* I finish a picture
are the only aspect of my work that makes me tired." . . .

Fellini was taken to dinner at a seaside restaurant by a wealthy
Sicilian, a short, chunky gentleman named Franco Gorgone who
was wearing a black silk monogrammed shirt and a monocle. The
Sicilian made no secret of his intimidating and powerful connec-
tions with mysterious and powerful people. He said to Fellini:
"We will drive in my car. We will drive in the Jaguar."

Fellini was very quiet, but he nodded assent to the plan.

The Sicilian's girlfriend, a beautiful young blonde, designer-
dressed to the teeth, said: "Franco is so proud of his Jaguars. He is
probably the only man in Italy who has two Jaguars. And he's the
only man in Sicily who has a Jaguar at all."

Fellini said nothing at all.

In another scene, Fellini's assistant, a young woman named
Liliana, tells him that their film producer wants him to go see the
Minister of Tourism and Entertainment about taking his new
movie to the Venice Film Festival. She offers to drive him to see the
Minister in her little Fiat.

Here is a scene from my piece:

INTERNO. Liliana's Fiat. As Liliana drives, Fellini is sketching
what could be a cross between an elephant and an anteater. She
leans over to see the drawing. Paternally, he turns her face back
toward the windshield. Then he briefly holds his drawing up in
front of her eyes.

Liliana: Ah, very nice, very nice!

Fellini: It is a lady I met at a party last week, eh? *(He attaches
the drawing to the visor above the windshield. He sighs.)*

Liliana: *(regarding the drawing happily, then looking to her driv-
ing)*: Will you take *Juliet of the Spirits* to the film festival?

*(Fellini gives a long mutter of dissatisfaction and falls silent. He
hunches himself up in the cramped space. Finally, he speaks.)*

Fellini: Liliana! Liliana! Italy is a very strange country. Success does not last long. Today they applaud. Tomorrow they kill you. We are a very ancient people. We have seen so much. Popes. Kings. Warriors. Merchants. Italy has seen so many gods appear and disappear. We have such a big, heavy story. Even the most ignorant man in Italy has something of our history in his blood. Italians applaud the Beatles, but they are really skeptical. They are friendly toward the Americans, but at the same time they are friendly also to the Russians, because they figure maybe the Russians will win. *(He lights a cigarette.)* Yet Italians know that the Americans are fundamentally loyal and naïve. But . . . Liliana . . . the movie society everywhere is very rich and full of vulgarity.

I kept in touch with Fellini—and with his movies, of course—and twenty years after I wrote about him in Rome, he came to New York to be honored by the Film Society of Lincoln Center. The morning after his arrival, Fellini invited me to join him and his entourage, in a cavalcade of limos heading for Darien, Connecticut, and the country home of Dorothy Cullman, Chairman of the F.S. of L.C. The entourage, it seemed to me, was there to help Fellini deal with one of those "things" he had to do after making a film, and it included Giulietta Masina, Marcello Mastroianni, and Anouk Aimée, all actors. There was considerable kidding around in the limos about what the visitors called "Conneckticut," and once there, the Cullmans gave the guests the obligatory tour of the remodelled old farmhouse. They listened respectfully to Mrs. Cullman recount that the original farmhouse, when it was first built around 1720, had only four rooms; now it had eleven. Everybody ate crab-filled apricot halves, curried chicken, seafood pasta, steamed mussels, steamed clams, green salad, white wine, three kinds of cake, ice cream with candied-ginger sauce, fresh fruit, and espresso. They talked:

"You haven't spent much time here, Mr. Fellini," Mrs. Cullman said.

"In 1957, I came for some producers, as the guest of them," he said. "They gave me people to show to me anything I want to see, and they said, 'Do what you want.' What I want was to go back

to Italy, so I left. In the plane, as we flew away from New York,
I looked down, and I felt very guilty that I was leaving."

In the limo going back to New York, Fellini was told how the
Tribute would go: "It will be pictures, people, pictures, people,
etcetera, and at the end you."

"I want the Rockettes," Fellini said.

The piece ended with what Fellini said at the Tribute:

"My dear American friends: You are truly a simpatico people, as I
always suspected since I was a child. . . . In the small movie house
of my village—with two hundred seats and five hundred standing
room—I discovered through your films that there existed another
way of life, that a country existed of wide-open spaces, of fantas-
tic cities which were like a cross between Babylon and Mars. Per-
haps, thinking about it now, the stories were simplistic. However,
it was nice to think that despite the conflicts and the pitfalls there
was always a happy ending. It was especially wonderful to know
that a country existed where people were free, rich, and happy,
dancing on the roofs of the skyscrapers, and where even a humble
tramp could become President. Perhaps even then it wasn't like
this. However, I believe that I owe to those flickering shadows
from America my decision to express myself through film. And so
I, too, made some films and gave life to some flickering shadows,
and through them I told the story of my country. And tonight
I am extremely touched to find myself here, together with my
beloved actors, and honored by the people who inspired me in
those old years."

There are always reasons for the particular organization of a
story, the sequence of the paragraphs, and, especially, the endings.
The last two sentences of Fellini's speech say it all and sum up what
I tried to show about him in the stories I wrote.

KUROSAWA AND
COPPOLA

IN WRITING the Profile, in 1981, called "Kurosawa Frames," I experimented with a modified screenplay style. Kurosawa, who did not speak English, used a translator. So the dialogue worked out better in this form:

MONDAY, JOHN F. KENNEDY AIRPORT.

The Japanese movie director Akira Kurosawa lands around 11 A.M., after a thirteen-hour flight from Tokyo, for a visit as the guest of the Japan Society, whose Film Center is about to put on a two-month retrospective of Kurosawa's movies—twenty-six, all told. Kurosawa emerges into the Japan Air Lines reception area: seventy-one years old, six feet tall, slightly stooped, gray-haired; wearing dark-tinted, horn-rimmed glasses, a dark green-and-tan plaid wool sports jacket, a tan silk shirt, a necktie patterned in brown and beige, wrinkled tan slacks, and well-worn brown shoes; carrying a small brown leather-and-canvas bag; and looking

expectant. Accompanying him is Teruyo Nogami, who has been his chief production assistant for the past thirty years—from the time he made *Rashomon,* in 1950. She is a short, chubby woman with wild, frizzy black hair, and her expression is dead-pan. She is wearing floppy gray flannel pants and a brown leather jacket with tassles. Greeting Kurosawa on behalf of the Japan Society is Peter Grilli, the director of the Film Center—a stocky, sharp-eyed, friendly, Japanese-speaking American in his late thirties. His father, Marcel Grilli, who is a music critic for the *Japan Times,* an English-language newspaper in Tokyo, took Peter there to live at the age of five. Peter attended the American School in Tokyo. Harvard University, and Tokyo University. He started the Film Center about three years ago. . . . Kurosawa, somewhat formal and stiff in manner, speaks only a few words of English. . . . The Americans bow to Kurosawa and he bows back. Everybody shakes hands. Grilli then gives Miss Nogami a heartfelt hug.

"*Yoku irasshaimashita, ne,*" Grilli says. Translation: "Welcome. It's great to have you here."

Bows and smiles all around. As they start outside, all three Americans say "*Dozo*" ("Please"), indicating that the Japanese should go first.

MONDAY I P.M. UNITED NATIONS PLAZA HOTEL ROOM 2301

. . . Kurosawa takes off his jacket and necktie and unbuttons his shirt collar, then sits down with Grilli to look over the schedule of activities for the retrospective.

Tuesday: 6 P.M. dinner at Japan House. . .

8 P.M. opening of Kurosawa Retrospective with screening of *Throne of Blood.* Francis Coppola will introduce Mr. Kurosawa. Mr. Kurosawa will introduce the film. . . .

Thursday: 6:45 P.M. William Friedkin dinner for Mr. Kurosawa, at his midtown apartment. . . .

Kurosawa asks Grilli how many people will be at Friedkin's dinner party. About twenty-five, Grilli says, and he starts naming them: Mr. and Mrs. Arthur Penn, Mr. and Mrs. Martin Scorsese, Peter Hamill, Linda Ronstadt, Bud Yorkin. . . . Kurosawa nods

affirmatively and says nothing, lights a Seven Stars cigarette.
Grilli resumes: Mr. Elia Kazan, Frances FitzGerald, Mr. and Mrs.
Michael Arlen, Mr. and Mrs. Norman Mailer, Mr. and Mrs.
Sidney Lumet—

"Ah, Sidney Lumet," Kurosawa says, interrupting. "I'd like to
see Sidney Lumet's film *Prince of the City*."

"We could go tonight," Grilli says. "If you're not too tired."

"Yes, yes, yes. I want to see *Prince of the City*," Kurosawa says.

MONDAY, 6 P.M., CINEMA III, THE SMALL THEATRE AT
THE PLAZA HOTEL.

An usher stands near the box office looking bored as Grilli hurries
over, followed by Kurosawa and Miss Nogami, and hands the
tickets to the usher, who gives no sign of recognizing Kurosawa.
. . . The film takes nearly three hours, in the course of which
Kurosawa's full attention never wavers. He doesn't ask for any
translations. A couple of times, Miss Nogami and he whisper to
each other, without looking away from the screen. The film moves
fast. Quick cuts. Lots of action: hitting, running, knocking about,
shooting, chasing, getting soaked in the rain, eating—moving the
story along. . . . End of the film. Lights go on. Kurosawa, Miss
Nogami, and Grilli stand, stretch, smile with obvious pleasure.
Led by Kurosawa, who seems to know his way around, they make
a beeline for the Plaza's Oyster Bar.

MONDAY, 9:30 P.M. THE OYSTER BAR.

Kurosawa is seated at a small square table with Grilli and Miss
Nogami. They are talking about *Prince of the City*. Kurosawa says
that he admires the quality of the color, the camerawork, the fast
cuts, and, especially, the way Lumet shot the scenes of the main
character driving in the rain, running in the rain, fighting in the
rain, and chasing around in the rain in order to get some drugs
to give to his addict informer. It is impossible to shoot in natural
rain, Kurosawa says. Lots of laughing from the three others as he
tells them how much water he had to use up in the last reel of
Seven Samurai, in the big twenty-minute battle scene that takes

place during a rainstorm, with both men and horses, when three
cameras were working simultaneously. Grilli says that the way
Lumet shot the scene reminded him of the way Kurosawa shot
the trees rushing by in *Rashomon*. He tells Kurosawa that Lumet
and other good film directors would be the first to say they had
learned much from seeing Kurosawa's films. Kurosawa grins and
nods in agreement. They order Bloody Marys and drink a kind of
toast to *Prince of the City*. . . .

TUESDAY. 3 P.M. ROOM 3701.
Kurosawa, without his jacket but wearing a tie, is having Japanese
tea. . . . Miss Nogami pours the tea into Japanese porcelain cups,
which Grilli has brought over from Japan House. . . . She hands a
cup to Kurosawa, and he takes a sip. With the tea, he smokes a
Seven Stars cigarette, holding it between thumb and forefinger.
Miss Nogami sits cross-legged on the floor facing Kurosawa, and
she lights a Seven Stars cigarette. Kurosawa says the tea is good,
and praises Miss Nogami for using warm tapwater to make it.
That's the best way, Kurosawa says—not with boiling water. He
looks at the cup holding the tea. In Japan today, he says, every-
thing is plastic. "In my home, I have all the old cups and bowls
and plates and spoons—everything I can—because I want my
children and my grandchildren to live with the old things, to
know them by living with them," he says. . . . In Japan today,
Kurosawa goes on, children grow up worshipping everything
from the West. The most painful thing in Japan today is the arti-
ficial democracy. After Japan lost the Second World War, Japan
became democratized from the outside. Democracy didn't devel-
op out of Japanese needs; democracy was just laid over Japanese
society. . . . "Television is a very harmful influence in Japan today,"
Kurosawa says. "University students only watch television and
read comic books. They don't read the classics. If I'm working
with a writer and I refer to a classic and find he hasn't read it, I
can't go on working with him." He looks distressed. "Japan today,"
he says. "It is all but impossible now in Japan for me to make a
film—even one film a year."

THURSDAY EVENING. BILLY FRIEDKIN'S
MIDTOWN APARTMENT.

Friedkin, the forty-one-year-old director of *The French Connection*, *The Exorcist*, and *Cruising*, had the apartment built to his specifications. It is comfortable, spacious, and handsome, with English oak floors throughout, and huge safety-glass windows. A large room given over to a billiard table has two nine-foot-high English oak panelled doors separating it from a sixty-foot living room, which is furnished with eighteenth-century and nineteenth-century English antique tables and chairs, and goosedown sofas with Porthault coverings and embroidered Japanese silk pillows. Over a marble fireplace in the living room hangs a nineteenth-century French mirror with a gilt frame. There's a lot of original art on the walls; a small Turner watercolor of Sidon fishermen drawing in their nets; nineteenth-century Japanese prints from the series *100 Views of the Moon*, by Yoshitoshi; a large Degas watercolor of horses and jockeys at Longchamps; a George Grosz; a Picasso. For this evening, Friedkin has placed small Japanese boxwood plants here and there in the foyer and in the living room.

Kurosawa, Grilli, and Miss Nogami have arrived before most of the other guests and are sitting with Friedkin in his study. The furnishings here include a nineteenth-century French table and black leather Charles Eames chairs. On the walls are a Matisse crayon drawing of a woman's face; a George Grosz drawing of a sailor kicking a woman; several Daumier prints; two large, signed photographs of Red Auerbach, the general manager and president of the Boston Celtics (Friedkin's favorite basketball team); a Boston Celtics pennant; and large, framed stills from *The Exorcist*.

Friedkin is a trim, volatile, friendly, good-natured and likeable man, his eyes alert behind glasses with thin gold frames, and his manner warm and hospitable. He is making a big effort to see that everybody feels comfortable. He is dramatically dressed in black pants, black boots, a black shirt, a beautiful tie of red Japanese silk embroidered in pink and red. Kurosawa has on his dark-blue suit and his tinted glasses. . . .

Drinks are served. Friedkin raises his glass to Kurosawa and says *"Kono go o-kampai!"* He translates, "Let's drink to the future," and adds, "What we all want is for you to make more pictures." Friedkin speaks precisely and clearly, like a confident student in an elocution class.

Kurosawa is nodding and saying "Thank you."

"Everyone owes him a debt. Everyone," Friedkin says. . . .

The doorbell rings. Friedkin gets up to admit new arrivals. Mr. and Mrs. Arthur Penn; Mr. and Mrs. Norman Mailer; Mr. and Mrs. Michael Arlen.

"The last time I did this was fifteen years ago—gave a whole dinner," Friedkin says from the doorway. "It was for Harold Pinter."

LATER. THE LIVING ROOM, WHERE THREE ROUND TABLES HAVE BEEN SET FOR A SEATED DINNER.

Sidney Lumet, wearing brown cords, a heavy white turtleneck, a tweed jacket, and black-rimmed glasses, enters and makes straight for Kurosawa. They shake hands, and Kurosawa, grinning widely, holds on to the younger director's hand and keeps pumping it. He tells Lumet immediately that he has just seen *Prince of the City* and thinks the film is wonderful.

"From you, that is very, very special to me, and I don't say that often," Lumet says. "Beauty many people can do, but beauty with meaning very few people can do," Lumet adds.

What impressed him so much, Kurosawa says, was the physical beauty of the cinematography in the movie and how it related to the story. Also, he was impressed by the way Lumet used light.

Lumet looks as though he were going to weep with joy. "For you to recognize these things!" he says. . . . "I've never seen one fake frame in your films." Turning toward the other guests, he adds, "To achieve the beauty he achieves without falseness is incredible."

"I don't feel I've yet achieved everything you describe," Kurosawa says.

"One always feels that way," says Lumet. "There were two directors after the silents who changed movies. One was Carl Dreyer, and the other was Kurosawa."

"Now I'd like to go back to making silent films again," Kurosawa says. "There's still a great deal to learn. How to make the words, the talking passages, shorter."

Billy Friedkin comes over and says to a guest on the edge of the group around Kurosawa, "In Japan, he's a prophet without honor."

Francis Coppola is a singular director to whom I am grateful beyond measure. In 1982, he opened the story of *One from the Heart* to me. For one thing, I was able to see the lengths to which he was willing and able to go. The piece about him ran with the title: "Some Figures on a Fantasy" (accompanied by a wonderful Saul Steinberg drawing of multiple rows of seated moviegoers off an aisle littered with popcorn, drinks, snacks, etc.).

The piece about Coppola—unlike *Picture*, which told about the dramatic relationships between John Huston and the other characters during the making of one movie—enabled me to show one character in relation to a movie of his creation that was particularly significant to him. The ending reveals his philosophy as an artist.

Francis Coppola, the talented, original, volatile forty-three year-old moviemaker, who is a movie writer (*Patton, The Conversation,* and other pictures), a movie producer (*American Graffiti, The Black Stallion,* and others), a movie impresario and distributor (Abel Gance's 1927 epic, *Napoleon,* and others), and a fan of other people's movies (Michael Powell's *The Thief of Baghdad,* Andrzej Wajda's *Ashes and Diamonds,* Akira Kurosawa's *Yojimbo,* Stanley Kubrick's *Dr. Strangelove,* and about five hundred others), started working on his movie *One from the Heart* in 1980. The year before, Mr. Coppola had bought Hollywood General Studios, built in 1919—one of the oldest movie studios in town. The studio occupies almost nine acres of land in the heart of Hollywood, one mile from the Goldwyn studios and two miles from Paramount. Mr. Coppola spent seven million two hundred thousand dollars (some cash, many mortgages) for the studio and renamed it Zoetrope Studios—after his production company, American Zoetrope, which he had founded in 1969, in San Francisco, as a center for young filmmakers.

"The Zoetrope was an early device to create the illusion of a motion picture," Mr. Coppola explained recently to a visitor in his studio. "In the eighteen-sixties, it was a popular toy—a revolving cylindrical box with slits in it, making pictures appear to move— but I'm sure it was used much earlier. In Greek, *zoe* means 'life,' and *trop* means 'turn,' or 'movement,' so the word really means 'life movement.'"

At Zoetrope in Hollywood, Mr. Coppola had nine sound stages; several one-story and two-story buildings; four bungalows, including one that was used by Harold Lloyd and is still named for him; and plenty of wardrobe space and rehearsal space. He borrowed an additional three million dollars and spent it repairing and renovating the place, with new roofing, new air-conditioning, new lighting, new carpeting, and a large assortment of the latest kind of electronic equipment (some of it designed by him, for making movies in a new way, which he called "the electronic cinema." He gave the studio streets and parking area new names, among them Federico Fellini Lane, Akira Kurosawa Avenue, Buster Keaton Boulevard, Raoul Walsh Alley, and Sergei Eisenstein Park. . . . One of the most dramatic components of Mr. Coppola's technology was a custom-designed twenty-eight-foot-long image-and-sound-control van, complete with kitchen and bath. "The concept behind this unit is that movies are like music and should be composed along the same lines," Mr. Coppola said, when he introduced his van to people. The system enabled Mr. Coppola to edit *One from the Heart* while it was being shot. . . .

Coppola, a notably unpretentious man, is burly, untrim, over-weight—two hundred and thirty-five pounds at five feet eleven inches—and he has none of the health-conscious, life-preserving habits, disciplines, or self-indulgences, of many of his Beverly Hills, Pacific Palisades, or Malibu peers, who diet, exercise, get plenty of sleep, and have an obligatory daily massage between work and dinner. Mr. Coppola eats too much and is always short on sleep. He has a three-inch-long curly black beard and long, wavy black hair, and he wears horn-rimmed glasses for nearsightedness. His clothes invariably look rumpled and slightly out of

season. He has remained untouched by most of Hollywood's social patterns, including the need to go to A parties, to sit in special seats in restaurants, and to get there in the most expensive cars. On the infrequent occasions when he has free time, he likes to stay home and practice on one or the other of two musical instruments he plays: the tuba and the string bass. He also likes to cook; his veal Marsala and his spaghetti with his own marinara sauce have a great reputation among his friends.

He does not measure his words. He is not cautious in expressing his ideas, or his uncertainties about them. He likes to throw out his ideas—to try them out on people who he thinks might share his deep interest in motion pictures. Using a tape recorder, he often makes oral notes to himself in the middle of the night, after his co-workers are asleep. . . . "I worry about content," he said, in one of his messages to himself. "I worry about story. . . . The talent for writing a good tune is especially admirable when we think how long composers have been arranging and rearranging those few notes into something that sticks as a melody. A story must be like that—a specific talent to come up with the sequence of events, the unfolding of information that captures us and has us eagerly awaiting the outcome, as though we were children. And even if we already know the story, we enjoy going through it again.". . .

Not long ago, in the Harold Lloyd bungalow at Zoetrope Studios, sitting alongside a newly purchased bass that he had not yet had time to practice on, Mr. Coppola said, "The adventure of *One from the Heart* was simply my trying to own the rights to my movies." By then, *One from the Heart* had come and gone on public screens. Mr. Coppola was in Hollywood for a few hours, to see a screening of his new movie, *The Outsiders,* and was about to leave for Tulsa, Oklahoma, where the image-and-sound-control van—along with much of the other technological equipment and some of the personnel of his company—was waiting for him. . . .

"I think it's wise to separate the earning of money from the making of a movie, but I wanted to own the *rights* to my own movies—to be the one to decide what to do with what I make,"

Mr. Coppola said, giving his bass a wistful look. "At the same
time, I was trying to use new methods. Everyone seems to be
encouraging you to be ordinary, to tell the same old story the
same old way, package it this way, package it that way. Just get
the money. All that doesn't interest me. I like to experiment—to
push the techniques of moviemaking forward and simultaneously
find the most economical methods of making a film. . . . In mak-
ing *One from the Heart*, I was trying for something different. I
wanted the scenery, the music, and the lighting, for example, to
be *part* of the film, not just a background for the action."

 One from the Heart took about twenty-two months to make,
including the time Mr. Coppola spent working on the screen-
play. . . . Its cost came to twenty-seven million dollars. . . . Before
One from the Heart was withdrawn from distribution in this coun-
try, it had generated a disappointing one million two hundred
thousand dollars in gross box-office revenue. Zoetrope's share
of the gross revenue was almost negligible. . . . Mr. Coppola has
explained, "If there's anything left after you break even, it's usually
a small pool, and it's divided up among the people who own
shares of the movie. *One from the Heart* will have to earn from
two and a half to three times its cost, or—according to a broad
rule of thumb—about sixty-eight million dollars, before we
break even."

 One from the Heart runs for a hundred minutes. As Mr.
Coppola describes it, it is "a fable about love and show business."
As Columbia Pictures describes it, it is "a romantic comedy, a
musical fantasy, and an erotic love story." It takes place in Las
Vegas. Because Mr. Coppola wanted to get away from realism,
and achieve certain effects of fantasy, he decided to make the
entire movie at Zoetrope Studios—a procedure counter to the
pattern that most movies have followed for the past thirty years
or so, of being shot on location, and more like the moviemaking
pattern of the nineteen-thirties and forties.

 . . . *One from the Heart* was rated "R" by the Motion Picture
Association of America. It is the story of an unmarried couple,
Frannie (Teri Garr) and Hank (Frederic Forrest), who have been

living together in a small house in Las Vegas for five years and are
dissatisfied with each other. They have brief alliances with other
partners. Hank then wants to get together with Frannie again.
After some resistance and turmoil, she returns to him, and
that's that.

Because Mr. Coppola wanted the movie to be what he called
"theatrical" instead of "naturalistic," he decided against making it
on location in Las Vegas. Instead, he created his own, stylized
version of Las Vegas at Zoetrope Studios. "The real Las Vegas is
like Burbank," Mr. Coppola said at the time. "We're going to tell
this simple story in a fantasy way, so we'll make our own fantasy
of Las Vegas, which for me is a metaphor for America itself, and
like the 'Mahagonny' of the world.". . . Technically, Mr. Coppola
owns *One from the Heart*. (*The Godfather*—both parts—is owned
by Paramount. Mr. Coppola is a profit participant in *The Godfather*,
receiving six percent of the net profits of Part I and a larger per-
centage of the gross profits of Part II, but he has no say in what
Paramount does with the movie.). . .

"You need a lot of capital to start with in order to get close to
the box office," Mr. Coppola said in his studio bungalow recently,
with one hand on his new bass, which so far he still had not
played. "It's like the oil business. George Lucas, for example,
now has incredible wealth, in cash. I'm in a different position.
My home telephone has been shut off all this past year, because
I haven't been able to pay my telephone bill. I wanted to own all
my own pictures, I once owned the *Black Stallion* film rights. The
film will probably make a profit of three million dollars, but I had
to turn over my rights to United Artists in order to hang on to
Apocalypse Now. . . .

"I believe that an artist has a right to own what he creates, but
I can't get my hands on the capital that I need to do the creating. I
was running a movie studio that had no money. The day I started
shooting *One from the Heart*, I had no money. Every week, I had
to start out by wondering, Where can I get the five hundred
thousand dollars we need for this week's shooting? . . . Before
we started shooting the film, everybody at Zoetrope took a big

pay cut for a period of six months. They were wonderful. Assist-
ants to assistants came to me with ideas for raising money. All
these people were paid back in full eventually, by the way, but all
along the line, they were really great. At one point in February,
1981, the bank stopped advancing us money, and sent people to
California to review our case. We considered stopping production
of the picture. If we'd stopped, though, a lot of people would have
been hurt. So in April, I had to make myself personally liable for
any loans beyond that point. . . . I just put the money where it
needs to go. So three million dollars could be in the budget for
me as director of *One from the Heart*, but I'd put the money right
back into what was needed to go on making the movie. Whether
it's your own or someone else's money you make the movie with,
you're under pressure. I find that it's worse, however, when you
use someone else's money. Then you always have someone look-
ing over your shoulder."

In August of 1981, the Paramount distribution office in
San Francisco, in order to satisfy complicated state theatrical-
exhibition laws, held a screening for exhibitors of the rough cut
of *One from the Heart*—a version that lacked, among other things,
most of the movie's twelve songs. One of the exhibitors at this
screening lost no time in sharing his opinion, which was unfavor-
able, with a film critic on a San Francisco newspaper—an erratic
development that was regarded by everybody concerned as a
highly unprofessional violation of privilege. The film critic then
reported the irregular and premature comments in the newspaper,
and they were read and resented by Mr. Coppola. He objected to
what seemed to him to be the casual way the distribution office
had held the screening. . . .

As 1981 drew to a close, details of the distribution deal
with Paramount were still up in the air. On New Year's Eve, Mr.
Coppola, who was working in the Technicolor lab in Rome with
Vittorio Storaro on the final touches on *One from the Heart*, sud-
denly decided that he wanted to hold a screening of his movie in
New York City. He telephoned Bernard Gersten and asked him
to try to get the Radio City Music Hall for the screening. Mr.

Gersten got it, for one day and evening, at a cost of twenty-four
thousand dollars. In the *Times* of Sunday, January 10, 1982, at a
cost of twenty-seven thousand dollars, Mr. Coppola placed a full-
page ad: "On Friday, January 15th, at Radio City Music Hall,
Francis Coppola presents the final preview of his new movie. . . ."

On the day of the screening, people started lining up for general
admission early in the morning. The outside temperature was
about twenty degrees Fahrenheit. . . . Mr. Coppola ordered free
soup—split pea soup with sausage slices—delivered to the waiting
audience in the afternoon. Cost: three thousand three hundred
and fifteen dollars. Accoutrements of the evening included pro-
grams, posters, and buttons reading "I was at *One from the Heart*
Radio City Music Hall," which together cost fifteen thousand
dollars and brought the cost of the preview to almost seventy
thousand dollars. The Radio City Music Hall box office that night
took in slightly over fifty-one thousand dollars in gross receipts for
the two performances, which were sold out, with eleven thousand
people paying to see the movie. . . . The program for the evening
included a press conference and a big party for the guests—the
latter held, at a cost of nineteen thousand four hundred and ten
dollars, in the Tower suite at the top of the Time-Life Building.
An eight-piece dance orchestra played at the party, and the cele-
brators were offered a buffet with shellfish, cabbage soup, three
kinds of pasta, cold cuts, and desserts, along with drinks.

Backstage at the Music Hall around seven o'clock, Mr.
Coppola, dressed in a heavy, khaki-colored down parka, light
brown pants, brown jacket, a maroon-and-white checked shirt,
a pink tie, and worn-looking brown loafers, was surrounded by
family, friends, colleagues, and other supporters. Off to one side,
the Dingbats—Sofia Coppola and Jilian and Jenny Gersten—
wearing rented tails and top hats and clutching canes, were
practicing a tap-dancing routine. Mr. Coppola was greeting one
well-wisher after another. He was elated. "We finished mixing
the sound at 6 A.M. today," he said. "Final changes on the negative
were made in Rome last night, and the master print just got here.
I was all over the Music Hall this afternoon. Finding out how

the house lights work. Everything. It's the most beautiful theatre you've ever seen. Not one of those multiplex shoeboxes. And we've got this perfect big, big screen. . . . We made the movie, and now we're going to lay it on the audience. I feel as though I were back in college. In fact—" He called to all those around him, instructing them to form a large circle, to hold hands, to lift their held hands up and down three times, in a ritual, while calling out "Pa-wa-ba!" each time. "It dates from my time at Hofstra, when we put on plays. It exorcises the evil spirits and invokes the good spirits. I still do the 'pa-wa-ba' before we do the first shot of all my movies."

The house lights were dimming. Mr. Coppola hustled out, toward the back of the house, clasping hands on the way, calling out he would see the hands' owners at the party later on.

"Francis invites everybody," Bernard Gersten said, hurrying to catch up with Mr. Coppola and make a path for him. "There are no Hollywood-type A, B, and C lists for parties with him. Everybody's an A."

People in the audience, mostly under forty, and enthusiastic, also held out their hands for good-will shakes, saying "Thanks for the evening." Or "Thanks for making it," or "I love your work."

"This movie is different," Mr. Coppola said, a couple of times.

"Different?" some of the well-wishers repeated, looking put off. . . .

When the movie ended, Hank and Frannie were together again on the screen. The audience applauded. Not a shattering ovation—just appreciative applause. . . .

About seventy people were at the press conference, including many photographers and television-news cameramen as well as people who write about movies. Most of their questions carried with them heavily inside information.

No. 1 was "How do you feel, now that everybody dislikes the picture?"

No. 2: "Doing this the way you have done it, what is your purpose, and have you, in your opinion, accomplished your purpose?"

No. 3: "But will this film be commercially successful?"

No. 4: "How important is the success of this movie to your future ventures—to your future movie productions and movie ventures?"

No. 5: "Is this film your homage to Fellini?"

No. 6: "Is there an agreement with Paramount on this film as to its distribution?"

No. 7: "Mr. Coppola, do you feel you love this movie as much as Hank liked Frannie?"

No. 8: "Mr. Coppola, why do you take these kinds of chances?"

No. 9: "Mr. Coppola, you helped create George Lucas. Why hasn't he helped you?"

Visibly trying to remain calm, Mr. Coppola replied.

To No. 1: "A lot of people in there looked as though they *did* like the movie. They seemed to laugh throughout the picture; they stayed pretty motionless and intent throughout the picture; there weren't many walkouts. At the end, there was a play of emotion and enthusiastic applause that lingered throughout the titles and even after the titles. That's what I saw. If someone saw it a different way, then maybe that's so."

To No. 2: "A lot of people who spoke to me told me it was a very unusual and beautiful picture. When I make a film, I take a jump into something I'm interested in. In this case, in the film, I was interested in show business, in gambling. I was interested in love, and I was interested in fantasy, and I was interested in music. Those are the things I worked with in my film. I am very proud of it, and I imagine that years from now, just as in my other films, people will see something of these elements and see it as an original work. It's not a copy of anything. It entertains people, and it is innocent."

To No. 3: "How the hell do I know?"

To No. 4: "I know very specifically what I want to do and where I am going. It's just two different roads I can travel to get there, the result of the success of this film determines maybe an easier road."

To No. 5: "No."

To No. 6: "About a week ago, I saw the film in Rome and then in Paris. I showed it to a few friends, filmmakers, directors, people,

kids. I felt real good about their reaction, and more important, I felt real good about my own reaction to it, which is all that really matters, I guess. At that time, because of a series of business discussions going on with Paramount, I became frustrated, and I decided I didn't care whether Paramount released the picture or not. At that time, I terminated Paramount's release of the film. But Barry Diller, the chairman of Paramount, asked us not to announce the termination until we had a chance to discuss it further. I had to finish the film. I had to bring it to a stop, because we were involved with the bank and these various things that had to come to a close. I was very concerned about the sloppy way the film was shown to the exhibitors when it wasn't finished, and I was concerned about the way the film was being prejudged. And I just wanted a chance to show it clean to an audience. The thing with Paramount is a tricky situation, because I terminated them. I had hoped that that would bring us around to make an agreement. Whether that happens or not depends on the reaction of people to the film, so I don't really know what's going to happen."

To No. 7: "I love this movie, because I like to watch it, and I like the music, and I think it is beautiful."

To No. 8: "I'm a guy who's been around for twenty years. I've made a lot of films, and you know them. I've also produced a lot of films. You know them, too. I've written a lot of films, and I've discovered a lot of new talent. I was the one responsible for making Part II's, if you want to consider *that* something. Every time I want to make a movie, every time I want to make a film, every time I want to sponsor a filmmaker, I have to go, hat in hand, to a series of studio executives who don't have my background and my experience. So I find that frustrating. So, since I don't have any money really, to speak of, I use what little I have to try to get to the point where we can have our own studio, where we can make films like the films we've made over the last twelve years—all of the quality that this film has. I will stand by this film, because I know what went into the making of it. That's what I want. But I can't do it if I have to be controlled by people who say what film you can make and who's going to supervise what. So if I have my own studio, to keep the control and supervision

to myself, it is taking a risk. Taking risks like this one creates some excitement. You may not have been excited, but others were. I don't know, but it was something."

No. 9: "I don't need to be bailed out. My friendship with George Lucas is such that I know that's not his style of doing things. He would help me in other ways. George is a good friend, not in a money-lending way but more in the way of giving me a lift to the airport if I needed it." Without missing much of a beat, he went on, "I'm a guy who feels, Let's get out and take some chances. What I really don't understand is why you guys don't seem to like that. Why don't we all cheer the moviemakers *on?*"

A bit later, Mr. Coppola went back into the theatre, where the second screening of *One from the Heart* had started, and he moseyed around, observing both his movie and the audience reaction to it. Then, along with six hundred and forty-seven guests, he went to the party celebrating the event. . . . Guests told Mr. Coppola that they had enjoyed his movie very much. Norman Mailer told him it was "an extraordinary film." Joseph Papp told him it was "a pioneering film, as big in its way as *Star Wars.*" Robert Duvall told him it was "a lot of fun and technically dazzling." . . . Andy Warhol told him "It's really lovely." Carly Simon, Richard Gere, Susan Sarandon, Christopher Walken, Robert De Niro, and Martin Scorsese all told Mr. Coppola they enjoyed and admired the movie.

Mr. Coppola did a lot more kissing and gave a lot more hugs. The orchestra played "One," from *A Chorus Line,* about fifty times, and the Dingbats did their dance routine to it a couple of dozen times; many of the guests rewarded their efforts with generous applause. Everybody seemed to have a good time at the party, and most of the guests, when they left, kept their "*One from the Heart*—Radio City Music Hall" buttons on. . . .

Mr. Coppola held a meeting with about a dozen of his associates at his New York apartment, which is at the Sherry-Netherland—four rooms with a kitchen. . . .

"It looks as though the press is lining up against the movie," said the publicity woman for the New York area. "*Variety* will do

a long interview with you any time you say, and you will have a platform for what you want to say."

"I don't want a *platform,*" Mr. Coppola said. "From what I saw last night, the audience was interested in this picture. They could see that this picture was different. I think this picture will be like *Apocalypse. One from the Heart* will change the way people look at movies. Just as *Apocalypse* did. In my opinion, the people who liked the movie least were the critics—the people who want to tell you how you should work, what you should do. . . . When a good film comes along, one that they think will work out with the public, they act a little bit like Danton, who, when the rabble rushed past his house to make a revolution, ran out behind them to lead them. . . ."

"I'm tired of making films so that people can come out and shoot them down," Mr. Coppola said. "I don't know whether I want people to see this picture. Why can't I just put the studio up for sale? Liquidate everything. Can't a guy opt out? Can't I just liquidate? All I have to do is give the bank back twenty million bucks. Right?" There were some uneasy laughs all around, but Mr. Coppola looked serious. "I think the artist still has a right to show his work or not to show it," he said.

. . . Mr. Coppola did not appear bothered by the bad reviews or by other negative comments on his movie. "It's like the first reaction to *Apocalypse Now,*" he said, on hearing about the reviews. "Everybody talked against that one, too. At first, they didn't like what I had done. A lot of them wanted me to go on making *The Godfather, Part III,* or something. Then everybody came around."

The ending to this story has Coppola talking:

"I'm bothered by the nagging idea that I failed in what I was trying to do. . . . I doubt whether many people knew the depth of my feelings on this subject. I have no doubt that I have the energy and the resourcefulness to keep going with the studio. But sometimes I wonder whether it's worth it in such a cynical and frightened world." He paused again and pushed his glasses up on the bridge of his nose. "I love *One from the Heart* not only for what it

is but for where it was going," he said. "I love Zoetrope Studios for the same reason. We were doing all sorts of things for the first time. I'm sure that we have profoundly influenced other moviemakers, and we deserve the opportunity to go on.

"Every once in a while, I feel a bit down, but I'm really enthusiastic about the future. My head is percolating with new ideas about everything. You know, some of those Chase bankers told me *they* liked the movie. I told the bank I'll make the first payment with the money we get from the sale of the studio and the money owed us from the foreign distribution of *One from the Heart*. For the second payment, I'll use the money we get from the cable sale of *One from the Heart, Hammett,* and *The Escape Artist*. In the meantime, I'll be finishing everything on *The Outsiders* and *Rumble Fish*. So what if my telephone is turned off again at home? Or my electricity is shut off? Or my credit cards cancelled? If you don't bet, you don't have a chance to win. It's so silly in life not to pursue the highest possible thing you can imagine, even if you run the risk of losing it all, because if you don't pursue it you've lost it anyway. You can't be an artist and be safe."

HARVEY, JEANNE, WES
AND THE DIAMONDS

T THE START of the year 2001, I used the third-person
approach in creating brief scenes to tell a story, this one
entitled "Harvey et Jeanne," in The Talk of the Town:

Harvey Weinstein and Bob Weinstein, the co-heads of Miramax
Films, were made Chevaliers des Arts et des Lettres, together
with three other movie specialists, at the French Consulate, on
upper Fifth Avenue, the other evening. In the former Whitney
mansion, designed by Stanford White, Harvey Weinstein milled
about with the other honorees . . . and their guests. Catherine
Verret, of the French Film Office, had brought the French actress
Jeanne Moreau. Weinstein's guests included his mother, his wife,
his three- and five-year-old daughters, and a number of Miramax
employees.

"I never got a medal before," said Weinstein, burly and smiling
and attired in what looked like his best, though rumpled, blue
suit. "I got the Oscar, but the Oscar is not a medal."

"At school, maybe?" someone asked.

"Maybe, can't remember," Weinstein said thoughtfully, and turned to Jeanne Moreau, who looked back at him with her large *Jules et Jim* brown eyes. She was wearing the tiny rosette that is given to recipients of the French Legion of Honor.

"I had the Ordre des Arts et des Lettres previously, and I have also this one," Moreau said in a slow, deep voice, fingering the rosette.

"And she was the first woman to be voted into the French Academy of Fine Arts," Catherine Verret added.

"Have you seen my new film, *Chocolat?*" Weinstein asked Jeanne Moreau.

"No," she said.

"There's a screening of it tonight," Weinstein said. "I'll have to leave early to make it."

"Paul Newman is hosting the screening," one of his aides said. "In the Woody Allen screening room."

Jeanne Moreau nodded graciously at the names. . . .

Escorted by Pierre Buhler, the *conseiller culturel*—a sharp-faced, sure-of-himself young man in gray flannels—the honorees and their guests went into a room set up with chairs and a podium for the presentation of the medals. Someone asked him what perks he thought the recipients of the medal would get in France.

"Free meals—just kidding!" a deputy counsellor said, and gave a long, loud laugh at his own joke. Then, at the podium, Buhler got to work, reading from his notes. "Along with *liberté, égalité, fraternité,* a Frenchman will defend to the bitter end good cinema," he said. He called Harvey Weinstein to the podium and said that Weinstein would accept the award for himself and for his brother Bob, who couldn't make it. "Siblings have been most influential in films," the consul said. "It all began with the Lumiére brothers . . . and then the Marx brothers . . . and the Coen brothers. I don't usually do two at once, but I am happy to make the exception tonight.". . . He stepped closer and on Harvey Weinstein's jacket pinned the medal, which was suspended from a ribbon of white stripes against a green background. He

said, "Au nom de Ministre de la Culture, je vous fais Chevalier
dans l'Ordre des Arts et des Lettres." He then pulled Weinstein's
head in turn against the sides of his own head. No kissing of
cheeks—no kissing at all. Both men seemed to be taking pre-
cautions against catching a cold.

"Chevalier means 'knight,'" somebody in the audience said in a
loud whisper.

Then Harvey Weinstein spoke. "I love France and French
movies. . . . When I was fourteen, I went to see François Truffaut's
The 400 Blows. . . . It changed my life. . . . We can protect Euro-
pean culture no matter what." He added, "Any room that has
Jeanne Moreau in it is a great room." Then he apologized for
having to leave to go to Paul Newman's showing of the movie
Chocolat, in Woody Allen's screening room. His mother and his
wife and his little daughters and his aides and helpers arose and
decamped, too.

Perhaps this little story reveals the essential meaninglessness of
what should have meaning. After all, the action takes place at the
French Ministry of Culture, in a Stanford White house where a
Michelangelo sculpture of an angel stands in the lobby. The char-
acters all have something to do with culture, the young *conseiller
culturel,* a famous French actress, an American movie mogul,
accompanied by his family. How do they all interact culturally? I
do not tell you how, explicitly. But if you read the story, you'll find
out for yourself.

In the spring of 2001, it gave me a good deal of pleasure to write
a Talk story about the film director Wes Anderson—the theme of
which was the unanimous appreciation of his entire cast, during
the filming in New York of his movie *The Royal Tenenbaums,* of
what this thirty-two-year-old man was giving *them.* The story was
entitled "Wes Anderson in Hamilton Heights":

> "He's the first director who doesn't scare me," Anjelica Huston
> said. "This is the first time a director asked me what I think of
> something. I suggested wearing my grandmother Rhea Gore's
> locket in the movie."

"Most directors only want it their way," said Bill Murray, who appeared in Anderson's last movie *Rushmore.* "This guy wants it to be right."

The object of their ruminations may be the most waifish-looking film director since François Truffaut. He has, from the top, nondescript brown hair, sharp features, clear-frame glasses, shoulders permanently hunched in behind-the-camera position, and no noticeable hips. On the set, he was elegantly clothed in mauve corduroy pants, a maroon corduroy sports jacket, and red sneakers.

Bill Murray said: "This guy has his own tailor. It's so nice, for a change, to like a guy and not begrudge him anything."

"There aren't even restrictions in his clothes," Anjelica Huston said. "His pants are custom-made with the crotch coming down about four inches above his knees. He's so skinny, and he gets skinnier by the day. We all want to hold him and mother him. We're so proud of him."

"The movie," Anderson said, "is about a family of talented people who peaked early and got short-circuited. They fell apart, and then they try to get together again in new ways. It's not about my own family, but I use tons of stuff about us. I'm the middle of three boys. My older brother, Merl, was a doctor in the Air Force. Eric, four years younger than me, is an artist, the concept illustrator of my movies. We're from Houston, Texas. My parents are divorced. My mom is an artist and an archeologist, but now she works as a real estate agent. My father was an amateur race-car driver, but now he's in public relations.". . .

"Wes can tell a personal story in a moving but still comic way," Bill Murray said. "Usually, these stories are sentimental or vicious. He makes me feel different, almost like I'm not obliged to be entertaining. I don't find myself pushing or selling my scenes. My own persona is greatly diminished."

"He's so stylized," Gene Hackman said. "This picture has a sense of fable."

An old Indian man named Kumar, who moved from Bombay to the United States as a juggler during the Second World War

("I can still juggle twelve or thirteen plates at a time"), is in the movie, too. He met Anderson in Dallas in the early nineties. "I ran the Cosmic Cup, a health-food restaurant and yoga center with jazz," Kumar said. "As a college student, Wes used to hang out at my Cosmic Cup with Owen Wilson. Now he puts me in all his movies. I play Gene's buddy in this movie. Wes lifts me up. He has trust, an interesting mind, and humility. That's the beauty of him."

Anjelica Huston said, "I've started smoking again. When I stopped smoking, I was so depressed, I cried for months. Now I'm happy. This picture gives me license to be myself. I'm fatalistic."

I offer the excerpt about Anderson mainly because I'm at one with his actors in feeling grateful to him; somehow, perhaps inexplicably, they know that this young director has given them something special in line with what they try to do in their work. This kind of thing is always worth noting.

Whether people are talking in singles, doubles, or multiples, humor in their talk will invariably bring them to life. Here is another example, from my Talk story of January 14, 2002:

"Diamonds for Dinner"

Attempts to pump up sales in high-end (a.k.a. expensive) merchandise took a bit of a surreal turn the other night when Yves Piaget, the jeweller-watchmaker, flew in from Tokyo to host a dinner party for thirty friends and clients in a private dining room at Le Bernardin. It was called Une Soirée Exclusive. The atmosphere was dreamlike but charged with purpose, as guests streamed in accompanied by a guitar-and-bass duo playing elegant melodies. "Luxury music, for luxury," a Piaget press aide said.

"Piaget has names for everything," Ellen Akwa, the company's boutique director, said. "We've got five tables tonight, named for the sentiments: Love, Wisdom, Joy, Passion, and Time."

Philippe Bonay, Piaget's vice-president of marketing, said, "Asia is our No. 1 market in the world. I hear we're putting a Hong at the Love table, a Tang and a Yu at Wisdom, and a Wei and two Wongs at Passion."

M. Piaget was seated at the Time table, which, like the other four tables, had a centerpiece made of assorted Piaget watches and jewelry, with price tags attached. The pile on the Time table was worth $1,197,300. "We've got four million dollars' worth of Piaget on the tables," the press aide said. *"Bon appetit!"*

"Bon appetit," M. Piaget repeated proudly. He is a short man with white hair, dark bushy eyebrows that recall Henry Luce's, and large, new-looking teeth. He was attired in a blue Brioni suit and an Hermès shirt, tie, and matching pocket square. He fondled his wristwatch. "My baby," he said. "It's my new, upgraded Piaget Polo. So pure." He smiled and put his teeth to the watch.

M. Paiget's table companion, Baroness W. Langer von Langerdorff, a large woman, with foot-high flaming-red hair and brightly rouged cheeks, regarded the centerpiece with a jolly, tolerant manner. She wore huge sapphire-and-diamond earrings and a giant sapphire-and-diamond necklace.

"Piaget?" one of her table companions asked.

"Harry Winston," the Baroness replied.

"No watch?"

"I never wear a watch at night," she said. "I don't want to know what time it is at night." The Baroness raised a hand that supported a ring with a diamond the size of a prune.

"Piaget?"

"Harry Winston," she said again, and giggled. "I loved Harry," she said.

To the right of the Baroness, a small, bald, spectacled gentleman, who introduced himself to the Time table as the sculptor Armand Arman, stared at the baroness's diamond ring, nodded to his wife sitting across the table from him, and said, "We call that a fuck-you stone." The baroness looked tickled.

"My watch is a Franck Muller," Armand Arman said. "I do not like the quartz. I like the mechanic."

"Well, I go to Monte Carlo," the Baroness said, as though to soothe him. "I see Yves at his home every summer in Monte Carlo."

"Monte Carlo magic," Armand Arman said. "If you spend a year in Monte Carlo, you lose two points on your I.Q."

"I don't go for a year. I go for July and August," the Baroness said.

Another Time-table guest, Joan Granlund, a pale, attractive blond woman, held up a hand adorned with a white-gold ring in the shape of a cube, encrusted with diamonds.

"The Sugar!" M. Piaget said, and plucked a similar ring from the centerpiece ($10,700).

"I was on the treadmill at home in Greenwich and bought it while running," Joan Granlund said. "Then I bought the watch to go with it." She displayed a diamond-covered white-gold wristwatch ($49,500). "It's the Diamond-Square Dancer," she said. "It's like the old days, when you bought the shoes and then you bought the handbag to go with it. The problem is, there are so many diamonds on the face, you can't tell what time it is." That stopped the conversation for a moment. Then M. Piaget came to the rescue.

"Our motto is 'Toujours faire mieux que necessaire,'" he offered.

Piaget's president, Robert J. Filotei, stood up and said that M. Piaget "is like a rock star with all the Chinese communities in the United States." Guests Hong at the Love table, Tang and Yu at Wisdom, and Wei and the Wongs at Passion laughed and applauded. "And Yves knows the Sultan of Brunei and the Sultan's sister and the Sultan's brother," Filotei said. "In Hollywood yesterday, I found out he knows Quincy Jones."

M. Piaget was called upon to say a few words over dessert. He smiled and said, "I really feel confused talking about myself. It's not my name, not my family, it's our *artisans* that make Piaget contemporary." He paused, as though he were searching for a conclusion. "I believe in world determination for peace and prosperity," he said. Everybody applauded.

Facts are wondrous things. When you stick to them, no other writing can beat reporting. From the beginning to the present day, every new story, short or long, that I embark on has been a thrill for me. In setting out, I always have a sense of happy expectation. As a child, I moved from Syracuse to New York, and I've never

lost the sense of excitement at having been let out of a constricted, small area into the open, free, boundless breathing space of the big city.

Curiosity has never left me. "The story" has always been all-important. "The story" comes first. It always comes first.

CHRONOLOGICAL
ORDER OF STORIES

T HESE STORIES BY Lillian Ross are included in this volume, and are listed below in the order in which they were first published in *The New Yorker*.

August 4, 1945, "One Man's Family" (Saudi Arabian Sheik), pp. 26–27
September 1, 1945, "Collars and Cuffs" (Harry S. Truman), pp. 53–54
February 21, 1948, "Come In, Lassie!," pp. 29–35
October 23, 1948, "Rugged Times" (Norman Mailer), pp. 147–151
October 22, 1949, "Symbol of All We Possess" (Miss America), pp. 104–108
November 12, 1949, "Man for Man" (Herbert Hoover), pp. 54–55
March 4, 1950, "Quick Bash" (Benny Goodman), pp. 130–132
May 6, 1950, "Feeling Lost" (Charlie Chaplin), pp. 168–171
May 13, 1950, "How Do You Like It Now, Gentlemen?" (Ernest Hemingway), pp. 142–147

May 24, 1952; May 31, 1952; June 7, 1952; June 14, 1952; June
 21, 1952, "Production Number 1512" (John Huston in
 Hollywood), pp. 159–166
May 9, 1954, "Playwright" (Lorraine Hansberry), pp. 180–183
August 14, 1954, "You Dig It, Sir?" (Newport Jazz Festival),
 pp. 113–118
November 20, 1954, "Young and Happy" (Julie Andrews),
 pp. 201–203
February 11, 1956, "Ageless" (Benny Goodman), pp. 132–133
September 28, 1957, "The Strong Ones" (Chanel), pp. 96–98
February 20, 1960, "On Film" (François Truffaut), pp. 246–247
April 16, 1960, "Movement" (Mailer and the Beats), pp. 151–155
August 20, 1960, "The Yellow Bus," pp. 22–25
January 21, 1961 "Dame Edith" (Dame Edith Evans), pp. 194–196
June 24, 1961, "Attorney General" (Robert Kennedy), pp. 64–67
October 21, 1961, "The Player" (Michael Redgrave), pp. 189–191
October 28, 1961, "The Player" (Zero Mostel), pp. 203–206
October 28, 1961, "The Player" (Henry Fonda), pp. 209–212
November 4, 1961, "The Player" (Walter Matthau), pp. 217–219
1962, *The Player* (Sidney Poitier), pp. 183–187
1962, *The Player* (Warren Beatty), pp. 206–208
1962, *The Player* (Jane Fonda), pp. 212–214
March 31, 1962, "This Season's Man" (Paul Scofield), pp. 215–217
May 25, 1963, "Thursday" (Adlai Stevenson), pp. 43–46
October 12, 1963, "Director" (Tony Richardson), pp. 191–192
November 30, 1963, President John F. Kennedy, pp. 60–62
December 7, 1963, "Fugue" (Glenn Gould and Yehudi Menuhin),
 pp. 136–140
December 14, 1963, "Rededication" (Adlai Stevenson), pp. 46–47
October 24, 1964, "Campaigning" (Robert F. Kennedy), pp. 68–70
October 31, 1964, "Truffaut" (François Truffaut), pp. 247–249
July 24, 1965, Adlai Stevenson, pp. 48–51
October 30, 1965, "10 1/2" (Federico Fellini), pp. 255–257
February 25, 1967, "Two People in a Room," pp. 196–197
August 12, 1967, Hubert H. Humphrey, pp. 71–73
December 7, 1968, "Nixon's Walk" (Richard Nixon), p. 56
October 17, 1970, "Truffaut" (François Truffaut), pp. 249–251
January 1, 1972, Ralph Johnson Bunche, pp. 74–76

June 12, 2000, "Naked and Truthful in the Bronx" (Gus Van Sant),
 pp. 200–201
August 21, 2000, "Jogging" (Sports Edition), pp. 124–125
October 9, 2000, "After the Pageant" (Brandi Burkhardt),
 pp. 108–111
November 13, 2000, "An Analog Toast to the Digital Age,"
 pp. 36–37
January 29, 2001, "Harvey et Jeanne," pp. 278–280
May 14, 2001, "A Cinderella Story," pp. 92–93
May 21, 2001, "Wes Anderson in Hamilton Heights" (Wes
 Anderson), pp. 280–282
June 18, 2001, "First Niece Steps Out," pp. 93–95
July 9, 2001, "Bill and George," pp. 57–59
September 24, 2001, 9/11/01 Story (P.S. 6 Principal Feigelson),
 pp. 39–41
December 10, 2001, "Girls and Dolls," pp. 88–90
January 14, 2002, "Diamonds for Dinner," pp. 282–284

"Mazie," by Joseph Mitchell was first published in *The New
 Yorker* of December 21, 1940, and reprinted in *Up in the Old
 Hotel* (Pantheon Books, 1992) and *McSorley's Wonderful
 Saloon* (Duell, Sloan and Pearce, 1943, subsequently published
 by Pantheon Books in 1992).

Acknowledgements

SINCE CHILDHOOD, I've been the lucky recipient, in my undertakings, of helpful and generous response from a long list of loving, smart, and gracious people. All of them, one way or another, have contributed to the emergence of this book, but it is impossible at this point to sort them out by name. For what I have been given specifically over the past few years for these pages, I thank my inspirational colleagues and friends at *The New Yorker*. Susan Morrison has given me generous and invaluable help beyond measure. I'm grateful in many ways to Marshall Heyman, Nick Paumgarten, Christopher Shay, Erin Overbey, Brenda Phipps, Dana Goodyear, Betsy Judelson, Françoise Mouly, Perri Dorset, Mauri Perl, Pam McCarthy, David Remnick, and the entire Checking Department.

Counterpoint's modest, heroic, and steadfast staff—Dawn Seferian, Trish Hoard, Norman MacAfee, John McLeod, Keltie Hawkins, Heather McLeod, and Jack Shoemaker—contributed mightily and patiently to my purpose here. So did my agent, Jane Gelfman, and her noble assistants, Cathy Gleason and Kelly Gillespie.

I've been given moral and practical support by Carol Matthau, Al Miller, Marsha Williams, George Sheanshang, Peter Parcher, John and Debra Schreiber, Dot McCleary, Fernanda and José Sousa, Tina Brown, Mary-Elizabeth Gifford, David Michaelis, Andrew O'Hagan, Judy Siegman, Lola Finkelstein, David Kuhn, Sheila McGrath, Stan Gibson, and, as always, my son Erik—with or without his invaluable computer expertise.

Lillian Ross
March 4, 2002